THE INVISIBLE PARENT

Published under licence by Brown Dog Books, 10b Greenway Farm, Bath Rd, Wick, nr. Bath BS30 5RL

ISBN printed book: 978-1-83952-398-4
ISBN e-book: 978-1-83952-399-1

Cover design by Kevin Rylands
Internal design by Andrew Easton

Printed and bound in the UK

This book is printed on FSC certified paper

FSC
www.fsc.org

MIX
Paper from
responsible sources
FSC® C013604

THE INVISIBLE PARENT

The Dark Art of Parental Alienation

ANONYMOUS
with Andrew Keith Walker

Foreword
By Andrew Keith Walker

Writing *The Invisible Parent* was supposed to be a typical ghostwriting project. I never expected to put my name on it. That became necessary as the project progressed and we realised there was a need to anonymise the author. Similarly, I never expected to write a foreword for it. Again, it is simply necessary to add credibility to chapters that follow. Typically, a ghostwriter puts the words of the named author down on the page in a form that reads well. The ghostwriter is invisible and uses their writing skills to turn conversations, interviews and the author's notes into a readable, coherent narrative. This project however, took a different turn.

That turn was the decision to make the author anonymous in order to protect the identities of the people in this book. Anonymity for the author means he can speak freely and openly about the events in his life regarding the deeply painful experience of Parental Alienation. It also means he can quote verbatim from documents that are normally prevented from publication by law, in this case, the many court reports and assessments in the author's private hearings in the Family Court. The decision to make the author anonymous protects his privacy and that of his children, which feels wholly appropriate given the pain and trauma they have already experienced as a result of Parental Alienation.

I approached this book as a research project in the following way – I interviewed the author many times over a three month period, sometimes daily. I also interviewed friends and former employees who witnessed the events in the book. The mandate for this book was to be evidence-based and to take a documentary approach to the issues – in terms of events, statements and so on - everything written here is supported by some kind of documentary evidence or correspondence. For each point the author makes, my job was to find at least one – and usually more than one – other source corroborating the claim from the mountain of court papers and testimony. This means the narrative couldn't become a half-remembered slew of anecdotes and accusations, it is a documentary account of the issues we cover in the book.

All the events and exchanges between individuals in this book come from real text messages, emails, legal letters and court reports. Email threads, screen grabs of text messages, WhatsApp messages, hard copies of letters, court reports, correspondence between lawyers, police statements and witness affidavits have formed the basis of this book – over 100 documents in total, produced over three years of court action – plus around 12 hours of recorded interviews and conversations with people who were there at the time.

The end result you will read from here onward, is a thematic analysis of the events of the author's life, with a particular regard to the period of his Family Court applications to re-establish contact with his children, during which the author experienced alienation from his children and fought to re-establish contact through the Family Court. The sheer complexity of the case made it hard to tell the story in a chronology, so we opted to explore the author's relationships with his ex-wife, his children and his fiancée, the court, the school and Cafcass in a series of essays. We also decided to unpick the many failings of the Family Court and propose reforms and improvements that would address the issue of Parental Alienation in a preventative, practical manner.

I can confirm that this book is factual with the exception of necessary changes to maintain anonymity for the author and his children. We considered this anonymisation in great detail to ensure we did not substantively alter the facts of the case or the events discussed, but we have made appropriate and significant changes to make it impossible to identify any of the people involved.

Ultimately, the book you are about to read could be the story of any one of thousands of UK parents claiming to be alienated by their ex-partner, regardless of gender or income bracket. Perhaps the most poignant aspect of this story is the fact most alienated parents will recognise themselves and their own experiences on the following pages. In that respect, the Invisible Parent isn't just about one person, it is also about the devastating impact of Parental Alienation on the lived experience of thousands of estranged parents and children in the UK.

Andrew Keith Walker, 26 October 2020

Contents

Chapter 1:
The Invisible Parent

Before I begin telling my story, let me share this extract from a court-ordered assessment from my case by an expert on parent-child relationship breakdowns, a highly qualified psychiatrist and well-known expert witness in my Family Court case and countless others like it.

'The mother is somewhat passive, and the children absolutely do not believe that she really wants them to see their father.'

It sums up the impossible bind an alienated parent is caught in. My ex-wife cut me off from my kids, and influenced them to hate me. I hadn't been abusive. Never been violent. I wasn't a criminal or an addict. I was a successful businessman, we had a beautiful home, and they had the best schools, holidays and every opportunity that someone in my privileged position could give them. My ex-wife, who received millions in our divorce and lived a very privileged life herself, hated me. And then, suddenly, so did my kids. Just like that, they were gone.

The expert court reporter I quoted above suggested family therapy, to bring us back together. This was aligned with the UK family law statute that mandates the Family

Court to ensure children of divorce or separation maintain a relationship with both parents – because it's considered to be in the child's best interests. My kids proved that to be true. Their welfare suffered as a result of our estrangement. They were depressed and anxious after years of non-contact with me. The court expert recommended the following approach:

'The focus of the work should be to assist the children with their current level of despair, to help them think about their family issues in a more rounded way, and, with the strong and frank assistance of their mother, to question some key aspects of the narrative. For example, how is it that they blame father for …?' [The expert then lists events that occurred without my knowledge or involvement, which my children nevertheless blamed me for in their assessments with him.]

Again, there it is. How was it, they blamed me for a list of things that happened after they cut me off, and I knew nothing about until I discovered them for myself? I hadn't seen my children for over two years when that was written. The court appointed an expert who interviewed my children. They told him their mother doesn't want them to have a relationship with me. They told him I was to blame for things I knew nothing about. That is the basis of Parental Alienation. I was to blame. I wasn't someone to have a relationship with. And the source of those opinions – some might call it brainwashing – was my ex-wife.

At the time this report was presented to the court, I had spent years alleging my ex-wife was alienating me from my kids. It wasn't the first report presented to the Family Court that stated my ex-wife was influencing my kids to cut me off. It was another report, from another expert, appointed by another judge in another Family Court session, that supported my claim that my ex-wife was the cause of problems between me and my kids. And it made no difference whatsoever. One day, aged 11, my kids decided they never wanted to see me again. They had rooms at my house. They stayed with me mid-week and weekends. We went on holidays, we had friends, pets, sports clubs, piano lessons, we were a normal, loving family of two divorced parents with shared contact. Then it just stopped.

I lost my kids. Teams of lawyers and barristers argued my children out of my life, and kept them from me. I fought to see them, tried everything to get us into some sort of mediation, counselling, family therapy, anything I could think of to get us back into each other's lives, but it was all blocked and fought by my ex-wife.

You might think you know about this subject. About people like me, or cases like mine. But the truth is your kids could walk out of your life and never come back. And the only other person in the world who could help you, the other parent, could be responsible for it. You can cry victim, you can accuse them, you can find an army of lawyers who will back you and fight your case, you can demand justice, you can fight with all the legal options provided by the Family Court, you can get court-appointed experts to write court-ordered reports that support your claims and recommend counselling, family therapy or a whole host of other solutions to get you back together, and it makes no difference whatsoever.

Your ex-partner can simply take your kids and there's nothing you can do about it. They can make you disappear.

Become invisible. Erase you from the lives of the people you love most in all the world. And nobody will help you or your kids as you grieve and break under the strain of the abuse. That is the reality of Parental Alienation in the UK.

You might think it could never happen to you. So did I.

About this book

This book is about three things.

It is about the failure of the Family Court system in the UK to act effectively for the welfare of children. My case is one of Parental Alienation, however, I am not simply referring to the inability of the Family Courts to act in Parental Alienation cases. In this book I will argue the case and demonstrate how judges and social workers are incapable of putting the interests of children above the complexity of the legal process and experts, who seldom help the children who need it most or when they most need it.

This book is also about the ability of a determined parent to completely alienate another from their children's lives. I will show you how this is done, and how easily – with the help of the court – my ex-wife did it to me. In doing so, she abused me by proxy through manipulating my children. They suffered, as did I, to satisfy her anger and resentment towards me after our divorce. I believe cutting me off from my kids was the only way she could truly hurt me. Why she did it, I cannot say for sure. But I can show how she achieved it, and how the failing Family Courts and the people who intersect around Family Law, enabled her to do it.

Finally, this book will describe the toll that Parental Alienation takes on children. I will explain how my own children suffered mentally and physically as a result of being psychologically manipulated to cut me out of their life. Their experiences and problems are all too common and all too predictable to be a coincidence. The longer we were apart, the worse their lives became. Parental Alienation causes lasting damage to a child's wellbeing and self-esteem and in this book, I will show how those issues manifest in the children whose wishes and feelings purport to cut one parent out of their life completely for reasons that should be easy to resolve in a normal family environment.

Parental Alienation is domestic abuse. It will one day be as obvious a form of abuse as any other. Like all forms of domestic abuse it has spent years in the shadows of public life. There is always something on the fringes of public awareness that is tolerated or unspoken, the politics of race, gender and equality is a history of those abuses being brought into the light of public awareness and legal reform.

This book will, I hope, help to move Parental Alienation and the abuse of loving relationships a little closer to that light. It will, I hope highlight the dramatic and profound change in my children from being happy-go-lucky kids to falling apart. All this can be directly attributed to the point in time I was purposely removed from their lives by a relentless and dark campaign.

About my story

My name isn't important but I want to expose the secrecy and injustices of the Family Court. It is failing. Right now, it's failing someone, husbands, wives, children. It ruins lives and makes bad situations worse. It is completely unfit for the purpose and public service is supposed to provide, yet it persists. It persists despite calls for reform. Despite campaigns, every year, for meaningful change. It is also a growth industry, worth billions and rising every year for the legal profession. It's time everyone took notice, before you find yourself caught up in it, as I did.

I am not writing this book with the intention of invading anyone's privacy, or doing harm to anyone's reputation. I am writing this book to help people like me. I am writing this book to help parents who have lost their children through a form of domestic abuse called Parental Alienation. I am writing this story to lift the lid on the broken Family Court process. The only way I can do that, is to do it anonymously to get around the privacy laws that keep the endemic Family Court failings a secret.

People like me are gagged, while we use our names. Anonymity is the only way the bigger truth can be made public, and I fully believe it is in the public interest to do so. Trust me when I say, by the time you finish this story, you will be shocked by the Kafkaesque bureaucracy and capriciousness of the courts you place your unquestioning faith in as a citizen of the United Kingdom.

The chances are – if you are an alienated parent – you already know about the harsh reality of Family Court and the bias of organisations like Cafcass. For others like me, I hope this book can do something else. I hope it can help you realise you are not alone, nor without hope. If my story can help anyone relate to their own struggles, or normalise their experiences, then I will feel something positive has come out of the worst thing that has ever happened to me.

I also hope that if you read this and find yourself in the challenging position of working out contact arrangements for your children, you will devote every possible effort to ensure your relationship remains workable with your ex-partner. I make this plea for one reason – children who lose a relationship with one of their parents through divorce or separation suffer mentally, physically and academically. Their health, happiness and chances in life depend on you remaining in it, so you need to make sure you don't find yourself fighting a battle you can't possibly win. You also need to stay well, and stay alive, because you are no good to anyone dead.

My name is Anonymous, and I am an alienated parent.

I am not writing this book to hurt my ex-partner, or my kids. If I used my name, that would be the inevitable result. I don't want to sound disingenuous. I will be completely honest and say that after all I have suffered I wouldn't care if my ex-partner suffered as a result of the truth about her coming out – however because of the power she exerts over my kids and their wellbeing, it would inevitably hurt them too. Everything I have done, the years of effort and struggle to see my kids, was motivated by my desire to help them. I am not about to hurt them now by sharing the intimate details of their lives in this book. So they must remain anonymous too, like me. For that to work, so must my ex-partner, and all those people involved in my case.

Anonymity will inevitably make some people doubt the honesty of this book. It's something I have come to accept. I am willing to make that compromise because as much as I want to come out and stand by my account of events and convince the doubters and sceptics that it is true – and I have the proof in the exhaustive paper trail that years of Family Court action generates – I don't want to give my ex-partner more ammunition to influence my children against me or respond tit-for-tat. That fight has already been fought, and I lost it. I have come to accept that. However, if my story can help anyone understand the injustices of Parental Alienation and the obvious lack of legal or social support for the adults and children who are victims of it, then I will feel some good has come from it.

By the same token, I don't want to hurt my kids by talking about the dreadful things they have suffered as a result of Parental Alienation but I have to talk about those painful events and issues. To whitewash or sanitise the effects of domestic abuse only harms the victims further. It is in the public interest to know the truth of the damage that Parental Alienation does to the children as well as the alienated parent. I don't want my book to help others at the expense of my kids or their mental health. To that end I have decided not to reveal their whereabouts gender or names. My children are referred to as pronouns only – they, theirs, their.

I am a father and talk about the issues I faced as a father within the Family Courts, and so I have decided to refer to my ex-partner as my ex-wife because that is appropriate and doesn't make either of us identifiable. I have removed references to specific places, and where appropriate used aliases for the names of people in my story to facilitate the relating of events.

The steps I have taken to anonymise my story enable a free and frank discussion of the issue of Parental Alienation, using my own case as an example to help illustrate the mechanics of how this form of abuse works. My goal in all of this is to advance the cause of alienated parents and children. It doesn't matter who we are, what matters is what happened to us and what is happening every day to parents and children around the world.

I have used a ghostwriter to help put my story into words. I have also given him access to all the documents and papers of my case, plus access to interview witnesses. I had one request – nothing will go into this book that hasn't been recorded in an affidavit, court order, court assessment or professional report that was used in my court case. This includes all reports shared by both sides of the case – my ex-wife and mine. We have applied a simple journalistic method to the work – that means referencing all claims with at least two corroborating statements in court reports.

I have taken pains to explain this to you to acknowledge my concern that readers simply won't believe this story. That concern is also shared by most alienated parents. The reason for it is simple. It is possible, with little effort and almost no scrutiny by courts or child protection experts, to turn a child against their parent and cause untold damage to their mental health and wellbeing. It is also possible with little effort to drive alienated parents to depression, mental illness and in all too many cases, taking their own lives. I will show how easy it is in this book, and it will shock you.

The nature of Parental Alienation is challenging. My story, like many other alienated parents, will paint a picture of red tape and bureaucracy that will at times sound unbelievable. My story will present the facts of the case and show how the mechanisms provided by law to deal with Parental Alienation in the UK – matched in their systemic failings in many other countries – are unfit for purpose and incapable of addressing the issue. My story will show how my children deteriorated rapidly under the care of my ex-wife, who was never called to account or subjected to reasonable scrutiny for their mental, physical, behavioural and educational problems. My story will also show you how at all times, my children's wishes and feelings to cut me out of their life were justifiable, despite those wishes and feelings being influenced – quite obviously – by my ex-wife.

If I had never heard of Parental Alienation, I would have been disbelieving too, if I hadn't lived it first hand, I wouldn't have thought it possible. While I lived through the hell of watching my kids decline so obviously, despite all my efforts to get them the help they needed, it took me the longest time to come to terms with the fact I was being alienated from my kids. The truth is, while it is happening to you, the notion is so outlandish you can't really accept it. And by the time you do, it is too late.

If at any point in the following chapters you are sceptical, I would urge you to do your own research. There are many thousands of alienated parents, with Facebook groups, blogs and online publications in most countries. There are campaigns to change the laws on domestic abuse to include Parental Alienation in countries and jurisdictions worldwide, and many high profile campaigns to reform the Family Court system. If you have never been in a fight over contact, you might never realise it. At no point would I ask anyone to take my word for it, look for yourself.

Parental Alienation is an issue that is both persistent and deeply problematic. It also attracts a broad range of opinions – not all of which I believe to be helpful or correct. There are some very militant opinions and there are organisations that behave in aggressive or unhelpful ways that claim to represent alienated parents as well as other divorced parents. I would like to make it absolutely clear that I am not taking sides or aligning myself with any organisation. I am not campaigning for fathers' rights, or campaigning against mothers' rights. I am not campaigning for anyone, I am not taking sides, I am not trying to persuade you to sign a petition or donate to a cause. This is my story, I am not generalising it to apply to someone else's cause. I am sharing it to help other people like me, and the other kids who might be harmed through Parental Alienation. That is all.

What I will show, in the following chapters, is how the alienated parent faces an unfair fight from the outset. If you can't read any further into this book, then I will make the case now ...

Parental Alienation is a catch-22

Parental Alienation occurs when a child or children exhibit hostility towards the non-resident parent in a divorce or separation to the extent they refuse to see them, due to psychological manipulation by the resident parent. To be clear, that means there is no safeguarding concern, no history of drug abuse or alcoholism, no history of violence or molestation. Just an ordinary parent being subjected to extraordinary hostility.

That might sound simple enough, but it is a paradox.

A circular argument. It exists in name only when it comes to doing anything about it. It is recognised to be a form of domestic abuse, but it has no formal statutory definition or measure. It is acknowledged to exist, but it is impossible to prove or demonstrate. The effects of Parental Alienation on the adult and child victims of alienation are well documented, but those effects are generally dismissed by the courts. The paradox is this – if you and your kids are suffering through Parental Alienation the situation is indistinguishable from you being a bad parent and your kids hating you for good reason. Except you are a good parent, and your kids have no reason to hate you. However, those two crucial differences are not a matter the courts are prepared to consider. If the kids say they don't want to see you, that is all that matters. The *why* is never considered.

To make that even simpler: If you are a good parent and your kids have no reason to hate you, the courts won't take that as grounds to consider Parental Alienation, even if you claim it. In fact, the claim of alienation might be validated, as mine was, but nobody will claim it is Parental Alienation. In my case, I was even told I alienated myself through things I considered to be normal parenting, like making my kids do homework and getting them a tutor for their 11 Plus exams. I was told I alienated my kids because I took them on ski trips and to a West End musical when they wanted to go to Disneyland Paris.

It's barely believable, isn't it?

Whatever you claim is the reason for your allegation of Parental Alienation, it will be used against you in court. The case you make, the evidence you cite, the court-appointed experts and assessments, the witness statements, every shred of evidence you use to make your case will ultimately prove pointless and useless. If your kids, no matter how depressed or anxious, no matter how badly they are doing in school, no matter how upsetting their problems become, say they never want to see you again, that is all the courts listen to.

Your children can justify their wishes and feelings with reasons that sound capricious, or claims that are untrue. They can justify their wishes and feelings with opinions that have clearly been invented by your ex-partner and nobody will challenge them. They could recite chapter and verse from statements they have been told to memorise, like a kidnap victim or hostage, and nobody will challenge it.

Your children will suffer personal problems that can't be dismissed out of hand as being normal developmental issues. They will deteriorate mentally and physically and the judgement of experts in the field will be dismissed by people who aren't qualified to comment. It will make no difference to the court.

Your children can be exposed to situations under the care of your ex-partner which raise significant safeguarding concerns, and those concerns will not be subjected to scrutiny.

It's like banging your head against a brick wall.

You have no case and you have no voice.

At the end of the pain and heartbreak, you are left with nothing to show for your efforts. UK law states in section 1 (subsection 2A) of the Children Act 1989 (CA 1989), which was modified by section 11 of the Children and Families Act 2014 (CFA 2014) as follows in regard to child arrangements orders:

'Where the court is considering one of the following applications, it must, in relation to each parent, presume (unless the contrary is shown) that involvement of that parent in the life of the child concerned will further that child's welfare.'

That guiding legal principle will still apply and be referenced clearly by the judge and the Cafcass officer in the recommendation and judgement that cuts you off from your kids and cuts you out of their life forever.

That guiding legal principle will apply and be referenced when the judge and the Cafcass officer claim they are cutting you out of your kids' life to further their welfare.

It is double speak. Gibberish. Nonsense and at the same time, the law.

It's a catch-22 that renders you completely silent and invisible in the lives of your kids, invisible in terms of the fundamental human right to a family life, and invisible in your right to equality before the law. You become invisible in almost every way, except of course, for the money you pay out in maintenance and support for your ex-wife and kids.

The invisible abuse, invisible abuser and invisible victims

It took me years to realise that I was being alienated and to fully come to terms with what that means. The experience of becoming an alienated parent is like being stuck in limbo, trapped between the reality of alienation and the reality of a legal system that doesn't have a universally agreed definition or a standardised process to investigate it. It is a trap and once you are caught in it there is no way out. Alienated parents like me are desperate. We are isolated. We're unable to move forwards. We can't make ourselves heard over the noise of the experts and witnesses who opine on our cases with little understanding of Parental Alienation, and little compassion for the alienated. We are written off as collateral damage, the natural by-product of divorce.

Alienated parents are victims of a form of domestic abuse that is not recognised in any workable sense. The system designed to protect children and parents from Parental Alienation is not fit for purpose, in fact, it's virtually non-existent. Experts, therapists and social workers cannot agree on how to measure Parental Alienation and there is currently no requirement for professionals to be trained to either assess it or deal with it.

Everyone acknowledges it exists. It exists, but professionals aren't trained to deal with it. It exists, but there's no precise definition of what it is or how to measure it. The same applies to alienated parents. They exist too, yet in most cases, the courts can't define who they are or measure the severity of the abuse they have endured. Parental Alienation exists in theory but not in reality, it seems.

I would argue from my own experience that, in fact, if you allege Parental Alienation it goes against you in court. The opposing legal team devote their case to proving you have wrongly accused your ex-partner of domestic abuse, and because there is no measure of Parental Alienation or statutory definition, it's not hard to disprove it. All the opposite side need is to report your children's wishes and feelings. The case then hinges on you proving your children's wishes and feelings are the result of bullying or manipulation by your ex-partner. That is impossible to prove.

In my case, my children claimed they hated me for reasons that changed over time. At first, I was a bully and I said mean things about their mother, my ex-wife, and my ex-fiancée who robbed me. Later, they said they hated me for reasons they learned about from my ex-wife – concerning very private personal details of an estranged child with an ex-girlfriend – and because of things I had said in emails to her and her lawyers, plus a slew of issues regarding maintenance and finances that were quite untrue. My ex-wife claimed my children formed their own opinions, and went snooping about in her private files and emails, she couldn't stop them. The court accepted that without question and therefore, my claims of alienation were dismissed.

In the end, they placed my ex-wife in sole charge of my contact with my children, limited to a letter once a month, which had to be addressed to her and was at her discretion to pass on to my children. They put the person I had accused of abuse in charge of ending the abuse I had accused them of.

If that sounds unbelievable, it's merely the tip of the iceberg.

The Alienated Parent Trap

When you claim you are being alienated, the focus of the court-appointed social workers, expert witnesses, therapists, the opposing lawyers and ultimately the judge shifts. It shifts away from the real problem – your situation – to consider an entirely theoretical question, i.e. *how do we measure Parental Alienation?* And as I will show in this book, it is a theoretical question that has no answer because Parental Alienation has many definitions but no process to measure it.

This means you leave court with a stack of papers from experts that all consider your claim of parental alienation and not the facts of it. That is the experience of being alienated. It is the experience of having the fundamental facts that matter disregarded by the courts, namely the facts you haven't seen your children for years and they hate you for reasons that don't make sense.

In my case, which is hardly unique, I have reports from a court-appointed expert, a consultant child psychiatrist, recognised as one of the most senior in the country, that says I am '*alienated in the plain English sense of the word*' and that it was harmful for the children not to be in a relationship with me. His report stopped short of identifying Parental Alienation. This is because the senior court-appointed psychiatrist knows he is going to come under aggressive cross-examination by the opposing barrister. He knows that he would struggle to prove something that isn't recognised in the statutes or defined in medical texts. It would be impossible to argue something into existence on the witness stand of a court.

What is the plain English sense of the word *alienation?* He felt comfortable using that term specifically. In that case, he was referring to alienation, which comes from the verb alienate. According to the *Oxford English Dictionary* it means '*Make (someone) feel isolated or estranged. Make (someone) become unsympathetic or hostile.*' It expresses intent. You don't wake up alienated by chance, you are alienated by someone. That is what the word means in the plain English sense of the word.

I have another report, from a family therapist my ex-wife and I mutually agreed to involve in our case, that specifically says that in my case 'there are some elements of alienation' and recommends family therapy to re-establish contact with my kids.

And another report that was considered in the court proceedings from a children's charity mediator – assigned via my children's school to enable us to restart our relationship – that states that my ex-wife *'may be influencing my children's decisions'*. This was the first report, produced as the children turned 12, which recommended mediation with my ex-wife as the only way to re-establish contact with my children. This report stated my ex-wife was influencing my kids and not supporting contact.

My ex-wife was not prepared to attend mediation. She said the children did not want to see me, and she would support their wishes and feelings. She didn't think the problem was between me and her, it was between me and the kids.

And I have another report written when the children were 14, from the children's official guardian, a social worker from Cafcass (Children and Family Court Advisory and Support Service) that states categorically that *'this is not a case of parental alienation'* based on their own assessment.

Plus the two reports above that state *'alienation in the plain English sense of the word'* (children were 12 and 14 respectively) and *'there are some elements of alienation'* (children were 13) based on a measure of Parental Alienation that comes from a US standard. Those reports were considered within the Cafcass framework that concluded my case was not Parental Alienation when the children were 14.

What I am trying to show, and will explore further in this book, is the sheer confusion on the part of court-appointed (and non-court appointed but mutually agreed) professionals regarding alienation. The meaning of the term, the extent of it, the vagueness of the terminology and ultimately the fact there is no objective measure of what it is. In the final analysis, after all the confusion, a social worker with little time and too many cases expresses a subjective opinion that quashes the whole thing. It seems almost pointless to have highly qualified professionals involved if a junior civil servant eventually has the final word in the judge's ear.

The differences between these reports – and there are many to choose from – are laid bare by considering who wrote them. Two authors have doctorates earned over years of study in the fields of mental health. One of them is a leading consultant child psychiatrist at a major London hospital, and an acknowledged expert. One of the other authors is a full-time child counsellor at a children's support charity that works with schools. One is from a relatively junior social worker in a service that is known to be chronically underfunded and operating under calls for case supervision and safer processes. It was – predictably – that last one, the Cafcass report, that carried the most weight. That report was written by the person who had spent least time with my children, and at the end of years of alienation, when they were aged 14. Those 14 year olds had not had contact with me since they were 11. They had seen me only twice in three years, once at school, once by chance in the high street. The Cafcass report was the only report that unequivocally dismissed my claim of alienation. This report said that my children were capable of making up their own minds, aged 14 even though at that time they were both diagnosed with anxiety and depression and undergoing therapy at a private clinic.

Of course, the problem here is obvious. These reports set opinion against opinion, with no regard for qualification, no shared framework or guidance, and no specialist training in cases of alienation. More importantly, the most damaging characteristic of alienation is the psychological manipulation of children by the resident parent. This means if the case before you is one of Parental Alienation, the children don't have the ability to make up their own minds. They have been manipulated into hating the absent parent. It is a symptom of the abuse they are suffering. It should go without saying that in cases where Parental Alienation is claimed, the ability of the children to make up their own minds comes under greater scrutiny, especially if they are both diagnosed with anxiety and depression.

Even though Parental Alienation was alleged in my case, the children's ability to make up their own minds about cutting their father out of their lives forever was never challenged. If the authors of these reports were trained to spot possible Parental Alienation and measure it against a shared definition of it, they would have come to very different conclusions.

My children were undergoing therapy for anxiety and depression. One was self-harming, cutting words into their arm and their thigh. The other had been sending inappropriate selfies to an online abuser, who groomed the child and subsequently attempted to blackmail my child for nude pictures. One of my children had suffered a dramatic decline in their school grades. Both professed to hate me, primarily for reasons that they discovered through my ex-wife. These were not issues between me and my kids, they did not refer to our relationship or anything that had happened between us.

The reasons they hated me were personal issues that I had not shared with them. Those issues were treated like a smoking gun by my ex-wife's legal team, and biased some of the reports against me. The issues were, by the way, perfectly normal. Just not the sort of things I wanted to share with my kids. Don't all adults have some things they keep private? Don't we all have skeletons in the closet? Perhaps we all fear the prejudice or judgement of our peers, but we certainly don't discuss our sex lives, stress, mental health, old relationships and a host of other things with our kids until they are old enough to handle it, if ever.

My children also said they hated me because I was mean to their mother over money. This is not uncommon in divorces, but in mine it was absurd. I am a very wealthy man, my ex-wife received almost £7 million in our divorce settlement and lived in a £2.3 million home. I paid over £80,000 per year in maintenance and school fees. My children spoke of me like I was Scrooge.

My children, aged 14, were dealing with depression, self-harm and online grooming, yet at the same time were deemed competent enough to make a decision to cut their father out of their life completely? Really? I think they weren't capable of making a decision like that. Especially if they felt paying £80,000 per year to support their multimillionaire mother made me mean.

Cutting a parent out of your life feels like such a huge

decision, making it at a time when you are in perfect mental health as an adult would be stressful and emotionally challenging enough, but while you are undergoing therapy and recovering from child abuse? It makes a mockery of the person who wrote that report that said they were competent and the organisation that published it.

The Judge in my case was of the opinion my children had been through so much emotional difficulty arising from my court attempts to see them that – despite it being in their best interests to re-establish contact with me – it would better for them to end the court action and leave things as they were, with no contact with me. That is another catch-22 of Parental Alienation.

The Children and Families Act 2014, The Human Rights Act 1998 and many subsequent judgements all make it quite clear that the relationship between a parent and child is a fundamental element of family life, and almost always in the best interests of the child. And so it was in my case. Every report concluded that contact should recommence at some point in the future, but stopped short of ordering it because the children were emotionally exhausted by the court actions I was pursuing to re-establish contact with them. I was told to stop fighting. My ex-wife wasn't told to stop resisting. My kids were never told to offer a chance for reconciliation. It is the bias inherent in the system against the parent who alleges alienation.

Every statement is shrouded in debate, or opinion, and ends with a 'Yes but' statement. And so the parent trap closes. You haven't seen your kids for years, but you aren't alienated? They would be emotionally better off if you had a relationship, but not until they are emotionally better off than they are now without it? They think you are a monster but maybe one day they'll want to restart contact with you?

It's a circular, contradictory mess.

My story isn't exceptional, but it might help someone to hear it

In this book, I want to tell my story but I want to do more than that. I want other parents in my situation to find some comfort in the fact they are not alone with the pain of this. I want parents to know how to address the problem if they can. I also want to explore the many facets of marital break-up and life after divorce that can become weaponised against you by an abusive ex-partner.

In the following pages, I will show you how alienated parents usually have a stack of reports that reach all kinds of conclusions which are largely dismissed. To be 100 per cent clear on that point, the debate and lack of clarity that characterises most reports mean they are of little or no value when it comes to a Judge making a court order. If your children are emotionally distressed, the judgement is usually in support of their continued residence with the current resident parent. It's a one-size-fits-all judgement, which is true of the one-size-fits-all Cafcass report that preceded it, and it gets used all the time to keep the Family Court and Cafcass case backlog from getting any longer.

I will show you that even if the alienated parent hasn't seen their child or children for years, nobody will re-establish contact if the children don't want it. Parental Alienation presents as your children exhibiting unreasonable hostility towards you, but no judge will rule to re-establish contact if your children are hostile towards you because their wishes and feelings come first. Even if those wishes and feelings are unreasonable, they are in the eyes of the Family Court, unimpeachable. I will explore that in more detail, and show how the court process cannot currently deal with Parental Alienation for this basic catch-22 reason.

An alienated parent often appears anxious, desperate, aggressive and angry. You would too if your children were taken from you, and worse they suddenly say they hate you. This is another documented sign of parental alienation. In this book I will explain how the abuser can appear to be reasonable, and the abuse victims – the alienated parent and the children – are presented as the ones with the problems. This happened to me and my children.

Also in this book, I will look at the problem of fathers within the family court system. I will not campaign for them, but I have to be honest about my experience as a father who was subjected to significant bias.

There is a pleasant legal fiction that we are all equal before the law, however fathers in family court often claim an unfair bias against them. Of course, we know that it is usually the father – or a man – that is the abuser in cases of domestic violence or the sexual abuse of children. We also know that it is usually the father or the man in the relationship that is coercive or controlling, emotionally abusive or uses financial control to bully their spouse in messy divorces.

There are many good reasons why the legal protections of children and mothers are geared up to look for and address domestic abuse by men. I have no issue with that.

My issue is where no abuse or safeguarding concerns exist, the father is judged against the same yardstick measures as abusers. There is no presumption of innocence for a man in that system, it's impossible to receive an unbiased appraisal. It's an unintended consequence of the case law that has shaped the courts, but it does place ordinary fathers at a disadvantage when they are judged by the same rationale that judges bastards.

The history of domestic abuse is mostly a history of men hurting women and children, but that means as an alienated father, you have to prove you're not an abuser before anyone will take you seriously. The system is heavily weighted to identify abusive fathers, but lacks the necessary processes to identify abused ones. By that same token, abused mothers are easily detected by the system, but abusive mothers are not. Worst of all, where abused children are protected, the children abused by Parental Alienation slip through the safety net and face the life-changing consequences of the Family Court's failure to protect them.

What happened to me and my kids?

It is hard to explain precisely what the reasons are that wrecked my relationship with my kids, because they were mostly things two 11 year olds shouldn't have learned about one of their parents. They didn't learn them from me. As I said before, they were deeply private matters, personal things that are difficult to talk about. In this book I will be open and honest about them, things that I have been shamed for by my ex-wife whose attitudes towards sexuality, mental health and relationships are – for want of a better word – bigoted.

I also had a few subsequent relationships that have caused me a great deal of pain and influenced my kids' opinion of me. An ex-girlfriend of mine became pregnant. I learned about this after we split. She had the child, whom I support but I have no contact with. She is happily married now.

That child, and my distance from it, was one of the major reasons my children gave for cutting me out of their life. They thought I was cruel to abandon a baby, even though the relationship was ending as I learned about the pregnancy. My children's shock was the emotional reaction of two young children – they were 13 when they found out. I didn't tell them about it because it's very complex and I didn't know how to tell them. They were also only 11 the last time I saw them to talk like that. When they learned about it, they learned about it from my ex-wife and it made them very upset. It made them judge me, and hate me even more. We had been estranged for over a year at this point. My ex-wife claimed she had nothing to do with it, and my kids were snooping in her private files and happened upon the court report where my ex-wife had flagged the issue as being 'morally wrong'. I believe the revelation was deliberate, but I have no proof of that.

I was engaged also, but my fiancée who I will call Elle in this book – with whom I was living and planning to get married and start a family, much to the delight of my children – stole a very large sum of money from me and ran away to America. That is no exaggeration. She also stole the £60,000 engagement ring, and shipped a container of furniture. It was the shock of my life. Unbeknown to me she had mental health problems. It was tragic really, for both of us. It also nearly destroyed me. That was the original cause of the rift with my children, who adored her. Elle returned the money, I dropped the charges against her. We tried to reconcile but she left me, again. I later found out from the police and subsequent court papers, that my ex-wife had been involved in her leaving plans. Yes, my ex-wife was mixed-up in the worst heartbreak I had ever endured with a woman who was a mentally ill thief. Was I wrong to think my ex-wife, who also allowed my kids to learn about my estranged child, was trying to hurt me? I don't think so.

Needless to say, you don't want your kids reading court reports where your sex life is discussed. That happened too. My kids, through my ex-wife or snooping, learned about aspects of my life that were wholly inappropriate for a child to learn about. Those things were my private affairs.

You don't want your kids finding out they have a half-sibling without you telling them.

You don't want your kids to learn their new stepmother-to-be was a thief with mental illness, who had made arrangements with their mother to help her suddenly leave the country whilst suffering from paranoid delusions.

You don't want your kids seeing you hit rock bottom when the love of your life ends so badly.

That moment, at rock bottom, is where my alienation story began for me. Not for my kids. Not for my ex-wife. In truth, I was already being alienated but I didn't know it. But for me, that was the moment when I realised I needed help to get over the shock and grief of losing someone I thought I was going to start a whole new life with. It was also the shock of finding she had emptied my safe. Stolen the engagement ring I had made for her. Taken over £300,000 from our joint account and fled to America. Honestly, it keeps me up at night wondering if she ever really loved me or if she was just a gold-digger. It's a terrible feeling. I was a victim of crime, and a jilted fiancée with a broken heart and trust issues. I referred myself to a psychoanalyst who deals with extreme shocks like that. My kids didn't need to know about those details at 11, they needed to be older to understand it.

At the same time, my children reacted very badly to Elle's departure. We went through a bad patch. Nothing major. We had a couple of arguments about Elle, and my ex-wife helping her. I wasn't thinking straight. They were saying I was to blame, I told them that the police had informed me that their mother had been involved. I shouldn't have done that. I was totally in the wrong. However, I was broken and I told them the truth.

Then one of my kids told the school – after an assembly on bullying – that she thought I was a bully. The school took this to be a formal complaint and asked me to attend a meeting. At the meeting, they suggested a cooling-off break between me and my kids, so we could reconcile. This seemed like a good idea. We had argued the last few weekends of contact, things were difficult and I didn't know how to resolve it. I agreed to the cooling-off period, as did my ex-wife. We never reconciled. I never saw my kids again for a contact visit. I have seen them twice, since then.

In retrospect, every major judgement has punished me for taking that cooling-off break. I have it in black and white, time and again. I broke off contact. I took a break for three months after the emotional trauma of being dumped and robbed of a fortune by someone who was mentally ill with the help of my ex-wife. We live in a world where we are encouraged to talk openly about our mental health, told there is no stigma, told we need to be open. We are told we should work through our relationship problems and accept mediation and help. In my case that was bullshit. I hit rock bottom and sought help, and the courts didn't give me an ounce of sympathy or understanding. They said I broke off contact and so therefore I alienated myself. Even though I had spent the following two years trying to 'unalienate' myself.

By the time I tried to reconcile with my kids, just three months later, my children claimed to have panic attacks at the thought of sending me a text message. At least, that is what my ex-wife told the school counsellor. That is what my ex-wife told the children's support services charity worker who wrote the first report that I supplied in legal proceedings

I was blamed for my own alienation because I criticised their mother in front of the kids. Which I did. I wasn't in a good place. Every weekend I had contact with the children my ex-wife would call constantly, asking to speak to them, asking them to speak to her friends and family members. She sent my children messages all the time on their iPads and so on. It used to take their time away from me. My ex-wife also refused to do any travelling to bring my children to me. Sometimes we barely had time to chat before bed. It drove me nuts. I am not saying I am proud of myself or right to have said things, but I don't deserve to lose my kids over it. Nor did I share the intimate details of my ex-wife's life with them. Nor would I.

According to my ex-wife, my 12-year-old kids hacked her

email and read correspondence between our solicitors and angry emails about the fact she wouldn't support me in re-establishing contact.

According to my ex-wife, my 13-year-old kids sneaked into her study and read court papers from experts that detailed our sex life, and they made me sound like I'd cheated on her with prostitutes. My ex-wife made this claim because our own sex life was non-existent. She assumed, and stated it to anyone who would listen, that as a high-powered businessman I must therefore be having sex with high-class call girls because that's what cigar chomping company directors do, right? It was an ignorant cliché.

According to my ex-wife, my 13-year-old kids went through her private papers and found court documents where she revealed I had another child. That was something that only she knew about. She told the court. She felt it was important to show what a heartless bastard I was. She knew I didn't want my children to find out and we had agreed to protect them at the time.

According to my ex-wife, all she did was arrange for someone to look after a suitcase for my ex-fiancée. She had nothing to do with the fact that that suitcase was part of a massive theft and the worst break-up I have ever experienced.

According to my ex-wife, who walked out of court with a multimillion pound settlement and a seven-bedroom house in a wealthy part of the home counties I used money to control her and my kids.

The kids said I was a bully even though we hadn't spoken for years.

The kids said I was cruel to abandon the child they

discovered through reading papers in my ex-wife's study.

The kids said I controlled my ex-wife through money, even though we had a clean break divorce and my ex-wife was set for life, and wealthier than the other 99 per cent of UK households.

My children saw me as a bastard, an impression they formed by accessing highly personal information in my ex-wife's house, material that was wholly inappropriate and clearly damaging.

I ask you, the reader, if it is credible that my children snooped and hacked their way into so much information about me – between the ages of 12 and 13 – that they formed their own opinion of me as a bad person they wanted to cut out of their lives?

Is it credible to think at no point did those children receive any steer in their opinion of me from their mother, my ex-wife?

Didn't they confront her? Didn't they say 'Look Mum, we found out all this stuff about Dad' and what did she say?

I can never know. However, I do know from the court reports that my ex-wife did accuse my kids of hacking her email and going through her personal files regarding the divorce. She didn't hesitate to blame them for my alienation.

Is that credible? I don't think it is.

I hope this book will help you make up your own mind.

My name is Anonymous, and I am an alienated parent

Parental Alienation is on the verge of being defined, or at least, that process is beginning. It is currently in a draft bill – the new Domestic Violence Framework – which is passing through the UK Parliament as I write. If it passes, it will establish Parental Alienation alongside other forms of domestic abuse and set a statutory definition into law. If that happens, the long process of incorporating it formally into assessment procedures can begin. It won't be an overnight fix. It won't change anything for me or the thousands of alienated parents for whom the nightmare never ends. However, I hope it passes and what happened to me, and countless others, will stop.

For me, I lost my kids. Whatever happens in the future will be a relationship with adults. Their childhood is lost to me. It was lost for them. Not by me and not by them. We are both victims of a pernicious, invisible form of domestic abuse. I wanted to give my children so much more than they got. I wanted to protect them. I wanted them to get every chance to do whatever they wanted to do with their lives.

I am not sure that can ever happen now. They are damaged by it, as am I. I am sure they could be happy, but they will need a lot of help to get there.

I don't know precisely how I lost them. Not for sure. But I know I wasn't there to become the childish bogeyman they painted me to be in the court reports, any more than I was there to take them on holidays or help them with their homework. In a way, that's the cruellest irony of Parental Alienation. You lose your kids. Really lose them. You lose track of them. You aren't there. You are like some blocked internet troll on social media. Banished. Erased from the universe to all intents and purposes. You become the monster under the bed – invisible, non-existent, but frightening all the same.

It is almost unbearable.

I always claimed to be a loving Father. I provided for my kids within my means, which are extensive. I have never been a drunk nor an addict. I am not a criminal. I am not an abuser. I have never smacked them. I have never sent them to bed with no supper. I never missed a weekend of contact. I never missed a holiday. I never missed a parents' evening. I got them a tutor. I took them to shows. We have eaten breakfast in hotels with royalty. We have flown on a private jet. With me, my children lived a life most people only dream about. They are set for life with a trust fund. And I was the happiest father in the world.

Then I had a child I didn't know about with someone I didn't want to be with. I was conned and dumped by someone who broke my heart. I had low periods and I sought professional help. And then I lost my kids, forever.

They hate me. They think I am a bastard. I am not a bastard. And whatever happened in my life with them, I did not deserve to lose them forever.

I came to believe my ex-wife turned my kids against me. I realised, too late, that she was manipulating them, brainwashing them for want of a better word.

It was domestic abuse. Systematic, psychological abuse that caused me untold pain and caused my children mental and physical issues that have no doubt damaged their life outcomes and from which they will need help to recover, help they needed before, and almost certainly still need now.

This book will explain how their abuse and mine passed by undetected by all the experts. It was the invisible abuse of Parental Alienation. You can shout it from the rooftops, tell anyone that will listen, point at the obvious symptoms of it before they even happen, but when they do, it is dismissed. That is why we are the invisible victims of invisible abuse. Parental Alienation made my kids and me invisible to each other.

Parental Alienation made me an invisible parent.

Chapter 2:
The mechanics of Alienation

While I have written about Parental Alienation as invisible abuse, the mechanism by which the alienator abuses the alienated parent is not invisible at all. It's visible if you know how to look for it, which is the problem, because until you realise it is happening to you can't possibly know how to look for it. It is also not a series of events, a logical progression that can be traced from A to B and so on.

The Family Courts – like all courts – use basic processes that come from the need to deal with clear breaches of law, whether that is a breach of contract or a breach of criminal law. They use lawyers for both sides of the court action, barristers make arguments based on case law and statues, and use a judge to make a ruling. However, as I will show in later chapters, this approach works for contract disputes or criminal cases much better than complex family or relationship issues. This is because Family Law cases are about relationships, not breaches of law or contracts.

Court cases rely on events, times, places and above all,

specifics. However Parental Alienation is seldom about specifics like that. Sure, there are many events, times and places where alienation takes place, but the process takes years and assumes so many different forms, from the resident abuser parent's attitude and behaviour towards the children when they talk about the alienated parent, through to the abuser actively interrupting the alienated parent's time with the kids through non-compliance with contact agreements, or calling the kids frequently, or scheduling appointments or trips during contact.

At the time, looking back, I found my ex-wife's constant telephone calls to the kids very frustrating and annoying. I didn't realise it was part of a programme of alienation. At various events unfolded in their lives, I became deeply concerned about how well my kids were being safeguarded at home and at school, however I found out about the events in trickle of lawyers' letters or emails that took deciphering and chasing-up with my time to get to the bottom of the problems and find out what was going on. Looking back, I became aware of things my children did or said, or my ex-wife's comments, or my ex-fiancée's behaviour (who was in contact with my ex-wife, more than I could possibly know) that didn't add up. And as my case progressed over the best part of three years in court, I became aware that my ex-wife and her legal team were actively trying to block the work of court-appointed experts and assessors, or interfering with the process to delay proceedings to the point of sabotaging them.

I can see now that they indicate a pattern of behaviour towards me that typifies the abuse of Parental Alienation.

All of those things became clear over time, and with hindsight. However, at the time it feels like lots of different problems, taking place in no particular order, and applying to unrelated aspects of my attempts to see my children. It didn't occur to me, for example, that my ex-wife would instruct my children's school, or my children's GP or my children's therapists to refuse to share information with me. It didn't occur to me that schools, therapists or GPs could be so poorly trained in privacy law and data protection that they would withhold information I was legally entitled to. It certainly never occurred to me that my ex-wife's lawyers would use terminology that was intended to disguise the truth behind a smokescreen of jargon, and I never expected court-appointed experts to complain to the courts that my ex-wife and her team were obstructing them in their work.

Finally, it never occurred to me at the outset that I would see a different judge almost every time in court, or that judge would eventually make a ruling that basically set in stone the level of contact (non-existent) as the outcome of my case, that was the same level of contact that drove me to court in the first place.

What I have learned from all of this is the mechanism by which one parent can abuse the other, ruin their life and by proxy, the lives of children too. It answers an important question for people reading who haven't been alienated themselves, namely, 'Why didn't you stop it from happening?'

That is, of course, an obvious but thoughtless question. It is as pointless as asking any victim of abuse why they didn't stop it. The answer is different for everyone, and different in every different circumstance. In mine, honestly, by the time I realised I was being alienated I couldn't stop it. It's a slow moving car crash. However, my biggest challenge – the same that many alienated parents experience – is convincing the courts that what I can see so clearly, is the evidence they can't seem to see at all. If that sounds confusing, let me put it another way.

Have you ever seen a close-up magician, doing card tricks at your table at a wedding or a conference dinner? They are masters of misdirection. They are very adept and make you look where they want you to look, or play with the deck in such a way to steer you to pick a certain card and so on. If you don't know what you are looking at, you are easily tricked into thinking what they have done is all but impossible. That's the Family Court. Easily misdirected, distracted and tricked.

Now, have you ever seen a close-up magician when you have a friend sitting alongside you who is also a magician? Totally different experience. I have a good friend who is a regular performer at the Edinburgh Festival, doing street card tricks. He sat next to me at a trade show dinner once and whispered in my ear a running commentary at the table magician. This guy was good, my friend was impressed, but he could predict each trick by the book, as any trained magician can. That's an alienated parent. They know the tricks, so they know how it works.

So allow me, now, to explain how abusive resident parents and their lawyers trick the courts into permitting Parental Alienation to take place right under their noses.

The lawyers know how to work the system for profit

This is not a case of sour grapes. Consider the basic logic of the situation regarding Parental Alienation and court cases, as conducted through Family Law firms. Parental Alienation is not new or unusual. Most family lawyers will have experienced it or at least, messy and bitter children proceedings that come close. They all know one unarguable fact of these kinds of cases, they seldom address the issue to the satisfaction of the non-resident parent. They don't tell you that, of course, they will tell you that you have a case and you have a chance, but in reality, you are fighting an uphill battle from day one. In most cases, the non-resident parent runs out of money before the case receives a final ruling from a judge. In most cases that receive a final ruling from a judge, that ruling is in line with the Cafcass report, which is usually fixing the status quo of the contact level at the outset of the case.

In Parental Alienation, this means your state of non-contact is fixed into indirect contact orders or some such fudge that means you can send an email or a letter to your kids via the abuser resident parent. It's a joke. It is however, well known in the Family Law industry that you should go to court only ever as a last resort, the odds are against you and more to the point, the restoration of contact can take years even in the unlikely event you are successful in court. And of course, those years enable the abuser to manipulate your kids even further, which means the longer the delay the harder it becomes to recommence contact anyway.

Meanwhile, for the abuser resident parent, their lawyers have a large bag of tricks they can use to wreck your attempts to see your kids. Delaying tactics are central, however, so are using every opportunity to make counter allegations and appeal decisions, ask for supplementary hearings or argue over court-appointees. They also have a large vocabulary that is designed to hide major issues and massively distort innocent events to look bad. They also know – and I am certain make off the record advice to do so – that it is possible to completely sidestep the courts by missing appointments, claiming data protection issues, pretending to lose files and so on.

Rather than list all the ways I experienced these things, I would refer you to look at the Law Society's own work in the area, where senior judges in their Family Law working group have published recent reports about the rising use of Family Court in children cases. Senior judges reporting on the issue state the legal profession should be steering families away from court, not encouraging legal action in place of cooperative parenting and mediation. Yet cases continue to rise, without offering any improvement in the lives of the children, or the parents who bring cases there.

I go into these issues – and how we can fix them with a better, smarter system, later in the book. For now, let's break down the mechanisms lawyers and their clients use to misdirect the court and non-resident parents.

Obfuscation

Obfuscation means the action of making something obscure, unclear or unintelligible. It's a strange word to explain something that is very simple. Once you claim Parental Alienation, your abusive ex-partner will work with their legal team to hide information about the kids from you, or misrepresent events involving you and your kids to make you look bad in court. This twisting of events and words to make a case extends beyond the lawyers for sure. It's a bias. An axe to grind. I can recall one time, early in our divorced lives, when my ex-wife called me up and told me to stop telling the kids they had a great mother because it was giving them false hope that we would get back together. Imagine that. Saying nice things about the abuser resident parent is used against you. Supposing I hadn't? Would she complain I didn't support her or appreciate her? If I criticised her – which I did in a temper when I discovered my ex-wife had helped my fiancée steal money and flee the country – this was brought up in court time and again as some egregious character assassination.

Twisting words, twisting events: it's all predictable in the case of an acrimonious battle for contact I suppose, but in my case the lawyers took it to a new and quite unbelievable level. I have two examples to illustrate this point, which are linked but unrelated. I will explain that in due course, but it serves as an excellent illustration of the way that alienation through obfuscation comes at you from different angles.

The first is a classic case of obfuscation to try and prevent me from finding out about serious safeguarding issues that would undoubtedly have supported my case that the children were not being adequately supervised by my ex-wife, and would be better with shared care or residency with me. It refers to an incident of online grooming – where a sexual predator groomed one of my kids and a friend to share nude pictures aged 13. This predator then attempted to blackmail my child into sending more explicit pictures. There was a police investigation, it was a criminal offence.

I first heard of this from the school, who called me to make me aware there had been an internet situation. They didn't explain it, just that the kids had been told about the dangers of sharing information with strangers online, and it was all taken care of. It sounded like some sort of social media thing, like sending round adult jokes or whatever. They didn't give me details, merely my child and a friend had been involved in some sort of online incident and it was all over now. It wasn't. When I demanded more information, the school retreated behind data protection. I argued (correctly) that this didn't apply to a 13 year old in that sense, and they retreated behind the argument that my statutory right as a parent with parental responsibility didn't apply because they were a private school, and the legislation only applies to state schools.

They had, I believe, been told not to share the full story with me by my ex-wife who was chair of the PTA at the school. I had no choice but to ask her for information. She said much the same via email, so I was forced to resort to lawyers to write demanding the full story. The reply, from her legal team, said this:

'We write to inform you of an incident in relation to inappropriate use of the internet involving the parties' children at our client's home over the weekend'

The words 'inappropriate use of the internet' were used to describe an act of criminal sexual abuse, which at the time they used, that term was under investigation by the police. It is akin to describing a stabbing as inappropriate use of a knife or drug dealing as inappropriate sale of chemicals. Was this event inappropriate use of the internet? Sending around memes on the office email, or looking at porn websites in your lunch break is inappropriate use of the internet. Criminal acts of a sexual nature with children is something quite different – possibly even worse than some cases of murder or manslaughter from the point of view that most people couldn't imagine themselves doing it. Whereas you might imagine a scenario where you commit murder – for example, if you got your hands on the bastard who sexually abused your kids. We might regret it, but we know people lose their tempers and bad things happen. We also know people don't accidentally ask children for nude pictures. That is beyond inappropriate. This example shows how a lawyer could misrepresent information to a point where it is, to all intents and purposes, a lie.

My case is full of examples like that. It makes you wonder what motivated the lawyers, and my ex-wife, to hide behind a smokescreen of jargon like that. The grooming happened at her home, on her watch. I argued the kids weren't being properly supervised. This would have been a good example of what I meant. And so they buried sexual abuse. It is as dishonest as it is disgusting.

The second example of obfuscation is linked to this, designed to discredit me, or worse, incriminate me with false accusations of violence. I saw my kids after the grooming event. I hadn't seen them for nearly two years before, but we live in the same town, so it was highly possible or even probable that at some point we could bump into each other. There was no non-contact order or injunction against me seeing them, so it is not as though I had been told if I saw them I was to avoid them or anything else. There was never any question about my integrity or safeguarding concerns regarding seeing my kids.

So it was not inevitable, but highly likely at some point I could see them out and about, and in this case, I saw them coming out of the supermarket as I was going in. We said hi. They were fine. I hugged them. I especially hugged the one that had been abused online, and asked about how they were doing. It was emotional, as you can imagine, heartbreaking for me. It wasn't a big drama, or any drama, and it lasted a few short minutes. Too short. One of the last times I ever saw them.

My ex-wife's legal team were straight on me, with a letter that described my hugging the kids as follows:

'Your client approached them, held one child in a crooked arm neck lock, he then let go and held the other in the same manner. They tried repeatedly to pull his arm away and he put it back in the same position.'

This was then referred to later as a headlock. And then, when I demanded the supermarket CCTV was examined to prove it was nothing of the sort, my ex-wife's solicitors said that it was not a neck lock, nor a headlock, but 'excessive hugging'.

Again, what happens is the courts are presented with a court bundle that has letters from lawyers downplaying criminal acts, and exaggerating hugs into neck locks and headlocks. There is, for each false claim a pile of papers from my lawyers challenging it. However, what is the end result? A debate over which is right? No. There is the overwhelming impression that I was making accusations against my ex-wife, and I was bullying my kids. I wasn't. I was trying to learn the truth about one child and every parent's worst internet nightmare. I also saw my estranged kids and hugged them.

I experienced one more egregious case of obfuscation from Cafcass. The incident referred to a time I clipped one of my kids across the top of their head – as my mum did with me as a child – when they were jumping off their bed at midnight with friends and getting overexcited. After a few times of telling them to stop, I shouted upstairs and told my overexcited child to come downstairs immediately – I was not only responsible for my own children's safety but also for that of their friends. I tapped one of the kids on the head as I made myself heard. They didn't cry. They didn't shriek. It didn't hurt. It was not a smack, or a punishment. I am not saying it was good parenting, but it wasn't a big deal. This was described by Cafcass as a 'physical assault' and I had 'physically assaulted' my child. That is not what physical assault means, however it did huge damage. There were no safeguarding claims about me. No claims of abuse or anything else. It was an innocent act of disciplining a naughty child who was an inch away from breaking her collarbone with horseplay and was completely ignoring me. Turning a tap on the head into a physical assault is more obfuscation. It's like the whole Family Law courts speaks in a language of melodrama and exaggeration.

The point of the obfuscation tactic is simple enough to grasp. It casts a shadow of doubt over your case. It means when I argue there are safeguarding concerns the judge (as in my case) will refer to the court papers and acknowledge there were issues, but stop short of noticing how my ex-wife's legal team attempted to hide the truth or distort it. Parental Alienation requires both of those things – hiding the truth of bad care and safeguarding, combined with distorting the view of the non-resident parent to make them appear angry, violent, or at the very least not someone who should be in the lives of their children.

It works. It also makes the non-resident parent more paranoid than they need to be. Imagine if your child had been sexually abused and it was referred to as inappropriate internet use. That seems so far away from describing it properly, what else could be lurking behind their words? It throws you into a world where you have to write via your lawyers over every little thing that happens, in case you miss something major. It is abuse, and an abuser tactic that comes from the lawyers who are making fees from the situation as much as the abuser resident parent.

Misdirection

Earlier this year there was a high-profile resignation by a Family Court judge, I will go into that at a later stage in the book because the example sums up a lot of what is wrong about the courts. However, for this section, I want to focus on one of his parting remarks. He referred to Family Court processes as being characterised by 'a tendency to concentrate resources on the unnecessary, complicating the simple and pandering to agendas which are at odds with reality or a diversion at best.' In other words, misdirecting the court's attention to focus on the wrong issues. This observation feels very accurate in my experience.

Misdirection is more subtle than obfuscation. It doesn't misrepresent issues to give one side in a dispute over contact arrangements an advantage of some sort, instead the misdirection ties you and your legal team up in knots trying to deal with problems which are irrelevant to the crux of your case. For me, I was trying to get contact with my children, however, in order to complicate that process, my ex-wife and her legal team created all sorts of obstacles along the way which only served to divert my attention away from seeing my kids.

The examples I am about to give should be prefaced by one, clear, unarguable fact: I had a legal right to information regarding my children and their wellbeing, called Parental Responsibility. Parental Responsibility is the legal term for the rights, duties and responsibilities that parents have for their children. It means the parent is responsible for ensuring that the child is cared for and for protecting and maintaining the child. Parental Responsibility is not lost when you get divorced. It is not lost if you are non-resident. If you are married to your wife or named on the birth certificate as the father, as I was, you have Parental Responsibility. Unless that changes, due to a court ruling of some sort that prohibits you from exercising your parental responsibility – which it might if you are convicted of a crime or have problems like addiction that means you represent a safeguarding risk to your kids – you have the same legal right to information about your children and to have a part in important decisions as the other, resident parent.

In my case, that Parental Responsibility meant I had a right to information regarding my kids, which in many cases I was denied. The denials were a result of the school, GP and therapists involved in my kids' case being misdirected over the matter of data protection and consent to share data. Time and again, when I approached my kids' school, GP and various therapists and counsellors, asking for updates on their progress, they denied me on the grounds of data protection. Time and again, I asserted my legal right to the information as a responsible parent, a right that is enshrined in law. They refused me.

You might ask how that is even possible, but that question is as redundant as asking 'Why didn't you stop it from happening?' which I have heard many times. What are you supposed to do to stop it? It goes like this:

> **Step 1:** *You request information – the school refuses on data privacy grounds.*
>
> **Step 2:** *You ask again, explaining your rights – they refuse because they say your kids haven't consented to you having that information.*
>
> **Step 3:** *You explain you don't need their consent, because you have parental responsibility and they are minors aged 13 – the school claims they have the right to withhold consent over personal data.*
>
> **Step 4:** *You argue they do not have the right to withhold consent over information you are legally entitled to – the school argues they do, and refer you to the Information Commissioner's Office guidance on data protection, which doesn't apply.*
>
> **Step 5:** *Your lawyers demand the information – the school refuses and the cycle begins again.*
>
> **Step 6:** *After months of argument, you go to court to seek a court order to share the information requested. The court date takes a year to come through, during which time the school continues to withhold information. They are then ordered by the court to release the*

*information, which they do, almost two years after
you requested it, by which time your kids are worse
off and your relationship with them has deteriorated
beyond the point you can hope to recover it.*

I was arguing that there were safeguarding concerns over my ex-wife's care for my kids. I needed the information at school regarding their own safeguarding records which showed – as we know, criminal internet abuse, and also self-harming incidents. I was denied this information long enough to mean when I got it, it was useless because the events were in the past and the judge decided they were over and done with by the time he ruled against a change of residence.

The issue of self-harming, which affected one of my kids, was deeply disturbing. However, when I approached the GP to get their assessment of the reasons why, the severity, and the underlying mental health of my child I hit the same data privacy roadblocks.

Of course, bound up in the concept of data protection is consent. My children were deemed competent and capable of consenting to medical treatment or interventions (called Gillick Competent) and also capable of having their own legal representation, which I agreed to. At the time, I believed that if they had their own lawyer it would mean they could speak up for themselves without my ex-wife's legal team turning everything into jargon and half-truths.

However, this was more misdirection.

The children were never assessed in terms of their ability to consent (Gillick Competence) by the GP, or the therapist, or the counsellor or the school. There was never a risk assessment made over their situation regarding the online grooming, or the self-harm. There was never a formal procedure of any sort that found my children to be competent, and therefore granting them the right to consent or withhold consent over their GP records, or therapy notes, or anything else. The truth is at each turn, with my kids aged 13, their lawyer did not advise their GP, school or any other professional that there was a court order to the effect they were to share all the information I requested and more with a court-appointed child consultant psychiatrist who was ordered to assess my kids, specifically with regard to my claims of Parental Alienation and my children's psychological state.

To be clear, my kids, who were diagnosed with anxiety and depression and were by that point attending a private clinic, who had been abused by an online predator and had self-harmed, were subject to a court-ordered assessment by an expert in the field. The expert was granted authority to provide a risk assessment of the kids and a psychiatric assessment, however, despite this he was denied access to my children's GP and therapist on the grounds of consent.

The court-appointed expert complained, asking how they could refuse consent when they don't even know what is being asked for? After all, they hadn't seen the court order, so how could they refuse it? He eventually wrote to me, with the most astonishing email:

'In almost 30 years as a consultant I have never previously been asked to write psychiatric reports on people to whose records I have been denied access. These children are not yet 14. They have not seen the LOI, and nor has the GP. How can their Gillick competence be

assessed when neither they nor the assessor is fully informed about the issues to be determined? I need you please to go back to Court and get me full access to the GP records and counselling records of both …'

This man was a leading child consultant psychiatrist, an expert on Parental Alienation, and my best hope for getting the kids the help and support they needed. They were in a bad way, depressed, anxious, harmed. This man was ordered by the courts to help and like me, was denied the opportunity through data protection issues and theoretical arguments over consent that were never proven, never assessed and wouldn't have stood up in court. However, it would have taken me many months, maybe over a year or more to get the court to order the GP to hand over records. Meanwhile, the kids were deteriorating mentally and being brainwashed by my ex-wife. Time is a luxury alienated parents don't have. Which is the final key mechanism for abusers to alienate the non-resident parent.

Incidentally, the practice of using consent and data protection arguments to block a non-resident parent is a well-known facet of Parental Alienation cases. It is called Information Gatekeeping. It is a means by which the non-resident parent is prevented from being present or engaged in the child's life when they need it most. In my case, if my kids turn around and ask me, 'Where were you when I was being abused and needed protection?' The answer is what? Your mother didn't tell me? The school wouldn't tell me? What can I say? They needed me and I wasn't there. And there is nothing I can do to make that right. I had to fight for everything, just to know how my kids were doing.

Information Gatekeeping is abuse. I was wracked with worry and almost consumed by stress trying to find out what had happened to them.

Blocking the process to run-down the clock

The example above, where a court order is refused on grounds of data protection or consent that wouldn't stand up in court, is a classic way of playing for time. It is one of the ways an abuser resident parent can use the Family Court process to their advantage. It's easy to see why this is so effective. Your children are growing up, and they get older so their ability to consent or be deemed competent increases. By the time they are 14 or 15, it's very hard to argue they don't know their own minds. And if they have made up their minds that they never want to see their mother or father again there is not much that can be done about it. A six year old can be ordered into mediation or family therapy, or even a change of residence because they aren't capable of consenting to care in complex disputes. A 14 or 15 year old can refuse and their ability to run away or resist is strong. So the abuser resident parent – and their lawyers – know winning their case is as much about time as anything else.

There is an old saying, that justice delayed is justice denied and this is never more true than in Parental Alienation cases. However, whereas we have laws in place to prevent the delay of justice in criminal cases, in Family Law, the overburdened courts run at a glacial pace. This means that each time you win the right to a court order or an assessment or another avenue that will advance your case, you lose another chunk of time. The more time passes, the more alienated you become. The harder it is to reconnect with your kids, and the less likely they are to see you. This is based on the simple principle that once they have been away from you for long enough, regardless of the reasons why, seeing you again is deemed to be more traumatic for them than keeping the status quo. In other words, the damage is done, and the court won't rule to address it. When my case ended, my kids were nearly 15. If I had carried on fighting, they might well have become adults before a resolution was found, but even if not, there is a point at which the stress of repeated court interventions is deemed to be worse than whatever caused them. In my case, whether I had been alienated or not became irrelevant, after three years of court cases and assessments, the judge put a stop to it because the Cafcass Guardian said the case had gone on long enough.

The scenario time and again is like this:

1. *You make an argument in court, the court upholds it and orders an assessment or an intervention. The other side insists that both sides reach an agreement on the process, i.e. the person making the assessment or the nature of the intervention (therapy, fact finding or whatever).*

2. *The assessment or intervention delivers a report back to the court, the outcome of which is more legal arguments which prolong the case by needing another hearing or more assessments.*

3. *A new date is set for 6–12 months' time.*

4. *Repeat as long as the court allows you to, unless the kids are old enough now for the court to rule that regardless of what has happened, it's too late to do*

> *anything about it because they have been in their*
> *current situation for years and the stress of legal action*
> *is worse than alienation.*

Now you might expect me, at this point, to say that in the end the reports were all written but it was too late. However, that wasn't true. In Family Law, a court order might be legally binding but it doesn't mean people comply with it. Quite the reverse. As I have noted, the consultant child psychiatrist felt he was being blocked and asked me to get a new court order forcing my kids' GP, counsellor and therapist to hand over their notes because he couldn't fulfil his obligations to perform the court-ordered assessments without them. However, I couldn't do that because it would have taken even more time, which I didn't have. With the court date fast approaching, in the end, the expert wrote a report based on a large amount of missing information which in his own words meant 'I will have to complete my report without the information that I need.'

I have correspondence between the expert and my children's lawyer, their therapist, their GP and their counsellor. In each case, he says he had court-ordered authority, and in each case they make some indirect reply like referring it to their legal team, or arguing consent, or in one case the counsellor saying she will have to talk to the children's lawyer to check what she can and can't say. That last one was a real eye-opener. The court order is the law, it is the mechanism by which the law orders people to comply with processes, the idea that someone would refuse to comply with a court order without consulting one of the legal parties' lawyers is as absurd as a witness in a trial refusing to answer questions without consulting with the defendant's lawyer first.

This is the effect of misdirection, but it speaks to another tactic which is running down the clock and blocking the court. Nobody refused to hand over information without a reason – they cited data protection, consent, referring to their own line manager or legal team for confirmation – however in each case it was using a lower authority to challenge the court. There's no way to escalate it, without seeking another court order. There is no enforcement either. You can simply refuse to comply with a court order for some credible yet wrong reason, and there is nothing much that can be done there and then.

The same is true of non-appearance at assessments or interviews ordered by the court. In my case, my ex-wife didn't come to the Cafcass meeting we were both ordered to attend. She confirmed it, twice, by phone and writing. She then simply never showed up and never answered her phone. This meant the Cafcass assessors never asked us both questions about our situation, and I never got the chance to raise my concerns with her in person, before someone who was supposed to be assessing my claims that she was alienating me through my kids. I believe if she had come, she would have said things that raised doubts and were recorded as such over her claim of simply supporting my kids' own wishes, as she did in every other interview she attended.

Similarly, the court ordered the consultant child psychologist to interview the kids with me, so he could assess the way they related to me. They refused to attend that session, and so there was never a chance for him to assess their attitude towards me or judge their hostility in person. Remember, Parental Alienation is measured by children displaying unreasonable or unjustified hostility against one parent. That can't be assessed unless they can be seen with that parent. In my case, whenever I saw my kids they were fine. They weren't scared of me, they didn't panic. They said they did, my ex-wife said they did, but they didn't. How could I get a witness to that? A court order! An assessment where an expert could see them with me and make a decision that they weren't having panic attacks or whatever like they claimed. However, by refusing to attend the assessment, there can be no witnesses to validate the non-resident parent's testimony before the court.

I wonder what my ex-wife's lawyer said about it. Did they advise her to turn up to that meeting at all costs, or did they suggest if she missed it that would be fine? I wonder if my kids' lawyer (appointed at my ex-wife's suggestion) advised the counsellor, the therapist or the GP involved to comply with the court order or refuse on the grounds of competence or data protection? It is impossible to know, however, what I do know is the clock never stopped ticking and when the final assessments were considered by the court, they had been compiled without the notes and testimony that was ordered by the court. Which renders them useless, or at least, questionable. These assessments became expensive wastes of time, expensive in terms of the legal fees that were charged and the time they cost me.

When I hired my first barrister in this case, we discussed a fact finding order. The idea was simple, it often happens in cases, the judge can order an investigation to establish the facts of a case – in my example, the fact I hadn't seen my kids for months and they didn't want to see me for some trivial reasons, which my ex-wife supported. My barrister advised me against it. She said it would waste too much time and explained to me that in cases of family breakdown and alienation, it was critical to re-establish contact as quickly as possible. She told me that a single divorced father was already 'two-nil down at half time with no goalie' and the best thing I could do was get into family therapy asap. Fact finding would cause delays.

What happened in the meantime was my ex-wife's team proposed more delaying tactics, including family therapy which didn't include me because of lengthy wishes and feelings work with the kids that merely took up more precious time. Then I learned of more problems, grooming, self-harm, therapy I didn't agree to, information was denied to me despite my rights, and so on. When it finally came to the crunch, my kids refused to be assessed, my ex-wife missed a critical assessment, and the court ordered expert hit a wall of bureaucratic time wasting that all but killed my last, best hope at resolution.

The mechanics of Parental Alienation – the triumph of the letter of the law over the spirit

A Family Law expert – Oliver Cyriax – advises people 'Do not expect anything in the court process to be true, or subjected to conventional or meaningful scrutiny … The general pattern of court cases is deferral, to roll the case forwards still unresolved to another hearing … The issue of proceedings does generally make things start to happen. More usually, it stops things from happening, i.e. it tends to freeze contact at whatever level it was before the issue of proceedings – until the main hearing which is likely to be a good six months distant.'

Six months, and then another deferral, and another. In my case I saw six judges over almost three years, overlapping in some cases where I was seeking an order for information that was withheld by the school.

How many deferrals before your kids aren't kids anymore? Not many. My kids were 11 when we broke contact, 14 nearly 15 when we received the final ruling that fixed contact at the level it was before I started the court case, or even worse.

There was no scrutiny.

The issuing of court orders stopped things from happening in many respects.

What happened to me was a blend of obfuscation, misdirection and blocking to run down the clock. This is what happens to every alienated parent, one way or another. This is because there is no good reason for a complete cut-off from your kids, so there can be no good reasons for the court failing. It's down to flawed processes and lawyers who know how to work the system to keep the case from resolving quickly or clearly. They know that unless you run out of money, the case will eventually be ruled as too much for the kids. All they have to do is make sure whatever you try to make happen, they try to delay it from happening. All they have to do is scare witnesses with data protection rules or concepts like consent, and they know it's over. In these days where data privacy and GDPR are commonplace issues, where every website has cookies and consent, and where the news is full of people claiming they have been abused regarding consent in some way, there is a climate of fear that is easy to exploit.

Obfuscation, misdirection, blocking until the time runs out.

That is how I was alienated from my kids.

Working the system and lawyers getting rich from a growth market? Does that sound cynical? It does if an alienated parent says it, perhaps, but when the top judges in the country more or less say the same in a report – as the Law Society did earlier this year – it's a call for reform of an archaic system that doesn't work.

To put that another way, the letter of the law in the Family Court beats the spirit of it. The Children Act clearly states a relationship with both parents – where there are no safeguarding issues – furthers the welfare of the child. That is the spirit of the law. Refusing to share information about sexual predators exploiting the kids in one parent's home, is the letter of privacy law perhaps. It is not in keeping with the spirit of the law if it is used to stop an alienated parent from seeing his kids. An endless round of court orders and missed meetings might be the letter of the law, but not in the spirit of the law if you haven't seen your kids for months or years. Ruling to end contact because the endless merry-go-round of court orders and appeals is stressful for the kids is not in keeping with the spirit of the law, because parental alienation is bad for them. Their welfare is not furthered by never seeing one parent in a normal healthy relationship.

My kids suffered because of our alienation. I suffered. And when the court ordered an investigation, the people who were supposed to be helping didn't want to know. They refused to help the court resolve the problem, and perhaps without realising it, sided with my ex-wife, who was abusing me and the kids. That isn't justice, it's paying by the hour for lawyers to help you commit domestic abuse against your ex-partner. They are experts with incredible skills and tools at their disposal to ensure you run out of time, or money, or both before you can restore a parental relationship. That is a broken system. And that term is apt because the system breaks relationships, lives, hearts and childhoods.

It isn't just a broken system, it is a system that breaks.

Chapter 3:
There is no smoking gun

I wish I could look back over my story and say, *'That's it! That's the moment when it happened! That's where my ex-wife turned my kids against me and I became alienated.'* You know, like one of those *A-ha!* reveal moments at the end of an old Agatha Christie story when the killer is unmasked by Poirot or Miss Marple.

Things don't happen like that in real life.

In real life events are blurred and obscured by emotions and time. In real life you don't experience the story as a logical sequence of events, you can't know how one thing leads to another while they are happening. You might look back one day and think you see the smoking gun moment, but the next day it's different. As more of the pieces fall into place, the moment where it all went wrong and the evidence of your alienation seems to move around from one time or event to another. That is because with hindsight, you realise Parental Alienation isn't a single event, it is a sequence of events. A dynamic, a relationship gone bad. There is no singular moment when it all went wrong.

The one thing that doesn't change as you sift through events in your mind, however, is the pain of losing your children. That sick feeling in the pit of your stomach. Not just for yourself, but for your kids. They might not experience the pain of loss like you do, the raw grief of a parent, but they experience the effects of their pain in their lives. It is what experts in child mental health refer to as *externalising* and *internalising* behaviours. Externalising behaviours are things like anger issues, behavioural problems at school and extreme thrill-seeking or substance abuse. Internalising behaviours are things like anxiety, depression, self-harm, anorexia and getting into abusive relationships and so on.

My children have experienced things you wouldn't want for your own kids. Self-harm and grooming by an online predator and blackmailer. They have suffered anxiety and depression. They have been aggressive and antisocial – shouting fuck off at their former academic tutor and me in a café. These are typical internalising and externalising behaviours brought on by the emotional trauma of Parental Alienation.

Seeing your children go through that is shocking, and I blame the abuse they suffered. It has to come out one way or another. A hugely influential study from the University College London (UCL) Centre for Longitudinal Studies looked at over 19,000 children over a period of 13 years from 9 months to age 14. This study showed a hugely significant correlation of increased anxiety, withdrawal and dysphoria (general unease or dissatisfaction with life) in girls and increased aggression, impulsiveness and disruptive behaviour in boys as they reach adolescence. What happened to my kids was, for want of a better word, predictable.

I warned the school, I warned my ex-wife of the risks.

They ignored me.

I raised it in court.

My concerns were largely dismissed.

Bad things happened to my kids. Things that shape their experience of life now.

I can look back now and clearly identify moments where the Parental Alienation began, but they aren't a smoking gun so much as glimpses of a lighthouse in the fog. What I mean is just like that, they are just a glimpse of what was really happening. To see the bigger picture, you have to consider the evidence of my children, their mother and the other voices who spoke up for and against my claims of alienation at the time.

I realise that at this point, you have just my word to go on. And my words are as subject to cognitive bias as anyone else's, it's impossible to be objective about your own lived experience of events because that is a subjective experience. So how can I write a credible book about my experiences. Isn't it all just subjective?

How could I prove Parental Alienation, which is by definition something that happens when I am not there to witness it, to children I am not in contact with by an abuser I can't see or prove is abusing them? It is all but impossible to prove, at least, that's certainly how the courts saw it. In the eyes of the courts, my claim of Parental Alienation was completely lacking in substance, it was conjecture and that was that.

My answer to that challenge of eliminating perspective, or cognitive bias, or whatever you want to call it is simple. You can't know what you don't know. You can't witness things unless you witness them. And anyway, that sort of proof doesn't work for Parental Alienation because it can't be reliably proven within the court process anyway. I will discuss that in a later chapter in more depth, but for the moment, let's just remember there is no statutory recognition of Parental Alienation as domestic abuse. Without that, it can't be proven. You can't prove something in a court of law if you can't even define how it works at anything other than a very abstract level.

It's like saying you acknowledge that drunk drivers crash cars, but you can't define the reasons why they crash and sober people don't, or how to measure if someone is drunk. It is impossible. You can only prove drunk drivers crash more if you can define the cause of the crash, the effect of alcohol consumption on driving ability and measure how much alcohol the driver has consumed. In other words, you need a process to work out what happened. For Parental Alienation, that process doesn't exist in the UK courts. It is just one person's word against another.

There is no one definition of Parental Alienation that is recognised by social workers, medics, psychologists, therapists, lawyers and judges. Without a shared, singular definition there can be no measures or scales applied to make accurate assessments that can be peer reviewed. Without some sort of clear-cut, generalisable assessment or measurement that all parties can agree to abide by, there can only ever be a circular debate over the meaning of terms. Parental Alienation needs a practical assessment that can only come after everyone agrees on what it is, and how to measure it or test for it in some way. Like my drunk driver example. That milestone is a long way off for alienated parents.

It is deeply ironic that it's only once a judge has ruled that you and your children haven't been the victim of Parental Alienation, then you finally have enough information to make the strongest case that you have. The reason for that is as obvious as it is shocking. It is only at the end, when the Judge dismissed your allegations of Parental Alienation, when you can see the totality of reasons your children have given for cutting you out of their lives. It is also only then, when you can compare the reasons they gave when it all began have grown or changed - something which can only happen under the influence of the parent they have seen, not the one who is estranged from them.

The Hug-Headlock Test

I call this framework for measuring the degree of Parental Alienation influence that my ex-wife exerted over my kids *The Hug-Headlock Test* because it's always easier to turn around in hindsight and see if something innocent has been turned into something sinister. It shows how psychological manipulation can change events from one thing to another in the mind of a child, and the courts. In order to understand how this thinking tool works, you need to understand the nature of the Family Court process in cases like mine. My experience of the *Hug-Headlock* is of course, the experience of obfuscation, however in the mind of a child it is more than that. It is telling them their memory is wrong, and brainwashing them into believing their experience of life is somehow faulty and their own judgement is unreliable. They know I didn't headlock them, but they were told I did.

The Family Court process is not – as people often imagine – like other more widely understood court procedures like

criminal or other civil trials. In those cases there is an event –
or a sequence of events – that are very clearly defined in law.
However, in the Family Court process things are less clear
cut. It is about relationships, which inevitably means relying
on the opinions and testimony of the people involved about
complex, ongoing situations.

This is why the judgements of the private Family Courts
are expressed through different kinds of mechanisms from
other public court proceedings. The Family Courts use
court orders, and various other legal mechanisms – like
child arrangement or contact orders – that may be enforced
in extreme cases by the police or social worker intervention.
However, where the process breaks down is the court orders
themselves are inherently weak and often fail to bring about
positive change. The Family Court is heavily reliant on the
opinions of the people involved in the process – the authors
of the court assessments who may or may not be an expert
or qualified to give an opinion – and slow to change because
they rely heavily on previous judgements and case law.

There are many complaints raised over the inequalities
in the system and bias against certain groups, not just by
alienated parents or fathers but people of colour, trans men
and women, LGBTQ parents and so on. There are many
groups that claim an unfair bias or a system that isn't fit
for purpose. I'm no expert and I can't comment on the
experience of other people in the process, but I can say this
is my experience and often raised as a common experience
of other people alleging Parental Alienation.

In my case, the years of court action ended with an
indirect contact order. In this order, I was denied permission

to contact my children directly. I was told I could write once per month only, however I had to send the letters to my ex-wife and she would decide what happened to them. I still can't quite believe it. I had claimed Parental Alienation which is a form of domestic abuse. The court ordered solution was to make the person I had accused of abuse responsible for facilitating measures designed to address the alienation I was claiming?

It was actually even worse than that. In a previous ruling which led to my final hearing, the judge had ordered my ex-wife to write to me monthly to keep me up to date with what my kids were doing. In the final case she argued that writing to me was 'onerous' and so the judge changed it to quarterly. So not only was she put in charge of contact with my kids, she also was only obliged to write to me every three months to tell me how they were doing.

Think about the real-world practicality of that for a moment. It doesn't make sense. It's not a question of assuming my ex-wife's guilt or innocence, it's a simple question of fairness. Is it fair to ask someone who was unfairly accused to help their accuser? No. That's placing them in an unfair position because they might have good reason to object to helping the person who had unjustly accused them and dragged them through the courts. Or, if they were an abuser, who was deliberately trying to break contact between me and my kids, putting them in control of contact between us would be absurd. In either case, the judgement has a high chance of failure in practical terms.

My ex-wife was not proven to be the abuser. My claims of Parental Alienation were dismissed. However, think about the absurdity of the big picture of the court ruling. Guilty or not, I had accused her and she had fought me over it for almost four years. We were either side of an acrimonious legal battle. Worse, I had claimed to be a victim of abuse, along with my alienated children, a form of abuse where the abuser destroys the relationship between a parent and their children. The court-ordered response was to place the alleged abuser in sole charge of the relationship between me and my children, someone who at the very least was the wounded party in nasty legal battle that had run on for years.

It is hard to imagine a situation where anyone else accused of physical abuse would end up as the court-ordered person responsible for the physical health of their accuser. Or a situation where someone accused of child sex abuse would be placed in charge of bathing the child who accused them. It might shock you to learn that there are many tragic cases where court-ordered unsupervised contact with parents accused of abuse have resulted with the death of children at the hands of the abuser, even with the involvement of Cafcass, social services, schools and charities in those cases. The system isn't just impractical and unworkable at times, it is sometimes negligent and ends in tragedy.

These reasons explain why, as I write this, over 120 MPs have called for an urgent review of abusive parents' access to children. Reforming the Family Court processes regarding domestic abuse is the reason why a new Domestic Abuse framework is passing through Parliament, and why for the first time, Parental Alienation is included in the definitions of abuse.

I raise these points to explain one simple aspect of my Smoking Gun Test. There are many cases currently influencing campaigns for urgent reform of Family Court processes and they all rely on evidence and arguments that are arising from cases that have ended. It is in the nature of Family Court cases that their obvious failures to protect abuse victims are only measurable in hindsight. In each case where there is an obvious failing, that failing wasn't addressed or necessarily even visible while the case was ongoing. It is only when the worst possible outcome is realised that people sit up and take notice.

By comparing why my case began – an application for contact with my children, with why it ended, it is possible to see the alienation and how it worked.

How it works

My Hug-Headlock Test takes the final assessment of my kids and compares it to the first report in the timeline of events that started my Family Court struggle to restart contact with them.

By the time my case ended I hadn't seen my children for nearly three years, except for bumping into them coming out of the supermarket. I hugged them. This was reported as me putting them into a headlock. I received an angry letter from my ex-wife's lawyers alleging assault. I responded by asking them to review the supermarket CCTV footage. They subsequently withdrew the allegations and said it was – in their view – '*excessive hugging*'. I had excessively hugged my children whom I hadn't seen for months, one of whom had been groomed and blackmailed by an online abuser. Yes, I hugged them. Damn right.

The headlock accusation was typical of the kind of attacks that happened every time my ex-wife sent a letter. It came to nothing. However, it does show one crucial thing. If I hugged them and it was reported via my ex-wife to her solicitor as assault and a headlock, it shows how the children were having events reframed for them by my ex-wife. A hug becomes a headlock, so then homework becomes slavery and so on.

In order to make the claim – which I maintain – that my children had become hostile towards me through psychological manipulation, it should be reasonably simple enough. We shall apply the hug-headlock model to it. If the reasons my children give for not wanting to see me can be put into a timeline we can see if they were reinvented from a hug to a headlock in some way.

We can look at the way their wishes and feelings about me change. Were they there from the beginning before they broke off contact or did they only emerge after contact stopped?

Similarly, we can look at the reasons and opinions of the professionals involved in the final reports and final judgement and ask if they are referring to issues we experienced as part of a parent-child relationship or issues we experienced while estranged from each other. Those things that happened when we were estranged are created by their environment and influences they are exposed to, not me.

If there is a smoking gun moment, it will become visible depending on how large the discrepancy between the reasons used to justify non-contact at the end of the process (the headlock) compared to the reasons given at the beginning (the hug). Or to put it another way, was my Parental Alienation judged to be merely justified estrangement by children who were capable of making up their own minds on the basis of things I had done to them? Or was it things that happened to them when I was cut out of their lives? Were their opinions of me formed when we were together or when we were apart?

Applying the Hug-Headlock Test

I will start the test by looking at the first report on the children by a counsellor from a children's charity organisation working with the school. It had been about three months since we had started a cooling-off period – which the school had suggested would be a good idea as my relationship with the kids had broken down into arguments over the break-up with my fiancée – Elle – and my subsequent discovery of my ex-wife's involvement with her. The cooling-off began in late January 2015. My fiancée had left and robbed me in July 2014, she returned later that month, only to leave again for good in August.

My fiancée and I had tried to reconcile but it proved impossible. I thought we were making progress. She returned the money, I dropped the charges, we got back together but she was a wreck and so was I. Then she left me, quite unexpectedly. She also told the police she feared I would be violent, and so arranged for removal men to come and take away some of my bedroom furniture with a police escort. It was as bizarre as it was unwarranted. I complained to the police, who investigated my complaint of heavy-handed behaviour, there was never any threat of violence. They reported back to me in December and apologised for the behaviour of the PC who attended. They also told me that my fiancée had assistance from someone close to me. They couldn't tell me who precisely. On the record. They could tell me, however, not to rule out my ex-wife. I later learned – in 2016 – from reading my ex-wife's own testimony to the court that she had helped Elle to leave me. To be clear, what Elle did was criminal. My ex-wife was an accomplice, in a criminal act. I will deal with that issue in a later chapter.

For the purposes of the Smoking Gun Test, I mention my break-up with Elle to explain what I believe caused the argument with my kids that in turn led to our relationship breakdown. They said I was a bully. That I was mean to Elle, like I was mean to their mother. That I had locked Elle in my home gym, which had no lock on the door. I told them – and I wish I hadn't – the truth. That Elle stole from me and Mummy helped her. It was a meltdown. I regret it.

The next weekend the children came as usual, but one was very upset. The two siblings were very different characters. One was upset and wanted to go home early. The other wanted to stay. Later that afternoon I got a call from school asking me to go in and see them because one of the children had made a complaint about me to the school. They wouldn't talk to me about it. I couldn't handle it. Elle had broken my heart and robbed me, my ex-wife was involved and now my child was raising complaints about me to school? It felt like the sky was falling in.

They went home the next morning, my housekeeper took them to their trampoline lesson and then home early. She was close to the kids, she had spent Christmas with us just a month before. They trusted her. She was very supportive of both them and me – and tried to help us resolve things.

For the three months after Elle left, I had been seeing a therapist – a psychiatrist who specialised in interventions for people under extreme emotional stress. Therapy for that kind of shock is hard. Elle broke my trust in people and relationships. It made me a little paranoid about everyone – when someone that close to you robs you and betrays you so deeply, it is earth shattering.

The sudden accusation of bullying by one of my kids, and the sudden involvement of the school in my private life was deeply challenging. I was still getting over my broken heart. I asked the school to help me resolve the issue. They suggested a cooling-off break from seeing my kids while they involved a local children's charity that specialised in mediation between divorced families and child-parent problems. It felt like a sensible, practical approach. I was convinced it would work. The school told me they had already agreed the idea with my ex-wife, which in retrospect makes me suspect it was her plan all along.

The report that came from that initial cooling-off break from that is my starting point. That report is the one with all the reasons for the split with my children. Those issues are the ones I needed to resolve.

Time is the problem in Parental Alienation cases. The longer you don't see your children, the harder it is for them to see you. They dread it. The longer time passes, the more they dread it. They lack the emotional maturity to address it, they hide from conflict. They were 11. How could I blame them? Three months when you are 11 is a long time. However, the school had recommended a cooling-off period, and they recommended counselling with this charity. I took that in good faith. I shouldn't have. If we had never had a cooling-off period, perhaps we would never have suffered such a devastating split.

What is really important to note at this point is I am not challenging their reasons. They felt how they felt, and whatever the reasons. This book isn't a he-said-she-said argument, nor is it a chance for me to make my case. I have made that already, nobody wants to hear it. This book is an attempt to explain what happened to *us*, my children and me, and in that case their pain and their abuse deserves to be validated – just the same as mine. The words are taken verbatim from the report, which was considered by all the later assessments and by the Judge. They weren't all reasons given by both children, most were from just one of them, but for the sake of simplicity, I will aggregate them. Even my ex-wife said there were no safeguarding reasons for them not to see me. She brought them to my house on alternate weekends with no worries or concerns over care. This meant my children's reasons weren't anything serious like abuse or neglect.

Reason 1: I 'had spoken unkindly about their mother'.

Reason 2: I had 'involved them in adult issues – discussing the recent break-up with his [my] fiancée'.

Reason 3: I spent 'too much time on his [my] phone, watching the news and not doing anything "fun"'.

Reason 4: One of the children found an email 'from her father to her mother, that she had managed to access on her mother's laptop which had stated "congratulations, you have successfully destroyed my relationship with my [kids]"'.

Reason 5: The other child felt like '"a puppet on a string" and didn't want to feel controlled by the father'.

Reason 6: They 'feel time with father is more "strict" than with mother whereby they are more "relaxed"'.

Reason 7: They 'gave examples of father booking West End shows and offering to take them on adventure holidays but that they would have preferred to go to Disneyland instead as they are young and want to do young, fun activities'.

Those seven reasons were given after a series of sessions with a counsellor from the charity, and one meeting with the author of the report who was a senior member of the charity. One of those reasons as well, clearly, was something private that they read about on their mother's email, at the mother's house.

Before we consider the last professional assessment to see how it compares with the reasons given two years later, one final thing. What did the author of the report think? Bearing in mind this was almost six years post-divorce.

'I advised Mr XXX that Ms XXX may be influencing the children's decisions, perhaps by "omission" rather than by "commission", given the pain and hurt she appears to still feel, given this, meaningful mediation may be more beneficial than adversarial court proceedings in terms of moving forward. The conflict type relationship between both parents appears to be an integral part of the current dynamic.'

Just to be clear, a full six years after we split, a report into my ex-wife's attitude toward me clearly picks up on pain and hurt over the divorce? There is an ominous quality in that when I read it now. At the time, it was upsetting. Now it is menacing. Was this a whiff of gun smoke? I think in retrospect, it was.

Two years later, what was different?

When you look at the reasons given for not wanting to see me two years later, it should be more of the same. I mean, we hadn't recommenced contact, or spoken about the argument or the reasons why we split. We hadn't managed to reconcile. We hadn't addressed those issues. So it's perfectly reasonable to assume they still applied – even if some of them (like going to West End show instead of a theme park) feel like strange reasons to wish someone was out of your life forever. I have to accept that for them, it was an instance of their feelings. However, I suspect they were not their own views as much as the view their mother had influenced.

The assessment that came last was from Cafcass, the court-appointed social workers. They met me at their offices for an interview which my ex-wife was meant to attend but didn't come. I found them to be hostile. They had met my ex-wife and children beforehand at a home visit. One month later they delivered this report on the situation and again, I will quote verbatim the reasons my children – now aged 14 – gave for not wanting to see me.

Reason 1: '[they] spoke about many of the allegations already before the Court, such as [Father] physically assaulting [one of them]'.

Reason 2: 'displaying preferential treatment towards [one of them]'.

Reason 3: 'involving himself too heavily in their school lives'.

Reason 4: 'speaking negatively about their mother to them in an attempt to influence them'.

Reason 5: 'having another secret child whom they consider he has potentially abandoned'.

Reason 6: '[they] maintain a degree of being frightened of their father'.

Reason 7: 'They consider their father has treated them badly and so these feelings are reinforced by their perception that he has abandoned his youngest child'.

The reasons have shifted considerably. Bearing in mind I haven't seen my children, nor had I discussed the complex issue of the child I had fathered. That was something they discovered at the mother's house – allegedly by accident. And it went on in the report to warrant three paragraphs about its importance in their decision not to see me. I didn't abandon a child. I didn't want to start another family with the mother of that child, I didn't want to become a part-time father to a baby, and I didn't want to pay the claim of a million pounds to the mother, who is now happily married with a family of her own.

And what did the report author think?

'It is right that the children have been exposed to adult information and information regarding these proceedings by their mother. This is not appropriate. However, there is also evidence before the Court that the children have shared that their father has shared information with them about their mother, negative information which was intended to influence their views. This is equally as inappropriate.'

I haven't seen them for over two years. I said to my kids that she helped my fiancée leave the country, in a temper, it was a mistake. Compared to letting them access a court assessment with adult detail of allegations, emails, lawyers' letters and information that they had a half-sibling it is not equally as inappropriate as that. Is it?

The results

What is really plain to see comparing the views of my children aged 11 (nearly 12) and aged 14, is the reasons they have given have changed in tone and severity. Parental Alienation does that, it compounds the reasons for the alienation in the child's mind, and changes the reasons as it does so. It is part of the child's coping mechanism for the loss of the relationship – in effect, they make the lost parent sound worse and worse to lessen the loss they feel. The real shock is how menacing the final report makes me sound.

Two years later I am frightening to them. The 11 year olds weren't frightened of me, but after two years of not seeing me, they are? How did that happen?

I physically assaulted one of them? No I did not. This was referring to an incident where I did, in a moment of temper, give one of them a light tap on the head. The sort of thing teachers used to give me as a kid for running in the hallway. Not a punch, or a slap. A tap on the head, towards the back of it, near the top. It was not smacking. It didn't leave a mark or cause a tear. It was one of those 'Oi! Stop jumping off the bed!' moments. To describe it as a physical assault is like describing a smack on the bum (which also was common when I was a kid) as a beating. However, something must have happened in those two years to make that event loom large enough in my children's heads to make them fear me and accuse me of assault. This is a classic *hug-headlock* retelling of events and manipulation by another force.

Displaying preferential treatment? That was never mentioned before. I treated them the same – I love them both equally. Every sibling claims preferential treatment at some point – it's not fair etc. – but it's not something that belonged in a court assessment as a reason to cut me off forever.

A secret child I abandoned? They discovered that via my ex-wife. And it is so large and significant in their assessments – which I will cover later in the book – that it was pivotal in their view of me. Pivotal enough for the Cafcass guardian to raise it multiple times in the report. Most significantly, I think, here:

'[They] cannot comprehend how their father could not want to have a relationship with this child, which is interesting as they are experiencing difficulties with their father's persistence in his relationship with them … They consider their father has treated them badly and so these feelings are reinforced by their perception that he has abandoned his youngest child, which is another negative behaviour.'

The Cafcass guardian never discussed the child with me. I was never offered a right of reply or a chance to explain myself. I was judged without any hearing with regard to that child. The 'secret child' issue (Cafcass called the child my 'secret' but I had not made it a secret at all) they learned about via my ex-wife comes up time and again in all the later assessments. It appears alongside the emergence of their fear of me, their view of me as a bad man. It was straw that broke the camel's back, in many respects. They had already rejected me, this merely compounded it and became the new focus and further justification for their hatred of me.

It is also a glimpse of the smoking gun barrel. My ex-wife says, in various interviews with court-appointed experts, that she was very conflicted over my other child. She was concerned about what my children would think of her if they discovered she knew about it. In her assessment with the court-appointed consultant child psychiatrist, she noted *'it was morally wrong not to tell the children'*. It feels a little more than a coincidence that they discovered it quite by chance at her house, in court papers in her study, which were left lying around apparently without concern.

I must fully acknowledge that at many points along the way, experts cited the litigation between my ex-wife and myself made things worse for my kids and affected their view of me. My children blamed me for the court action. I have to acknowledge that it was for their own good – they were falling apart and not being properly cared for.

Their mother supported their wishes to have no contact with me for reasons that changed considerably between the break in our contact and the end of my legal attempts to see them, two-and-a-half years later.

Their mother, my ex-wife, accidentally allowed them to learn things about me – their estranged sibling – that destroyed me in my children's eyes. The children I took to Mustique, as well as backstage at a London theatre and skiing at a resort where they ate breakfast with pop stars.

As I said at the beginning of this chapter, there is no smoking gun. No moment where you can point and say *'A-ha! That's it, that's where it happened'*. But in cases of parental alienation there is no one specific moment. There are only relationships. Relationships are complex and spread over time. However, consider the logic of it. How could our relationship change so dramatically without seeing each other? How did my kids come to hate and fear me without contact? How does one side of that relationship become afraid of the other? How did the reasons my children gave for not wanting to see me get so much worse over the time we spent apart?

I did not abandon any child.

I did not physically assault my child.

I did not involve myself too heavily in their school lives.

The only thing that is consistent between the first account and the second is the fact I spoke negatively about their mother. Which I did. In divorce cases, this is common. It's human. I am not proud of losing my cool and speaking negatively about their mother, but I learned from the police investigating a theft of over £300,000 – at a rock bottom moment in my life – that my ex-wife had helped the thief, my fiancée, to escape abroad and leave me in pieces. That doesn't make me a monster does it? Have you ever lost it and said mean stuff in front of your kids, or to them? It happens. You assume you can fix it, too. Is that enough to make my children so afraid of me they never want to see me again? I apologised.

Even that reason changed in the court assessments, though. It changed from 'speaking negatively' to me 'sharing information to influence the kids against their mother'. That shift may seem subtle, but on the other hand, I claimed Parental Alienation which has to include children being influenced by one parent to be hostile toward the other. Suddenly, when I claim my ex-wife is influencing them against me, they claim I am influencing them against her. I haven't had any contact with them. They live with my ex-wife. They see her every day but won't see me at all. How was I influencing them against her? How is that even possible after two years without contact?

The thing I can't understand and the aspect of it that keeps me up at night even now is the events my children cited as the reasons they didn't want to see me ever again all happened years or months before the split. And we were fine.

The tap on the head – the physical assault – happened long before.

To read my children's testimony after two years of not seeing me, they make me sound like a child beater and a cruel, heartless bastard who abandoned a baby. Not even a cruel heartless bastard who abandoned a pregnant ex-girlfriend with a £1 million claim for maintenance, which would be to misunderstand the nature of the relationship but would at least be more accurate.

So there is no smoking gun. But there is a question to be asked about what happened. My kids aged 11 said they didn't want to see me because I had said mean things about Mummy, spent too much time working and taken them to the ballet instead of Disneyland. My kids aged 14 said they were frightened of me because I physically assaulted them, involved myself too heavily in their school lives and because I had cruelly abandoned their baby half-sibling.

Except I hadn't abandoned the baby. In court, the baby's mother was moved to write a letter of support for me on that very subject. We were cordial, polite but not close after our relationship ended and she demanded money, however, we worked it out and to her credit she wrote this which supported my reasons – agreed by my ex-wife – for not discussing it with my children until the time was right:

'I was his girlfriend for just over a year in 2011/2012 and had his child in 2013. The pregnancy wasn't planned and he chose not to be involved in our child's life at that time. He does support our child financially. He mostly kept our situation private, but I know he discussed it in depth with his ex-wife. They mutually agreed not to tell their children about their half-sibling. I consented to this and at his request, I agreed not to keep in touch with his children. These things normally come out eventually, but the presentation/delivery of such a delicate matter would be crucial to its interpretation.'

It was crucial, in my mind at the time. And look at where it left me years later. It became one of the central reasons for my kids hating me. That discovery, disclosure or whatever else happened in my ex-wife's home was a crippling blow to my relationship with my children, and that was something we all predicted – me, my ex-wife and my ex-girlfriend – years before it happened.

How my kids formed that view of me that decided the judgement of Cafcass and the courts is Parental Alienation exposed for what it is. The children didn't see me in that period. They lived with their mother, on and off with their maternal grandparents, on holidays in the Spanish villa I paid for with their mother and her friends and family. They experienced my attempts to see them as an acrimonious court case between me and their mother and family. They knew nothing of our divorce settlement, or the subsequent financial dispute action their mother brought against me. I kept that a secret from them as any good parent would.

However, in the eyes of Cafcass and the courts, they experienced many problems since the alienation as things that happened because of the court case and therefore, because of me.

Again, this is the impossible catch-22 of Parental Alienation. If I try to see my kids – the court is my only route – but it means I lose my kids because they are emotionally worn out by the court process. If I don't try to see them, I lose my kids because they don't want to see me and my ex-wife won't maintain the relationship.

As I said in the first chapter of this book, Parental Alienation is abuse. If there is even a hint of abuse, it has to be properly investigated. Safeguarding must be central to all contact cases. There should be no hint of violence or sexual abuse that passes by uninvestigated. Yet in this case? Didn't the dramatic change in the reasons my children gave about not seeing me, and the obvious fear and disgust they expressed about me enough to raise suspicion? Remember, these weren't healthy, happy-go-lucky kids, they were having therapy. One was cutting words into their thigh and the other had been groomed and blackmailed by an online pervert. Didn't any of that count as a whiff of something more than just having a bad father? Didn't that say something was amiss in the mother's house and care of them?

The catch-22 is this: I try to see them when they are 11, my ex-wife says she will support their wishes and feelings if they don't want contact. When I try to see them when they are 14, my children say that the things they have learned about me in the interim period have made them frightened of me. In between those times, the children go through all sorts of problems, and they discover things about me in their mother's email, in their mother's court papers and overheard the mother, grandmother and grandfather discussing her friends and family. None of that is even a hint of alienation? Even the reports that say it's present to some degree? And none of it could have come from me. They haven't had any contact with me since they were 11.

Everything by the end was so much worse, but in the end the judge decided it was just all coincidence. That the acrimony between my ex-wife and I was the reason my kids hated me. Nothing to do with the information they learned about me in my ex-wife's home. Or the strange way that after two years without seeing me, the children had formed a view of me they didn't have when we split.

In the report from when the children were 11, my ex-wife was assessed by the counsellor as influencing the children. My ex-wife, who three years before the split, refused to do any travelling for contact arrangements. My ex-wife who was involved in the break-up with my fiancée that broke my relationship with the kids. Those things alone make a decent case to investigate her role in the split with my kids with a greater degree of suspicion than she was – at the very least – capable of alienating me from my kids and involving herself in my personal relationships.

There is a point at which you realise the process is as broken as your relationship. By the end I saw it for myself. I thought I could find a way through the maze of catch-22 traps and loopholes. I thought that someone, somewhere would look at the evidence and say that we should have an intervention to bring us back together. Of the four court-ordered assessments, each one said it would be better for the children if we could get back onto speaking terms. Even the damning Cafcass report said that contact could resume in the future. Even the judge – who relied on the Cafcass report more than any other, despite it being written by the person who spent least time with my kids, my ex-wife and me – agreed it was a shame and we should resume contact in the future. Everyone made a case that contact could resume, and it would be a shame if it didn't resume, and that it should resume. But none of the rulings or recommendations were to that effect.

Here I am, writing this, my children are now virtually adults.

Here I am, as even more alienated now than when they were 11.

Cafcass defines parental alienation as *'when a child's resistance or hostility towards one parent is not justified and is the result of psychological manipulation by the other parent'* and that expresses the sheer impossibility of my problem. You can't prove psychological manipulation. Worse, for me, the people involved in my case – with the exception of the consultant child psychiatrist – felt that my children were actually justified in their view of me. The justification was simple enough – I had a baby I didn't want and didn't have any contact with, I had been through a personal crisis over my break-up and robbery with Elle, and so therefore was unstable. They justified my kids' wishes on the grounds I was desperate, angry, anxious, all the things I admit I was as my kids slipped further and further away from me. And finally, of course, I was a rich banker, and everyone hates them right? Especially social workers earning less in a year than I made in a week. I was a bastard waiting to happen for them.

It was a shame nobody looked at the reasons my children gave for the split, and how those reasons changed as a result of information they learned through my ex-wife, either by design (she did it deliberately to alienate me) or by accident (she neglected to safeguard them from information that was deeply damaging for children to discover). The former shows evidence of psychological manipulation, the latter could show that or simply neglect. What else could you call it if one person exposes children to information about another to affect their view of that person? It's pretty clear-cut to me. I agree that I appeared anxious, angry and highly stressed by the fight to see my kids. I am sure that the professionals I encountered, I appeared to be an angry man at times, frustrated at others. I also made a huge effort to remain calm as well. This is something experts in Parental Alienation cases have documented time and time again. To someone who isn't trained to spot alienation Alienated parents just look like pushy, angry, anxious people. In my case, an angry, pushy, anxious rich banker who physically assaults kids. That was me as far as they were concerned. A caricature of a villain, like so many abuse victims who are 'asking for it' by being who they are. It shows a complete lack of training on their part to understand how domestic abuse – psychological abuse – presents in its victims.

There is no smoking gun, but there is also such an imbalance in the reasons my children gave about me, you can't help but wonder what would need to happen for someone to ask the question whether my claim of Parental

Alienation was valid or not. The reasons they gave changed from hug to headlock within a year or so of our split. The evidence is clear, the change is clear, it is easy to see. It should have prompted a proper investigation into my case. At the least, a court-ordered fact-finding investigation to establish whether there was any validity to my claims of abuse. Of course, fact-finding means more court delays and even more time away from the kids, and so it's not necessarily effective and delays just amplify alienation.

The real scandal here is nobody, despite claiming to put the wishes and feelings of the children first, looked at the way their opinion of me changed so much and asked if that was a cry for help from two children who were themselves abuse victims, because in Parental Alienation, the children are victims too.

Chapter 4:
What did he do to make his kids hate him?

One of the hardest things to deal with as an alienated parent is the assumption you are to blame. It's a knee-jerk response. If you are an alienated father, the assumption is you're either a wife beater, child beater or abuser. If you are an alienated mother, you're usually assumed to be mentally ill or an addict. These are the clichés you are forced to live with as an alienated parent, the same stereotypes that make Parental Alienation possible in the first place. If we didn't believe so easily that behind closed doors practically any man could be a violent abuser or that any woman is a nervous wreck propped up by booze and pills, claims of Parental Alienation would be taken more seriously.

Parental Alienation is a social stigma. You have to live with it and it never goes away. For example, a few weeks before I started writing this book, I played golf with an old friend from my time working in the City of London – the surprisingly small worlds of property and finance in the nation's capital. It's a place where high-profile city players are always the subject of gossip. As we played our round my associate – alienated parents don't use the word 'friend' lightly – told me that there was a rumour amongst my old work community that I must have *done* something. My old friend calmly went on to say that a couple of people had asked if I had been abusing my children.

'And what did you say?' I asked. I was furious.

My friend was evasive.

'Well I know it's not true, but that's what people are saying.'

'Who was it?' I asked, 'I want to know who is saying this about me.'

He wouldn't say.

'We have seriously different views of what friendship means,' I told him, 'If someone said that about you to me, I'd tell you. And I'd put them straight.'

I am not sure if we are really friends anymore. Not after that. However, I wasn't shocked to hear it, after all, that's what people think – if you are alienated from your kids, you must have been asking for it, right? It's easier to believe that than to believe abuse could happen so easily to an innocent man or woman for most people.

When you are an alienated parent you go through so much outrageous abuse. It puts a distance between you and your friends. Between you and everyone. Your trust is damaged. Worse, what does it say about people? What does it say about casual assumptions and lazy clichés if your acquaintances can calmly have conversations behind your back? That people would talk calmly while playing golf with a potential child abuser? It's unthinkable to me. If I thought someone I knew was playing golf with a man who had abused his kids, I'd ask them why the hell they were doing it.

The assumption that you are to blame for alienation is common in Parental Alienation cases. It comes from what is known as a cognitive bias – a way of thinking – that psychologists call a *fundamental attribution error* (sometimes called a *misattribution error*). It describes how people form assumptions by attributing the wrong reason for an event. In studies at the University of Texas, they showed people generally assume someone's personality or behaviour is responsible for what happens to them around 65 per cent of the time – as opposed to what happens to a person being the result of events around them, or someone else. It explains why people often think the victims of crimes were 'asking for it' in some way.

There have been many studies into this very common cognitive bias, we all have it. We all have unfounded assumptions. We assume politicians are in it for themselves and can't be trusted. We assume teenagers in hoodies hanging around the street corner are up to no good. We see homeless people and assume they're sleeping in a doorway because of something they did. And people often assume the reason you lost your kids isn't Parental Alienation, it's something you did. I probably thought the same before it happened to me, too. It's human nature.

What did you do? Well, what's the lowest common denominator for being cut off from your kids? Sex abuse, mental illness, violence and addiction. The assumption makes an association between the strongest reasons for being cut off from your children and the likelihood of those reasons applying in the majority of cases.

There is another common thinking pattern called a *proportionality bias* that applies here too. Proportionality bias means we tend to assume big problems have big causes. It's the bias we find in conspiracy theories. It was easier to believe something big like the CIA or the Mafia killed John F Kennedy than it was a gunman acting alone. Millions of people still think so. It's easier for some people to believe the Chinese invented the coronavirus in a lab (something big) than it was just a random event caused by bad animal welfare in a market (something much more ordinary). Big things need big explanations in most people's minds, it's a normal proportionality assumption that is usually wrong, but we all do it.

This applies when people think about Parental Alienation. Losing your kids is big so therefore, you must have lost them for a big reason. What reason? In my experience, it's easier for people to believe alienated parents are all abusers or wife beaters rather than victims of a vindictive ex-spouse. They assume it is something you did (fundamental attribution) and they assume it was something very serious (proportionality bias).

In reality, sex abusers, violent abusers and addicts are the tiny minority of divorced parents. However, they are newsworthy and interestingly they are disproportionately overrepresented in Cafcass cases, which is why Cafcass often appears to exhibit bias against non-resident fathers. We also hear many stories about abusive fathers who have killed or harmed their children during contact, or mothers who do the same, that we think it's more common than it actually is. This feeds the biased view most people have about Parental

Alienation and family litigation: that cases of alienation are somehow linked to these rare, disturbing abusive parent-child relationships. We don't hear stories about the many parents who become estranged from their children for less shocking – less newsworthy – reasons.

Most cases of estrangement are a result of divorced parents remarrying and starting new families with a second partner, or cases where a divorced parent moves away. I am mindful here of the fact I fathered a child I have no contact with. However, that isn't parental alienation, it's quite different. We broke up and the mother had the child and moved on with her life and my financial support. It was a sad end for a relationship, however, it did end and there was nothing to be done about it. I didn't want to parent a child with someone I didn't love. I didn't want to make my life more complex than it was already as a divorced single father. You might judge that as selfish, but it wasn't meant to hurt the child or the mother – in fact some may argue I was a target all along.

I say that because the mother told me she couldn't have children. She told me she had given up on having kids, she had tried for years and it wasn't possible. Then, as we are splitting up, she suddenly becomes pregnant. Friends at the time asked me about the odds of that. After all, if you were about to miraculously get pregnant, what are the odds it would be with a multimillionaire just as you were splitting up? I felt trapped by it, but sometimes that's just how life turns out by chance.

It would be nice – comforting even – to think all the bad things that happen in our relationships are down to bad people or bad decisions. Junkies and abusers are reassuring bad guys in that childish view of the world. I say childish because reality is much more disturbing. If you are married and in love, it's unthinkable to look over at your loving husband or wife and imagine one day seeing them on the other side of Family Court. But this happens a lot. Almost one half of marriages fail.

Imagine the person who said 'I do' one day telling everyone in the court about your historic sexual preferences, or about aspects of your private life like an unwanted pregnancy. Imagine your children who once made you Father's Day cards with the cutest little drawings or videos saying 'I love you' standing one day in a coffee shop and shouting 'fuck off' at you as you sit in the car. Imagine your kids, aged 12, telling the court they think you need psychiatric treatment and they never want to see you again.

That's reality, for some people.

That's my reality.

Don't take my word for any of this. How many marriages end in divorce? How many relationships end badly? How many mothers end up looking after kids on their own? How many fathers don't see their children after divorce? How many kids have difficult relationships with divorced parents? Answer any of those questions and compare it to incidents of drug addiction, domestic violence and child abuse and you will realise those tiny minority of cases explain no more than a fraction of the real reasons why marriages and parental relationships break down. I make this point for one reason – my kids didn't stop seeing me because we had some dark secret. They stopped seeing me for other reasons of influence.

It's almost impossible to believe my alienation some days, even now. I wake up every morning and have to accept that reality. My kids hate me, or at least, can't bear me. And the reason for it is worse than me being some sort of monster who deserved it. I could accept it more if I was an abuser or drunk. But I wasn't. I loved them more than anything in the world and I tried as best I could to give them everything. A better life than I had, or than my ex-wife had. The best life I could give them.

The hardest part is accepting I didn't make them hate me. Someone else did.

Answering the wrong question – Why?

The assumption of domestic or sexual abuse is a cognitive bias, and it's also a sign of asking the wrong questions about cases of Parental Alienation. What did I do? Nothing. I didn't do anything to make my kids hate me. At least, not until I became aware of being alienated. You see, at the point where you start to suspect your ex-partner is cutting you off from your kids and manipulating their opinion of you, pretty much everything you do is wrong. If your kids fear you, they see your actions as bad regardless of whether they are or not. It becomes a self-fulfilling prophecy. You are a bad parent in their minds, so therefore every parental action you take is wrong. Everything you do is coloured by a false view of you, which has been created in your children's minds by your ex-partner. You're the bogeyman.

That is how Parental Alienation works. If the kids have enough steer early on in the alienation, it becomes self-sustaining and reinforcing. They see your actions in the worst light without question. It is similar to any prejudice, if you grow up thinking something negative about a person or group of people and your parents and family endorse that view, you don't challenge it. Intolerance breeds intolerance and once you alienate someone from their kids, they stay alienated in their kids' minds without you.

One clear example of this is my own children's testimony that I was trying to 'bump into them' in town or on my visits to their school to receive monthly reports on their progress – which I was entitled to as their father and the person paying their school fees. The concept of 'bumping into them' accidentally-on-purpose made me sound sinister, like a stalker. It is something that was used by my ex-wife's lawyers, and repeated verbatim in various court expert assessments. The scenarios that the assertion described was always the same – my children would be out in the town where they live, and they would see me. I would see them. Therefore I was trying to 'bump into them'. Except that happened only twice in three years. Also, my kids said they didn't want me coming to school for the monthly report from the teachers while they were in school, in case they saw me. That never happened. I never saw them. It's a massive school and there is no reason why they would see me unless they were waiting in reception at the precise time I was, which isn't something kids would do anyway.

Not one person raised the obvious flaw in these *'bumping into'* arguments.

I lived near that town too. I was entitled to visit the school for updates by law. There is nothing sinister about that. I went to the town when I needed to for shopping and such. I went to school at the time they offered me to visit. It was as simple as that.

The town where my kids live is my nearest town. I can be seen there a lot, by practically anyone else who lives in the area too, not just my kids. It's the town where we all lived together before the divorce. It's the town where I catch the train into London – and have done on-and-off for the last 20-plus years.

Post-divorce I lived in Central London, but I bought a family home mid-way between that town and the children's school a few years before our relationship broke down. I did it to make contact weekends easier, because my ex-wife refused to do her share of travelling and I did it to help my children with their education. As a result, I was losing a lot of precious time with my kids travelling to and from my home in Central London and their home in the home counties for pick-ups and drop-offs.

To see more of my children before the alienation accelerated, I chose to move near to them and their lives. It was the area I grew up in, the area I've spent most of my life in. The likelihood of me randomly intersecting with my kids in a town with a population of around 6,000 people is reasonably high without trying to *'bump into them'*. All I had to do was go to the shops on a Saturday or Sunday and it was possible. But I still needed to go shopping. I still ate out in restaurants with friends. I still drank coffee from the local café. Was I supposed to live like a recluse as well? What was I supposed to do? Move away and start over somewhere new so there was no risk of me accidently seeing my kids? The argument is absurd. You can't force someone to move town over a relationship breakdown.

Another reason they spotted me in town was they recognised my car. Of course they did. This means I am more conspicuous to my kids and my ex-wife. I dare say I could have driven past them many times in different car and they wouldn't have even seen me. Was I supposed to buy a new car as well as move town?

Parental Alienation puts you into this hostile reality where the only way you can prove you're not some sort of child stalker is to leave the area where you were born and grew up – where my ex-wife also comes from – and avoid your local town centre, train station, shops or supermarkets in case your children happen to be there. That means you don't just lose your kids, you lose your sense of belonging anywhere. You are hurting inside and traumatised by the grief. You are a victim of domestic abuse. Are you expected to sell-up and move on somewhere without any friends or familiar places nearby as well? That feels like more abuse.

It feels as though at every point, at every twist and turn in Parental Alienation, someone is asking the wrong question about you, or answering the wrong question about your situation. So what is the right question? How do you know what the right question even is? I can't imagine ever cutting off my ex-wife from my kids or turning them against her, I couldn't imagine why anyone would do that. How could I possibly explain why she would do that to me? Again, *why did she do it?* is the wrong question to ask, same as *what did he do to deserve it?* These are lazy cliché questions. There is an answer, I believe, but the question is *when?*

What was happening *when* I lost my kids?

I was moving on with my life.

I was moving on with a beautiful woman who was 12 years younger than my wife. We planned to get married and start a family.

When that relationship began, was that when my alienation really accelerated? I think so. In fact, I think every time I tried to move on with a new relationship, my ex-wife tried to alienate me from my kids.

Answering the right question – When?

The first moment I became aware of problems with my ex-wife regarding contact arrangements was in 2010, shortly after our divorce when my kids were just seven-years old. She said she wouldn't do any of the travelling for contact weekends. If I wanted to see my children, I would have to collect them and drop them off from her house in the country – those words still ring loud to me.

That might not sound like Parental Alienation and at the time, I didn't think so but it was very hard for me nevertheless. At the time, I was part of a very successful financial institution with over $25 billion in assets under management. That kind of job comes with a lot of pressure and very long hours. It's not a 9–5 job. I was regularly up at dawn on calls with Asia, and working late. It is a gruelling workload at times, but I loved it.

Post-divorce my home was in Central London, my offices were in Mayfair. My ex-wife lived in the home counties, about half an hour train ride outside London. In order to collect my children, I had to leave my office around lunchtime and travel across London and on to the home counties, collect the kids, then make the return journey. Or make the drive, which was significantly longer because of the famously congested London traffic. All in all, this round trip meant that by the time I got the kids home to my place and we had dinner, it was bedtime.

In effect, I lost half a day of work – which stressed my time because of the huge legal compliance and regulatory pressures placed upon senior finance personnel after the 2008 financial crisis. Worse, I lost one of the two evenings I got to spend with my children on alternate weekends. It was a real source of conflict for me. I got them on alternate weekends, but it felt like that time was being taken away from me unfairly. Plus, my work pressures kept mounting as a result. It felt like my ex-wife was doing it with intent.

Why did she decide to stop travelling for the contact weekends? Why then? We had been divorced for less than a year. We had settled amicably and my ex-wife was financially independent without needing to work with millions in the bank, a home with no mortgage and monthly maintenance payments. We had cooperated just fine over the kids and travel. We even spent Christmas day together.

There are two answers.

One complex, one simple.

The complex answer: A dispute over money

In our divorce settlement in 2009, my wife and her solicitors were quite adamant that I had to settle in cash. Without going into boring detail, most of my assets were in shares, investment funds and complex financial instruments, like derivatives and private equity which are very long dated in nature. Many of these assets were also mired in problems – the so-called toxic assets of banks and investment firms that were caught up in the financial crash of 2009 and the subsequent government bailouts across the world. Put simply, valuing my assets was difficult even for my accountants. Selling them was impossible.

Anyway, we had enough cash to settle with her agreement, for around £6 million – and a trust fund for the children of around £1 million. It was a final, clean break. As part of the agreement my pension was ring-fenced, i.e. we agreed that I would keep my pension and offset any share of that with cash from assets. I also agreed to pay monthly maintenance for the kids. This made my wife richer than most people in Britain – she insisted on a cash settlement, no investments, which meant I had to take all the risk on my share of the settlement, which was made up from assets that could go down in value – I was forced to take all the risk.

One year later, when the economy was recovering in 2010, my ex-wife stopped travelling for my scheduled contact weekends. She also took me to court for additional financial claims. In this second financial case, some of my investments that were worthless in 2009 had become more liquid, and the markets were strong after the financial bailouts and quantitative easing. This included a small pension fund that wasn't included in the assessment of my pension holdings before. This became relevant in the context of the broader case my ex-wife brought against me, after the news broke that my company was being acquired in a takeover and I stood to make a large profit as one of the firm's partners. The merger deal – for around $1.9 billion – was reported as one of the largest deals of its kind and it was all over the press.

In many respects, this is where the acrimony started. I offered to settle out of court with my wife for a very reasonable sum – £1 million. She rejected my offer. She demanded £10 million, and also demanded I pay the cash equivalent of the value of the small pension fund – around £200,000 – to her parents. She claimed her parents – who had been a rather invasive presence in our marriage and often stayed for long periods, holidayed with us and made use of our houses in the UK and Spain – deserved a payout. It made no sense to me. I refused but agreed to pay the £200,000 into my children's trust fund. I would rather they had it than my former in-laws.

After huge expense and months of legal letters the judge awarded my wife less than I had offered in the out of court settlement, however, he also ruled that the money from the pension pot should have been paid to my ex-wife and not placed in trust for my children. So, in addition to the £700,000 I was ordered to pay to my ex-wife, the £200,000 was taken out of my children's trust fund and paid over to her as well. That really summed her up when it came to money. She'd go to court to take money out of the kids' trust fund, even though she had millions in the bank already.

She had now, in total, received £7 million as a settlement, including the money she demanded from my children's trust fund – which angered me because it was taking trust fund money away from the kids. It is another example of the many failings of the court process that they have such a poor grasp of complex finance.

I advised my wife at the time of the divorce to wait for me to organise the finances and wait for the economy to recover a bit before insisting on a payout. I also advised her to take on the investments as securities, not cash, in order to maximise their long-term value. I couldn't help it – it was my job. I could see that she would have received more if she had agreed to that, however at the time her lawyers insisted that she was better to settle in cash, for less. So be it. This is the nature of legal advice when finances are being settled by divorce lawyers and not financial specialists.

This time, of my ex-wife's second court case against me for money, was the beginning of the alienation. The timing was the same, at least, however, that's not quite the whole story. The whole story involves a second, much simpler reason.

The event of my company being acquired coincided with something much more deeply damaging to my ex-wife's perception of me.

I had started dating again.

I had a girlfriend.

The simple answer: I started dating again

The acquisition of my firm was announced around the same time I began a romance with a woman (I will call her Polly in this book). Polly and I dated for less than a year. She was a very intense younger woman, we had a lot of fun but I was very cautious. She talked of marriage quite soon into our relationship; I wasn't keen on the idea. I'll be honest, she was very attractive and fun, we had some good times but I don't think I ever saw us getting married. I was rebounding from a divorce. I wanted to have fun.

My children didn't like Polly. They were naturally cautious of the new woman in my life, and in all fairness Polly tried to be nice to them but was young and not particularly experienced with kids. They were seven at the time, and that year I had spent Christmas together with my ex-wife at her house. As I have noted already, my ex-wife and I had a good relationship for divorcees, or so I thought. She had even helped me choose my house in London.

I had tried to do the same for her when she chose her large seven-bedroom house in an exclusive part of the town where we used to live. I advised her against buying that home because it would require a lot of upkeep and staff – like we had at our more modest home when we were married – however she insisted. Status was very important to her, and within our small community, it meant a lot to have the biggest house, the newest car and so on.

My ex-wife also began a new relationship of her own in 2009, with the father of a well-known local thug. This was a source of concern for me. The thug and his father were involved in a criminal trial, accused of racially aggravated assault. The case was deeply worrying. I found it hard to keep my calm, thinking my kids were around this family who were alleged to be violent racists. The father was alleged to have shouted racial abuse at his daughter while his son stood accused of biting her on the face and choking her. The daughter's boyfriend then stabbed the son. I was concerned that the father was around my children and people embroiled in that kind of lifestyle were part of my kids' life.

Despite my concerns, I gave my ex-wife plenty of space. At the time I met Polly my relationship with my ex-wife was friendly, and it stayed that way for a while. I didn't want to mess it up by complaining about her boyfriend. It wasn't easy to keep my mouth shut about it. But I did.

My ex-wife invited me for Christmas that year. After spending Christmas together, contact weekends resumed as per normal. We got into a routine. I took the children skiing. We were into a polite divorced relationship. Everything seemed fine.

But then it changed.

About three months into my relationship with Polly my ex-wife became difficult over travel arrangements. This was also the time when she took me to court for additional financial settlement. At the time, we had a child arrangements order, and my ex-wife was breaking it. It seemed like an open and shut case to me. It was not as though my ex-wife worked, or couldn't afford to bring them to my home precisely as she had done for the previous six months without problem.

At first, my solicitor suggested mediation.

My ex-wife and I attended one mediation session and it became quite clear she wouldn't budge. She told me that as far as she was concerned, if I wanted to see my children I would have to pick them up and drop them off. She claimed she was advised by her friends – other parents at school – that she had no obligations to travel to facilitate my contact weekends and that I should do all the travelling. The previous 50:50 travel arrangements were – in her words – damaging her social life. Our mediation broke down.

I couldn't understand it. Why was my ex-wife suddenly so obstructive about bringing my kids to London? I was starting to get my life back on track after the break-up of my marriage. I had been through a tough time for my industry, a major global crash. I'd been through a tough time emotionally – as divorce always is.

I thought things were good.

I thought my ex-wife and I were on good terms.

My children were happy.

I had a good business life and a girlfriend.

I had a real sense of optimism about my future.

Then I am being sued for more money by my ex-wife.

And then I was forced to resort to lawyers to try and restore the status quo.

It felt like as I began to move on with my life, she began to act out.

Our initial agreement was for alternate weekends and holiday time with the kids, and we had mutually agreed travel. I assumed it would be simple enough to fix it. How could my ex-wife make a case that I should do all the travelling? In the end, our legal teams reached an agreement over our travel relationship. My ex-wife agreed she would pick up the children from school and bring them to the train station 200 metres from her house.

I would travel for 90 minutes there, and 90 minutes back to my house.

She thought it was a compromise, I did not.

I wanted to take her to court to restore travel arrangements to our original 50:50 arrangements, but my lawyers advised me to settle her financial suit against me before we addressed the contact arrangements. I took their advice.

That Christmas – 2010 – Polly and I broke up. She wanted to marry, I told her I wanted a prenuptial agreement. She went berserk with rage. I wasn't prepared for how difficult things could become when you're divorced and trying to get back into the dating scene. It was tough. I felt very rejected by this younger woman who was keen to marry until I mentioned a prenuptial. It felt like I was being used. Or perhaps, I was just overcautious after my divorce? A good friend of mine warned me that a rich man had to be careful about young women who suddenly fall in love and want to get married. I guess she was right about that.

I took the children to California with me for Christmas a few years later. It was to visit with an old friend Uncle Matt, who my kids used to see on most weekend visits. A dear friend of mine, he was like a brother. He loved the kids and they loved him. He arranged for us to go on trips and arranged an au pair to keep my kids properly looked after as well. We had a wonderful time.

Fortunately, I had hired a personal assistant to manage my affairs and the house – Peter – and he was a huge support and helped me to juggle the kids and handle the difficulties with Polly.

Peter also helped me handle my ex-wife, who would call constantly while my children were with me. She would call all the time, to let them know their auntie had visited, or their grandmother was there and wanted to say hello. Or some friend from school had called for them. It was invasive. She would call several times, and stay on the phone for upwards of half an hour regardless of what we had planned or what we were about to do. I was losing hours of my time with the kids, again. It was a real source of frustration, Peter helped to handle the calls and keep her at a distance. He had a polite relationship with my ex-wife, and was wonderful with the kids.

My ex-wife started proceedings to claim additional money, and the settlement was finally granted in November

2011. The next month, I initiated Family Court proceedings to redress the travel issue. There was no negotiation. There was no compromise. Our attempts at mediation had failed. She simply stopped making any effort to facilitate my efforts to see the kids.

It was to my mind a very clear indication of how my ex-wife viewed the kids. They were hers. Not mine. In her mind, I had no rights. If I wanted access, I would have to dance to her tune. When we were married, she insisted I came home early to bathe and feed the kids a couple of nights per week. It wasn't easy, but at the time my bosses at the large US bank who employed me were supportive but confused. It was hard, in those days I was up at 5 am every day on the phone to Hong Kong and working into the small hours. My wife's additional demands on me for childcare felt spoilt and selfish. My wife didn't work. She had staff – including a dog walker and a nanny. She was hardly worn out by looking after two young kids part-time. I think it established a dynamic between us, though. She made the rules, and used the children to enforce them.

There was a hearing in January 2012, and the judge ruled in my favour to restore some equality to travel. The judge was known on the circuit as being hard on contact cases brought by fathers, something that is often talked about anecdotally by fathers in Family Court cases. However, she ruled in my favour. Not quite fairly, she ordered that my ex-wife had to bring the children to London, not my home. My ex-wife took them to the big London train station, which still meant I had to leave my office early to collect them – or send Peter to get them – and then take them to my London home, however

I could leave a couple of hours later at least. And get them home a little earlier so we had more time together on the Friday evening. It wasn't 50:50 travel, but I accepted it.

Peter had the arrangements sorted, he would make up their beds, make sure the fridge was stocked with their favourite foods and healthy snacks, and get them little magazines and games to play with too. Together, he and I tried to make their visits a real home from home, which is hard for a divorced dad sometimes. I think we made a really good job of it too. They were very happy at that house in London, for sure.

The way my ex-wife became difficult over travel arrangements when I told her about Polly, and introduced Polly to my kids, however, was ominous. It was a warning sign of what was to come. As I moved on, she made my life harder. It wasn't a surprise I suppose, as one side in a divorce moves on it often causes issues for the other, but in my case it was something much darker.

It was the beginning of my alienation.

Divorce is downhill all the way, sometimes

Between May 2010 and January 2012, as my children aged from seven to nine, the relationship between me and my ex-wife broke down completely. The breakdown started – as I have written – when I started dating for the first time after our divorce.

It also started when I was set to make enough money to retire in my forties and live out the rest of my days – with my children – as a man of leisure.

I made a decision when I first began working in the city,

aged 17, that I would work into my forties and make enough money to retire and spend the second half of my life doing whatever I wanted. I achieved that dream. I think my ex-wife envied that. She knew it was my dream. I think achieving a lifelong goal and moving on with my life made her green with envy. Envy is a powerful emotion. I worked hard and made my dream a reality. Dreams don't just come true by chance. And even if they do, it doesn't mean a nightmare isn't just around the corner. In my case, the nightmare of Parental Alienation. I would give it all away in a heartbeat to have my kids back in my life.

The events in my life in 2011–2012 were the catalyst that caused my Parental Alienation. I didn't realise it at the time, but looking back it is clear as day. I had moved on from being divorced to dating. My work had moved from being successful to being recognised at the top of my professional game. I was enjoying life to the full, while my ex-wife was standing still. She was a divorced housewife, with a new middle-aged boyfriend, in the same town with the same friends she had before. I think my success made her envious.

The court case to restore travel arrangements – which ruled in my favour – was just the tip of the iceberg. I think the signs of my wife's hostility towards me were there before. My ex-wife and I broke up in late 2008, she ended our relationship. It sounds passive of me, but I accepted the situation. We weren't sexually or romantically involved anymore, but we were in a holding pattern as parents. More like brother and sister than husband and wife. We were friends. It wasn't perfect, but I had settled for it. What happened to us was hardly remarkable, but looking back it is hugely relevant. She wanted to divorce me, and I was happy to move on.

She wanted to divorce me because I went through an identity crisis after two major emotional shocks in 2005 and 2006. The first was when my mother died quite suddenly from aggressive cancer. She kept it to herself, and by the time I found out, it was far too late to help her. I threw myself into those last few months with her, tried to make them the best she could have. The shock of the news was terrible. I had a poor relationship with my father. I idolised my mother. Mum's death made me question everything. Deaths – especially of your parents – can do that. It shook my sense of certainty about life. About everything. I would wake up and review my life, my own mortality loomed heavy in my mind.

The second shock came later. Not long afterwards I was walking home from the train station when I heard screaming. It was coming from my neighbours' house, an elderly couple I had known for years. It sounded like panic. I rushed around the house and through to the back garden where the elderly wife and two neighbours were trying to fish the body of the elderly husband from the bottom of their swimming pool. They were in a panic, the two neighbours were shouting they couldn't swim. I kicked off my shoes and jacket and dived in, dragging the old man from the bottom of the pool. He was dead, he must have been down there for a while. That scene haunted me. The dead weight of the man's body was shocking. The complete look of helplessness of the wife and neighbours, plaintively trying to hook the body with the net used for skimming the leaves out of the pool, plaintively explaining they couldn't swim. It all seemed surreal. So tragic. Such a sad, pointless death. To this day, I have never really spoken about it. It happened, and it shook my faith in the future and plans.

These events had a profound effect on me. I started to question my life choices. Was I really going to settle for a sexless marriage? Was I going to spend the rest of my life with someone who had such a different view of the world? My life had been all about trying to change, to grow, to create a legacy. My ex-wife's life plan was to marry a rich man and lay on a sun lounger with a glass of wine. It put us on different paths and we naturally grew apart, this was amplified by being parents. Then suddenly my mother dies and I find myself up close and personal with death in a very shocking way. I had spent my life with my nose to the grindstone. I suddenly felt like I had never questioned my choices, or my identity. I wasn't sure I had found myself, if that makes sense.

I married young. Threw myself into work. I'd never really had a chance to experiment like students or gap-year kids or whatever. I'd never gone travelling, or been to a pop festival. Never taken drugs. Never slept around. Never questioned my life choices, my sexuality, never dyed my hair, grown a beard or got a tattoo. It sounds silly now it comes to writing it down, but when I look at kids these days, they seem free and worldly in a way I never was. I was like most people born in the late 1960s a little naïve. Serious. I felt old before my time.

My wife was like me in some respects. Old before her time. Conservative with a small 'c'. She hadn't questioned her life choices either, but the difference between us was she never felt the need to. She had what she wanted out of life – kids, a big house, a holiday home in Spain, the latest top-end SUV to drive the 200 metres to school every day. She had always wanted to marry a rich guy, he'd work, she'd have kids and be a housewife. It was a working-class 1970s cliché of gender roles. Hubby commutes into the city, pays the bills, plays golf. Wifey packs the kids off to private school and watches daytime TV while the gardener mows stripes into the neat lawn, and the housekeeper makes the beds.

We were starting to argue over things like the kids' education and which sports car I was allowed to buy. I wanted to watch the news channels, she wanted to watch *Big Brother*. I wanted to move to another county to reduce my 90-min commute to work but she refused to leave the local town or the support from her parents, who had almost moved in with us. Yes. That old chestnut came back to haunt me. It was her gripe, my kids just repeated it. Stupid stuff, really, but a sign we were growing apart.

I disconnected which led to arguments, squabbles and a widening gap between us. She then asked me for a divorce and a final cash settlement. No strings. I didn't fight her – in fact I was relieved. I also decided it wasn't worth arguing about money. Life is too short for that, and we had plenty. I thought that would be enough. And it was, until I made a lot more money and started dating someone about ten years her junior. Then suddenly she's in court asking for millions more and I'm in court asking for her to bring my kids over and to support contact between us.

So the answer I give to the '*what did he do to make his kids hate him?*' question is what did I do to make my wife hate me?

That's the nature of the abuse. One parent acts against the other parent through cutting off access and ultimately the relationship with the children. Both the alienated parent and the children are victims of that. The abuser might believe they are doing it all for the right reasons, but the harm they do to the children is serious. The harm they cause to the other parent is deep and can't be repaired.

Each time I started a new relationship, the situation with my children got worse. The hostility my ex-wife exhibited grew worse. The timeline is clear.

2009 – We divorce, we have a clean-break settlement. We have a polite relationship.

2010 – I start dating again, my ex-wife refuses to bring my kids to my home for contact weekends.

2010 – I make a huge payday, my ex-wife sues me for more money.

2012 – Court rules for more equal care travel arrangements.

2012 – I dated a woman who 'accidentally' had a child.

2013 – I have a relationship with a younger woman, we plan to get married.

2014 – We get engaged, she steals from me with assistance from my ex-wife.

2015 – I completely lose contact with my kids.

What did I do to make my kids hate me? That is the wrong question. It doesn't have an answer, because in cases of Parental Alienation, the whole point is everything – and anything – can be turned around by the abuser to make your kids hate you. Including taking them to a musical instead of a theme park.

The right question is; what motivated my ex-wife to become intent upon inflicting pain and hurt upon the father of her children in such a dark and sinister way? The *why? The* answer is anybody's guess, why someone acts against you can only ever be supposition, but you can't argue with the timing. When they did it is objective. Provable. Time is a fact. The *when?* is about as close to the truth as an observer can get.

When? She began playing games with access to the children within a couple of months of my company making the news for the massive deal.

When? She began playing games with access to the children within a couple of months of me beginning to date other women as a single man.

After years of abuse, I don't believe it's a coincidence.

Chapter 5:
The Family Court is a slow motion car crash

If I had to sum up the experience of trying to prove Parental Alienation in the courts, I would describe it as being trapped in the backseat of a car while it crashes in slow motion. I spent years making my case to judges, experts and lawyers, all of whom failed to agree on what was actually happening between my ex-wife, my kids and myself. I saw six judges in total over the period, and we were assessed four times for the purposes of reporting back to the court, plus my kids saw three additional therapists who were not court-ordered. The judgements were inconsistent, the reports were both inconsistent and inconclusive. The whole thing felt like a waste of time in hindsight. At the time it seemed like I was constantly trying to prove a negative, to find a new direction to reach my kids, all were promising, all ended in expensive dead ends.

At every turn, my allegations of Parental Alienation begged the question of who was qualified to decide it. Was the word of one of the UK's leading consultant child psychiatrists enough? Or a psychologist and established family therapist? A young Cafcass social worker? An experienced child counsellor? What about all of them taken on aggregate? The sad truth dawned on me that judges are just not qualified to make these decisions. Neither the judge nor the opposing barrister had met my children, yet they were making life-changing decisions for them. The experts and reports can't compete with that. It all comes down to a contest of words, bias and luck.

I had experienced this before. In my Financial Dispute Resolution hearing 2011 when my ex-wife demanded more money, my barrister was delighted when the judge appeared. He told me the judge was a friend of his, and he was getting divorced and my ex-wife's law firm was also representing his wife. No kidding. He said the result was a foregone conclusion. The judge had a grudge, apparently. I have no idea if it was true or not. The outcome was more favourable than the out of court settlement I offered my wife, so perhaps he was right.

Although I benefited from that turn of events, it showed me – and to this day it still shocks me – how broken and subjective the court process can be. There should be no room for that kind of personal animosity before the law or within the mechanisms by which people's most personal issues are decided. As someone who has spent his life around the highly regulated worlds of public limited companies, property and financial services, the relative lack of oversight, conflict of interest and poor compliance procedures within the courts seems almost unthinkable.

I represented myself in the end. I wanted to cut through all the noise and legal waffle and get down to basics. I wanted to see my kids, I hadn't seen them for years. My kids seemed to hate me for frivolous reasons initially and latterly for deeply personal reasons that had been revealed to them by my ex-wife – which proved influence and manipulation. My kids were also suffering as a result of my ex-wife's poor safeguarding in her home, as evidenced by the fact they were victims of online grooming and self-harming. Their schoolwork was suffering. They were in a private clinic with a diagnosis of anxiety and depression. They needed help and my ex-wife and her family denied they even had a problem. These sorts of accounts are common in alienation cases, I had heard them dozens – hundreds – of times in my own research. I assumed, because it seemed so obvious, that everyone in the court process would see it too.

I had a case that was so open and shut, I didn't need a lawyer. I didn't need to represent myself. I could – like my ex-wife did – afford a top London barrister with a reputation for shredding experts in the witness box, but I didn't choose one. I wanted to get my kids back. I thought all I would have to do is present the findings of the experts that had assessed the children over time, and present my obvious situation of being cut off for no good reason. I thought the court would call my ex-wife to explain my safeguarding concerns, which would force them to at the very least restart contact in some small way. It was all there in the reports, after all. The facts, the problems, and my obvious estrangement without cause.

As you know from the previous chapters, that's not how it works. I have already written that claiming Parental Alienation goes against you, and it surely does. It is treated like a conspiracy theory and you are treated like you are wearing a tin-foil hat and claiming NASA faked the moon landings. In my case, the issue of Parental Alienation was dismissed out of hand by the final judge, heavily influenced by the arguments of my ex-wife's barrister and ruling in line with the Cafcass recommendations. The barrister was cruel. In my mind, a complete bastard who gets rich by legitimising abusive situations like the one my kids and I were in. He argued, having never even met my children, that their wishes and feelings to never see me again were valid. He argued that the consultant child psychiatrist had breached his remit. He won those arguments, and that was that. It felt like the judge was asleep at the wheel of a juggernaut.

He was very effective at steering the judge's attention towards the one report – the Cafcass Guardian's report – which dismissed alienation out of hand, not the other reports (multiples from three highly qualified experts) which all partially or fully supported my claim of Parental Alienation to a greater or lesser degree. Enough to warrant further attention and certainly contradicting the Cafcass Guardian report.

The barrister managed to discredit the other reports, which is to be expected because there is no standardised measure or statutory definition of Parental Alienation, which means the experts couldn't reach that conclusion in terminology that would be accepted by the court. The psychiatrist called it alienation – in the English sense of the word, the psychologist called it a hybrid case with some characteristics of alienation but used a set of measures that come from the US and aren't accepted by UK professional associations or the law, which the Judge stated he found useful. There was the initial report from a children's counsellor that laid the blame squarely at my ex-wife's door, but didn't use the word alienation. The only report that used the term was the Cafcass report and the Cafcass Guardian dismissed it in a single line.

However, none of the reports dismissed my claims in any way. Nor did they exonerate my ex-wife as being falsely accused of Parental Alienation. They also noted that my wife was not supportive of contact between me and my kids – and this was to the detriment of their welfare, as the Children Act states. However, none of those things are proof of Parental Alienation. And none of those things stopped the judge from ruling me out of the kids' lives forever.

The Cafcass report carried the most sway with the judge as far as the final ruling was concerned – from the person who was the least experienced, least senior and least academically qualified of the four. It was my children's Cafcass Guardian. My ex-wife had pressed for my children to be ruled competent, and then assigned their own legal representation and guardian. I realise now, this was a tactical move on her part. It removed her from the question and set me against my own children in the court process. It also introduced yet another lawyer – whose fees I ultimately agreed to pay – and introduced a Cafcass Guardian who without doubt assessed me as an angry, impatient man with a grievance. She assessed my ex-wife in very positive terms. My kids too.

My ex-wife and I were due to attend an assessment interview at the Cafcass offices, but she was a no-show. I was interviewed, alone, faced with the Cafcass manager, the

Cafcass Guardian and my children's lawyer (court appointed on the basis of consent). I was in a 3-to-1 interview between me and the opposing side in my Family Court proceeding. It denied me the opportunity to raise any questions with my ex-wife in front of them as witnesses.

My ex-wife, on the other hand, received a home visit and a cup of tea with the children's Cafcass Guardian and the children's lawyer – or in other words, her side of the Family Court proceeding. They had a friendly chat, I received a grilling. My ex-wife wasn't asked any difficult questions. She wasn't interrogated. The tone of the interview was different. More worryingly, whereas I was asked to justify my position, my ex-wife was never questioned about hers. I was asking to see my kids, she was never asked why I hadn't. I claimed there were safeguarding concerns arising from the events that had happened to my kids in her home, these were never addressed. It was taken as a given in her interview, and in the final Cafcass report, that my children didn't want to see me and my ex-wife was being supportive of their wishes and feelings – and by logic, therefore, I was not.

The matter of Parental Alienation was completely ignored.

The safeguarding issues were completely ignored.

The matter of my ex-wife exposing my children to all sorts of personal, private information was also completely ignored.

This is typical of the lack of agreed processes or fair due process of law within the Family Courts. The experts who play a part should be governed by a universal set of standards that mean everyone is treated equally and investigated fairly. We should all get interviewed with the same rights by the opposing side or we all get home visit with our legal team, but not one rule for one side and different one for the other.

Of course in this case, Cafcass would argue they were there to represent the children, not my ex-wife. However, in Parental Alienation – as we know – those two sets of interests are aligned. You can't claim the ability to represent the children's wishes when their wishes are the result of psychological influence by the resident parent. At that point you are simply representing the resident parent by proxy through the kids. This is why the consultant child psychiatrist interviewed the children not together but separately. He was supposed to interview them with me as well, to see how we interacted, but they refused. As a result, we never got the chance to engage in a dialogue before a court expert, which undermined the whole process of assessment in my opinion – again I suspect this was designed to stop any chance of us reuniting.

Why did I pursue the case the way I did?

When I first discovered I couldn't work through my ex-wife or the school to see my kids again, I was forced to resort to the Family Courts. I think the school was instrumental in making me choose that direction because they did not help to resolve the problem. After all, it was the school that suggested we take a break and cool off – and that became a major sticking point for the case against me because it meant I had effectively broken off contact. It made it look like I had alienated myself, when in fact, I was taking the advice of my kids' school. It later came to light that my ex-wife was heavily involved with the school as Chair of the Parent-Teacher Association, and the school was sharing information with her but not with me. I think that schools should be a fundamental part of ensuring good relationships between children and parents in the context of home life and particularly in the context of divorce. I will address that in the next chapter, but for the purposes of this chapter, I want to explain why I chose the route I chose in my case of Parental Alienation.

My view was heavily influenced by my own research into the field of Parental Alienation. I had never heard of it before my kids cut me off. I started looking into the topic when it felt like something was blocking my ability to reach the kids. I am well aware of the saying that *a little knowledge is a dangerous thing* and I have to be honest, I was shocked and scared by what I read. There are groups on social media with thousands of people, all alienated, all telling their own stories. Many are shocking. Many are shockingly similar to mine.

There are many accounts and descriptions of the way legal processes block access to children through diverting the alienation claims through counter claims like asking for more money, or accusations of abuse that are never followed through with by the police. I was fortunate that I never experienced that – my ex-wife was a multimillionaire and I was paying my share. My ex-wife and one of my children did make claims that were untrue about me, for sure, which influenced the judge in the final judgement, but they never escalated them to the police.

They accused me of *'physically assaulting'* one of the kids as Cafcass described it. I have mentioned this. I *'clipped'* one of the kids on the back of the head – a light tap to get her attention – the third time I had to go upstairs and tell them to stop before they brought the ceiling down on me by jumping off the bed with a bunch of sleepover friends at midnight, aged 11. There were no tears, no bruises, no lumps, no shrieks. It did get her to listen. It was not a smack. It was nothing like an assault. And were it anything else, why didn't anyone raise it – my ex-wife, or either of my children – at the time or at any time in the next two years?

In fact, on that point, turning *'clipped'* on the head into *'physical assault'* is more of the obfuscation I wrote about in chapter 2. However in this case, it wasn't my ex-wife's legal team doing it, it was the Cafcass Guardian who was hostile towards me. I was particularly shocked by this because it wasn't just a gross distortion of the facts, they never asked me about it. In my Cafcass interview, this was never raised. In the notes of the Cafcass interview with my ex-wife, it was never raised. As far as the legal paper trail generated by Cafcass goes, the issue of a clip or an assault was never discussed. It's important to note that in Family Court assessments, there is no reasonable expectation of scrutiny or consistency. A major accusation – and being accused of physically assaulting your own child is just that – can literally appear in a damning and influential report (like a Cafcass recommendation to the court) without any legitimate investigation or discussion with the accused. It's another example of the bias people associate with Cafcass, and the unfit processes of Family Court in general.

What really scared me about the potential disaster that my kids were facing came from the way all the accounts I read described the way the resident abuser parent and their team plays for time, and that the longer the time that passes, the more the courts and lawyers focus on the most recent issues raised rather than the original one – the fact one parent hasn't seen their kids for years. It scared me because the longer the Parental Alienation goes on, the risk of the children suffering mental health and behavioural problems increases. Their education suffers. They start acting out at school. They often self-harm through anxiety and depression. They often develop damaging sexual relationships or get groomed by perverts. There are increased risks of substance abuse and eating disorders. It's every parent's nightmare and it all hinges around time. The longer the alienation goes on, the worse things get.

I learned about the damage Parental Alienation causes to kids before my children suffered academically. Before there were behavioural issues at school. Before they became anxious and depressed. Before one of them self-harmed. Before the other was groomed by an online predator. I warned the school about it. I warned my ex-wife's legal team about it. I told the judge. I told anyone who would listen. Over the next three years, it all happened to my beautiful kids. I couldn't help them. I couldn't do anything. I couldn't even watch, I could only learn about it after the fact, through doggedly demanding the school and my ex-wife's lawyers share information with me – as was my legal right as a parent. This was why I was forced to go to court and demand my kids get help.

The huge negative impact of Parental Alienation on children was my first concern, and remains so to this day. This is why when my first attempts to re-establish contact failed, I asked to go down the child mental health expert route. I felt then and still do, that regardless of what lawyers say, we listen to doctors. In the case of alienation, where so much of the abuse revolves around the psychological manipulation of children, a specialist consultant child psychiatrist or child psychologist should be the authority of record. Not lawyers. Not social workers. Clinicians who specialise in children should hold sway over whether your kids are suffering from being manipulated and turned against one parent by the other.

The problem here is the pathway can be highly variable in quality. In my case, after an initial report by a very senior consultant child psychiatrist, our lawyers agreed to seeing a family therapist who was qualified but had only experience of one case of Parental Alienation. Also, she was located too far away from the kids so they resented that, and didn't like the therapist. Worse, her suggestion of spending years in therapy to resolve the issue just meant increasing the time I was kept away from the kids. I couldn't afford to wait that long whilst knowing how much the time away could lead to serious issues.

There was only one therapist recommended to us who specialised in Parental Alienation reports. This specialist was recommended by the family therapist. The specialist was too busy, with a long waiting list. She didn't even respond to my lawyers. This is typical. Parental Alienation has few experts, and those that do exist are hopelessly overloaded with cases.

When that process failed, there was another attempt to see a therapist – again, qualified but I was against it. The therapist refused to cooperate with me or share any information on the grounds of Gillick Competence, and one of my kids started self-harming shortly afterwards.

This made me wary of the private health route. It was too hard to know if the care the kids were receiving was effective or not. I wanted the kids to see a doctor. A normal, community GP. Someone who is the front line of referring people into the NHS psychiatric care pathways. My kids needed help and I felt an NHS solution would be harder for lawyers and my ex-wife to manipulate. In the end, the children entered a private clinic with another psychologist who recorded their issues as stress-related. Their anxiety and depression was a result of the acrimonious legal proceedings in her view – which of course was tautology. Their problems began before the legal proceedings, otherwise, the proceedings wouldn't have been necessary. The kids cut me off, for no good reason, and refused to see me ever again. That was the problem we faced. Parental Alienation was the cause, not stress, and the children's problems were the effect.

By the end of the process, realising that I couldn't bring that solution to bear while my kids were resident with my non-cooperative ex-wife, I applied for a change of residency. Too late. My kids hated therapy and hated therapists and experts. My kids were receiving therapy in a clinic, self-harming and had been the victims of internet grooming. My kids professed to never want to see me again, and they had their own lawyer and Cafcass Guardian who didn't question what was happening and referred to the kids as 'normal teenagers' despite everything they were going through.

That experience showed me there is no workable process for addressing Parental Alienation. At the end of it, I was still alienated. I still hadn't done anything to warrant it. My kids were in a mess and my ex-wife did nothing to help me or them, and insisted they were, according to the many reports and experts, just normal, average, anxious, depressed, stressed-out, self-harming internet abused kids like all average teenagers. It was ridiculous.

Why isn't there a workable court process to address Parental Alienation?

Parental Alienation is recognised by the Family Courts, social workers, therapists and lawyers. It exists. However as I have written before, there is no shared definition, no agreed way to measure it, no specialist training on how to recognise it or deal with it. So it exists in name only as far as doing anything about it is concerned. In reality, there are thousands of parents who are cut off from their children and can't see them, who claim to be alienated. However, there are no mechanisms to resolve it other than the same mechanisms that exist to resolve disputes over contact where there is no alienation. Parental Alienation cases can't be resolved in the same way as a judge would decide a child arrangement order in usual circumstances.

I was poorly advised on that front at the time. My lawyers recommended Family Court, hearing in private. However, that process wasn't the only one available. These days most lawyers will recommend a different kind of private hearing where both sides agree to a court arbitration hearing with a private judge called an Arbitrator – not a District or Deputy District Judge. Arbitrators are specially trained in conflict resolution. The option of arbitration became law in 2012, so in time for me to access it, but my lawyers didn't inform me about it. In 2016, specialist Family Law arbitration became an option as well. Again, I was never made aware of it – as I was also within the Family Courts at that point.

Whether arbitration is an option or not in alienation cases is debatable. Both sides have to agree to it, and agree to abide by the ruling of the Arbitrator. It also precludes then going to Family Court if you don't support the ruling. However, lawyers report the system is much better at getting resolutions because it forces people to compromise – whereas the Family Court is an adversarial battle where one side wins and one loses, in most scenarios.

In most cases, people claiming Parental Alienation lose in Family Court because no statutory definition exists. That means that the courts and judges can't decide if alienation is happening or not. However, in this bizarre catch-22 there is widespread recognition that parental alienation exists. It exists in cases where the children are turned against one parent and refuse contact due to psychological manipulation by the resident parent. However, the only legal mechanism available to resolve these cases is the same one used in cases where the children have not been turned against one parent and refuse contact due to psychological manipulation by the resident parent. It's a self-referencing paradox.

Consider that for a moment.

When determining whether to make a child arrangements order, a judge must consider the wishes and feelings of the child. Children are inevitably pulled in different directions by messy divorces, and depending on their age, a child's wishes and feelings can have a prominent steering on the resulting judgement. If the children want to see both parents, the courts will usually arrange contact and facilitate it in some way. However, in Parental Alienation, the child's wishes and feelings aren't reliable because of manipulation by the resident parent. Therefore they cannot be used as a guide for the court.

That means the same process that orders contact in cases where children want to see both parents, is the same process that denies contact in cases where children don't want to see one parent. So, if Parental Alienation is taking place, the courts compound the problem. This means there is an urgent need to find another way of assessing the best interest of the child in alienation cases. If the kids decided their wishes and feelings were to stop going to school, nobody would agree with it. It would be a life-changing decision with huge long-term consequences. Cutting your parents out of your life is the same, and yet wishes and feelings are enough.

That last point is crucial. The best interest – or *welfare* – of the child is defined in law as a relationship with both parents. Seeing one parent only isn't in the child's best interests, unless there is a safeguarding issue. In Parental Alienation cases where there are no safeguarding issues – like mine – the wishes and feelings of the child are therefore to the detriment of their own welfare. The concept of wishes and feelings only works if there is no alienation.

What this means is in Parental Alienation cases, the court becomes a mechanism by which the domestic abuse of Parental Alienation is administered. In other words, the court unwittingly becomes the channel that delivers the abuse to the victims of it. That is a clear institutional failing. The system only works if you can rely on the wishes and feelings of the child. If you can't rely on their wishes and feelings the whole system fails. This is why there are thousands of alienated parents – and a growing body of lawyers, judges and politicians – claiming the Family Court process is not fit for purpose and in urgent need of reform.

Without a widespread definition of Parental Alienation and how it presents, how it works and how to measure it, few professionals are willing or capable to support an alienated parent's claim. In Parental Alienation cases, there are only a handful of experts worldwide. The subject has not been widely researched, and in one very high profile case, Dr Richard Gardner's Parental Alienation Syndrome, for example, there are serious questions over the veracity of his research and findings. Parental Alienation is a legal and psychological grey area in almost every respect, but that doesn't diminish how serious or damaging it is.

Most experts in the field or adjacent fields like psychology and psychiatry will acknowledge a relative lack of research into the area compared to other child-parent issues, and an almost complete lack of training for court-appointed experts to spot cases of Parental Alienation based on the research we already have. Whether the expert is qualified to speak about Parental Alienation is therefore highly subjective. Whether their tools or assessments are sound and reliable is also highly subjective. As a result, if a social worker claims you are not being alienated, but a consultant child psychiatrist (with the most experience on the subject) says you are, the judge is blinded by the endless amount of mud being thrown and completely loses sight of the core issue while also having to adopt the Cafcass report as being the main road forward.

The social worker probably has the least training and the highest caseload, and possibly spent a few hours in total on your case as opposed to the consultant who might have spent days over the period and is medically trained. One should outweigh the other, and the process for deciding which report takes precedence over another should be transparent and clear for all to see. Without doubt, the final judgement of the family court is as highly subjective and unreliable as the reports is it based on.

Parental Alienation is a problem of expertise, or rather, a widespread lack of it. This fact, however, should also raise a number of red flags. The history of domestic abuse within the courts is very much a history of a lack of expertise. In fact, the history of law, especially criminal law, is much the same. There was a time when most of the protections we expect in law relating to racial abuse, sexual abuse and all manner of discrimination didn't exist. These are not consigned to ancient history either.

Within just my lifetime, concepts like workplace bullying, constructive dismissal, racial discrimination, age discrimination, gender discrimination, disability discrimination, sexual harassment and consent have all been transformed in the courts. They were unheard of when I was a kid in the 1970s. They were rare occurrences when I started working in the 1980s, and not that widely understood even in the 1990s. The changing landscape of social and personal rights and abuses have reshaped everything in our daily lives in the last two decades from criminal law to HR interviewing techniques and employment tribunals. The basic rights we expect at work and in society are constantly evolving.

One day the same will be true of Parental Alienation, its recognition and its resolution.

How should the courts address Parental Alienation?

Unlike other forms of domestic abuse, Parental Alienation is invisible to the naked eye, at least, for the alienated parent. The outward signs of domestic violence aren't there to be documented or questioned. Where there is physical harm – most usually on the side of the children – it is self-inflicted. One of my children began self-harming mid-way through my three-year battle to restore contact. Self-harm is common in cases of alienated children.

There are also obvious signs of mental distress for parents and children in alienation cases. Alienated parents often display signs of post-traumatic stress. They are often paranoid and anxious. Alienated children will suffer from anxiety and depression, or develop stress-induced behaviours like eating disorders, acting out at school or sexual promiscuity at a very young age. Again, these are often noted by experts in the field. The problem is the field is new, there aren't many experts, and although support is growing for more do be done the courts and professional organisations involved are very slow to react and change.

There are also regular tactics that the abuser parent uses in Parental Alienation cases. Often starting with refusing to comply with contact orders or agreements. They also interfere in contact arrangements by calling or intruding on time. They often ask schools to limit the other parent's access to their children or reports. They rely on schools and other organisations to be unsure of their legal obligations, and take advantage of that. They frequently agree to mediation and therapy only to end it without discussion. They will ask healthcare professionals not to share reports and records with the other side. They also often push for the children to be deemed legally competent and capable of Gillick consent (consent to treatment under the legal age based on individual competence) and push for children to be appointed state social workers and their own lawyers to represent them in court.

These tactics combine with one simple – but devastating – effect. They complicate the Family Court process and make it take longer. Time is an important factor in Parental Alienation. The longer it takes to resolve the lack of contact, the longer the children and the alienated parent are apart and the harder it is to re-establish relations. The Family Court is slow and busy, hearings are often set months away, and then interventions are booked in months more after that. However, the longer the child is away from both parents, the harder it is to stop the alienation. They are being manipulated and growing more distant from the alienated parent at the same time. Parental Alienation cases are usually stories of repeated attempts, and repeated failures, to re-establish contact. The thing that remains constant is the fact one parent hasn't seen their children for a long time, and the children don't want to see that parent and their hostility increases the longer the time they are estranged.

If the courts and court-appointed officials were trained to look for these signs, or apply an assessment framework to measure them consistently, Parental Alienation would be much easier to deal with. Perhaps one red flag or another might not be enough to raise a query about alienation, but if many of these hallmarks are observable, surely there should be some kind of intervention? Anyone who has taken a young child to Accident and Emergency will know that no matter how innocent the child's injury, the nurses check for signs of abuse like bruising or cuts. Parental Alienation could be preventable if children in Family Court were checked over like that, except looking for the signs of psychological abuse, not physical.

For the rest of this chapter, I would like to consider a few clear starting points to present a better pathway to diagnose claims of Parental Alienation than the almost non-existent one we have available in court today. This is the kind of work I am involved in these days, after my terrible experience in Family Court ended. I am working with experts in the fields of family law and Parental Alienation to bring about a better way of addressing the claims of alienated parents to remove the grossly subjective and highly variable opinions and judgements that characterise a Family Court process can't possibly work in cases of alienation.

A reasonable assessment process for the parents and children

Parental Alienation is a situation you can't really understand at the time it is happening. We experience most traumas – like bereavement or heartbreak – in small doses as we grow up and mature. Your first pet dies, first loves and high school sweethearts come and go. Grandparents and school kids get sick and so on. There's a sad but useful childhood exposure to difficult life journeys and emotional distress that helps us develop the resilience to deal with more acute, more painful, more distressing inevitable events in our adult lives.

Parental Alienation bears no relationship to anything else you have experienced in your life before. You are not prepared for it, you can't even recognise it until it's too late to do anything about it. When I share my own experiences with other alienated parents, the way it is often described is this growing sense that your life has taken on the menacing overtones of an old Alfred Hitchcock thriller. It is referred to now as gaslighting, after another old thriller with Ingrid Bergman from the 1940s, in which a malevolent husband tries to send his wife insane by messing with the lights.

Most of us will report the same sense of doubting yourself, to the point of doubting your own sanity. I certainly did. You find it hard to gauge other people's intentions, and find it hard to trust the advice and opinions of the professionals you are forced to seek help from. Alienated parents often use words like sinister and paranoid, with good reason. You can't be sure of anything other than the clock is ticking down and your kids are drifting further and further away.

I describe it like being a caged wild animal. Suddenly you are caught in something you don't understand, something you have never even imagined before. None of the life skills you relied upon out in the big wide world can prepare you for the claustrophobia of it. You are like an animal in the zoo, your most intimate details on display for all to see and discuss. And like all caged animals, you either submit to the reality of the situation no matter how much it wrecks your mental health. Or die.

The reason I raise this – and the fact so many alienated parents report similar experiences of the emotional and mental health trauma of this particular form of domestic abuse – is because it's not a question that factors in the court process. Specifically, nobody asks what is wrong with you when you appear paranoid, angry, stressed or desperate. None of the court officials, judges, Cafcass Guardians, social workers recognise your obvious distress. Most often, those people take a look at you and decide that your demeanour explains why your kids don't want to see you. Why would they? After all, you're angry and paranoid. You are clearly a short-tempered, argumentative person. You don't trust people. You appear abrupt, desperate even. If you parented like that, no wonder your ex-wife left and your kids are scared of you.

Nobody asks if you were like this *before* you claimed Parental Alienation. I have often said so myself, and heard from others, that surely if your claims of alienation were true but you appeared calm and serene about it, that would be abnormal. Of course you are climbing the walls with stress! You are scared for your kids. You fear losing them. Who wouldn't get angry at that?

As I have mentioned before in this book, it's another catch-22. There are many signs of Parental Alienation that make you look bad to people who don't know what to look for. By the same token, there are signs that make your children seem happy when they clearly are not. If children appear perfectly rational when they say they never want to see Mum or Dad ever again, that's abnormal. Children don't make that decision rationally and calmly. They don't decide to break off friendships at school or leave the football team without crying about it. Deciding you hate your parents is emotional and traumatic, so if they appear fine with it, that's a sure sign something is wrong.

There is a fundamental problem where the abuser resident parent seems to be able to get away with their abuse by using one infallible defence – they argue that they are only supporting their children. If their kids don't want to see the other parent, the abuser resident parent appears kind and compassionate by saying they will do whatever their kids want. That is not what parenting is about. My children, whom I love dearly, would have stayed up all night eating sweets if they could, but kids need sleep and a healthy diet and teeth. So I would send them to bed, make them brush their teeth and make them eat their greens. We don't support them to do things that are unhealthy. Again, I repeat the Children Act guiding principle that a relationship with both parents is in the best interests of the child. It therefore should follow that in the absence of safeguarding concerns a reasonable parent should strive to ensure contact for the welfare of their own child. To actively allow non-contact orders to continue in these circumstances is bad for the children. It is a form of neglect.

In my case, my ex-wife claimed to support contact. She was also cited by three of the court-appointed professionals in four reports as doing nothing to promote or restart contact. Omission, it was called by one, passivity by another. In the damning Cafcass report, it wasn't mentioned on the grounds they were happy for my ex-wife to support the kids in no contact because I was punitive, blaming and aggressive. No safeguarding issues, but you know, I behaved like someone who was climbing the walls with panic over their self-harming kids in the depression clinic.

Once again, this is a typical behaviour and an indicator of alienation.

So what would it take for the Family Court to change the approach? A framework designed around typical Parental Alienation cases, like mine, would look something like this:

At the point of divorce both parents should be warned of the risks to children if they do not support contact with each other, these include mental health problems, self-harm, eating disorders, anxiety and depression. This must be reinforced by lawyers and judges at every opportunity. It's not enough to simply quote the principles of the Children Act, it should be a fundamental part of every hearing.

When a parent claims alienation, lawyers must deal with this issue urgently and appoint an expert to opine. It is not acceptable for the resident parent to simply say they support the child's decision to reject the other parent.

A category of recognised experts should be defined and accredited. An untrained therapist will make the situation worse in most cases, so it should be someone with clinical expertise in dealing with children – like a consultant child psychiatrist or a clinical child psychologist.

Schools must be included in contact arrangements or child arrangements orders by the courts and made aware of the risks of harm to children. They must also maintain a neutral position with both parents at all times – especially with regard to sharing all information equally with both responsible parents. This would prevent abusive resident parents from hiding issues from the other parent – which is a way of alienating them.

The GP must also be included for continuity of care and oversight. The GP must share all records with both parents for alienated children and this should supersede *Gillick Competence* or *capacity to consent*. This would prevent abusive resident parents from hiding issues like self-harm or eating disorders from the other parent.

If there are no safeguarding concerns relating to the non-resident parent, then action must be taken as soon as possible. This should come from the judge who should be guided by statute to prioritise a speedy restarting of contact between the estranged parent and the child to minimise the danger of alienation increasing over time. The judge should also make it clear to the resident parent they must support contact and it is their job to resolve the issue within a reasonable time frame (e.g. next three months). Ultimately, the only effective way to end alienation is for the resident parent to be part of the solution to the problem. They must be court ordered to promote and facilitate contact, if necessary. If contact is not re-established within the allotted time frame, the judge must consider a change of residency or 50-50 shared residency by way of court order.

If there are safeguarding concerns, then these need to be defined and categorised by scale. It is evident that some parents are a risk to children, and this must be defined at the outset. Children should also be reviewed independently by the GP and school at regular intervals to ensure the court intervention is on track and productive.

The sad truth about the failure of the process

The reason we need a specialist assessment framework – and the one I outline above is a very simplified approach to it to convey my point – is simple. Identifying parental alienation is challenging for the courts. Judges and experts quite literally can't agree on what alienation is, or when it is happening.

If you describe a situation where one parent has gone to the Family Court because the resident parent has refused to comply willingly with a contact order, that doesn't immediately mean it's Parental Alienation. Indeed, if there are no safeguarding issues for the children, and the parent claiming alienation doesn't have any accusations of domestic abuse, domestic violence, addiction or criminality hanging over them, that should raise a red flag – but it doesn't automatically mean Parental Alienation either.

In cases where a parent moves away and makes contact arrangements more complicated, or begins a new relationship where there are other siblings or partners who have problems with the children of a previous marriage, there could be legitimate reasons for refusing contact. What we all have to acknowledge – especially alienated parents – is the Family Courts have to deal with a huge diversity of family situations and not all of them will mean contact orders remain fit for purpose or are workable practically.

What is different about Parental Alienation cases is the tell-tale combination of factors including but not limited to: acrimony between the parents, the children are conflicted and distressed, there is non-contact over a prolonged period of time which is deeply damaging to the parent-child relationship, and which keeps getting worse the longer the non-contact continues. The estranged parent is anxious, depressed, traumatised and at high risk of suicide. In that combined scenario, there should be a procedure to investigate the claim of Parental Alienation. Otherwise, the inevitable conclusion is the judge – as in my case and often reported – cannot decide what is going on and rules for non-contact because the children are showing signs of stress, and it is assumed the stress is coming from the acrimony of the court case and not for another reason like Parental Alienation. The tragedy of the ruling is that the cure is worse than the illness, so to speak.

In my case, the one thing all the expert reports agreed upon was the ongoing court case was bad for the children. Although the different experts all suggested different reasons as to why, and different remedies, the basic problem was the kids were depressed and anxious. Ending the court battles and cutting me out of their lives was the easiest solution – and the one that happens time and again. This is the ultimate catch-22. You lose your kids. You fight to see them because you love them. You fight to see them because you know their lives are going to suffer with all sorts of emotional, mental health and behavioural problems as a result of the abuse of Parental Alienation. You fight to see your kids because the alternative is to let them down and abandon them. To let them suffer.

So you fight. Of course you do! And the only mechanism you can access to do so – the Family Court – is a mechanism that is geared up to fail. In the end, the judge puts a stop to your case on the basis your kids have been through enough. In my story, the judge, the Cafcass Guardian, the psychiatrist, the therapist and the counsellors all agreed the best thing that could happen is my ex-wife and I work out our differences and cooperate in the interests of the children. Which would have been nice, but it was never going to happen otherwise we wouldn't be in court. It's like a doctor wishing someone would just magically get well from cancer. That would be nice but no, you need to operate. In the same way, they needed to intervene to stop the abuse my kids and I were suffering.

But what the judge ruled instead was to force me to stop fighting.

That was an outrage.

It is like asking the victim to drop their charges against the abuser.

It's like asking the victim to drop their charges against the abuser and expecting the abuser to spontaneously stop the abuse.

It's like asking the victim to drop their charges against the abuser, expecting the abuser to spontaneously stop the abuse and expecting everyone to magically be friends.

I was fighting to see my kids because I had been cut off from them, because my ex-wife was making them hate me and they were suffering as a result. I wasn't fighting to see them because my ex-wife was a reasonable person who wanted me to have a relationship with them. I wasn't fighting to see my kids because they were doing great, they were in a mess. My ex-wife was responsible for a child that cut words into their thigh? My ex-wife was watching TV on the sofa while some online pervert asks my 12 year old for nude pictures? Damn right I fought to see my kids. Damn right I wanted them to be better looked after than that!

If I had stood by and done nothing, I would have lost them. When I fought, I lost them. The system that was supposed to protect us from alienation, something I can never recover from, something that has ruined my life and theirs, that system became the reason why the alienation was allowed to go on.

I was left with the Cafcass Guardian's suggestion, an indirect contact order by the judge. I was not allowed to contact my children directly. I could write, no more than once per month, a letter to each one. Those letters had to be sent to my ex-wife, who would have the final say over passing them on to my children or not. There would be no requirement for my children to write back.

The judge and the guardian basically put the person responsible for cutting me off from my children – the domestic abuser – in sole charge of the only possible chance I had to reach my kids and end the abuse. It was nonsense. Nothing I had done, demonstrated or argued had made the slightest difference. The judge rambled on about it being a shame, about having a relationship with both parents is in the Children Act and the situation was bad for them, sure. But in the end, the court decision was leaving them in that situation was preferable to resolving it through further court action.

This is how the abuser wins. They run the clock down. There are only so many interventions possible before the children say they have had enough. As the time runs down, so your anxiety and panic increases. I actually saw where things were headed, when my ex-wife's barrister destroyed the expert witness – the consultant child psychiatrist – on the stand for suggesting my ex-wife had deliberately allowed the children to discover material that turned them against me. As I wrote at the top of this chapter, in the end, it's all down to a sensible judge. It's not a contract dispute, or a criminal trial. It's supposed to be a mechanism to protect our right to a family life, our fundamental human rights. It is treated like you're haggling over who is to blame in a car accident.

I asked to withdraw my case so I could regroup. I wasn't granted leave to do so.

The judge rules that unless they wanted to see me, I would never see my kids again. He even said it was a shame, but the court case was too much for them.

Which means if I had never tried to see them, or simply abandoned them, the result would be no different than if I fought desperately to see them.

That is not the outcome of an effective process, it is the outcome of a broken system that isn't fit for purpose. In the final analysis, my kids and I were the victims of abuse, a pernicious from of domestic abuse that was facilitated by the failure of the Family Court and Cafcass to determine the difference between a child's wishes and feelings, and the psychological manipulation of children by an aggrieved mother to cause pain and distress to their loving father.

Chapter 6:
Schools – the missing link in preventing Alienation

One of the hardest things about writing this book has been to work out how to tell the story of my alienation in any sort of order with a beginning, middle and end. That might sound strange, but the experience of alienation is like a hurricane of problems, legal correspondence and court appearances. You are constantly responding to urgent requests for information, having meetings and calls, rushing from one situation to the next. As a result, it's hard to form a big picture of what is happening in your case as you try to deal with so many things at once. It's even harder to get a perspective when your world is being turned upside-down and inside-out by the trauma of losing your kids.

One of the hardest things about turning all that chaos into a story is events happen in parallel with each other, particularly if you have two children because they have their own experiences that make up their sides of the story. I am not just telling my story, I am trying to tell the story of how I lost two relationships with two individuals and both of them have their own stories to explain their part in all of this.

The alienated parent with two kids ends up trying to manage a Family Court case for both children, but every report and every intervention or possible solution has to work for each one separately. It's a one-size-fits-all compromise, which is why it doesn't work – one-size-fits-all never works in relationships. You might see progress with one child, you might see a complete lack of it with another. Where one child might be open to reconciliation, the other might not. One might see you and shout angry things, the other might have a panic attack and cry. Both children might present their own versions of events, and both will have their own unique problems arising from the alienation. The story is like a pile of jigsaw pieces, like your broken relationship. Putting it back together feels like an impossible puzzle at times.

It's all but impossible to work out which bit fits where in that story because you don't learn about the emotional and personal crisis each child has endured in order, and it is always after the fact. It takes a long time to look back and see that A led to B and C led to D and so on. At the time, it's as much as you can do to keep up with lawyers' letters and the school reports. The mental strain and stress is huge. You have to become familiar, very quickly, with complex court processes and legalese. That would be hard enough if you were studying for a law degree, but while you are climbing the walls with worry about your kids? It's a truly dreadful experience.

The issue of both children having their own issues to deal with was brought home to me when the children got their own lawyer and Cafcass Guardian, who represented them as competent and distinct from my ex-wife. However, they were both represented by a single Guardian and a single lawyer. This meant their individual interests were rolled-up into one joint interest. Surely, if that system was a fair reflection of individual competence and representation before the court, they should have a lawyer and a Guardian each? If they had, maybe I wouldn't have completely lost contact with both children. There was no reason for them to have just one lawyer for them both, other than it was my ex-wife's suggestion. I agreed on the basis that if my kids had an opportunity to get out from under her influence, they might be more open to reconciliation. I was completely wrong. All it meant was my ex-wife could wash her hands completely of any responsibility and adopt a position – which she stated many times on the record – that she would support whatever the kids wanted, and whatever the courts decided.

My ex-wife's position is a neat legal tactic. The alienator wins by making the kids hostile, and then hiding behind their wishes and feelings. It meant that, in effect, I was now fighting my kids in court. It also meant that where my ex-wife was now submitting to the will of the court. She was assuming no position and making no case whereas I was fighting with my kids, against their wishes and feelings, and in effect fighting to make Cafcass and the Family Court reach a judgement in my favour. That meant the court case became all about applying scrutiny to my side, and none on my ex-wife. I was claiming abuse, but now I wasn't fighting a case against my alleged abuser, I was fighting it against the other victims of the abuse – my kids.

To put that another way, my ex-wife's position became one where she didn't mind either way what happened between me and my kids? She would accept any ruling? Really? Then why had she fought me so hard to block all attempts to restart contact for the two years previously? What changed for her? If she had no opinion either way then surely the whole legal battle had been for nothing. That fact alone makes her position totally unbelievable. Again, this is an area that should trigger a red flag – when the alleged abuser in a case of Parental Alienation suddenly has a change of heart and backs off, leaving the kids in charge.

In all the court reports – except the Cafcass report – one of my kids is described as conflicted, the other is quite definite in their opinion of me. In all the court reports – except the Cafcass report – one of my kids wants to avoid getting caught up in arguments with the other over the alienation, over seeing me and over working it out. One of my kids is – in all the Court-ordered assessments – more open to working things out than the other, but won't assert themselves. One of my kids was feeling like they had no power to change their situation, and was clearly showing more signs of distress and anxiety than the other.

That's a terrible position to put a child in. That also shows how the one-size-fits-all guardian solution isn't always fit for purpose. For the child that feels they are caught in an emotional tug-o-war between the abused siblings, the abuser resident parent and the alienated parent, it must be dreadful. Where can a child in that position find support?

There is one place – the school. The children attend school as individuals. The parents interact with the school as individuals, and schools have a legal obligation to share information about kids as individuals with both responsible parents, not just the one with residency. Schools also – in my children's case – offer access to counselling and pastoral services to try and deal with emotional or personal problems that affect the wellbeing of individual children. Schools also have an obligation to safeguard children in their care from the sort of problems that we see time and again in cases of alienation, like inappropriate sexual behaviours and exploitation, self-harm, anxiety and depression.

The school doesn't treat two kids as one package, unlike the Cafcass Guardian or their lawyer. The school doesn't offer a one-size-fits-all solution they both have to agree to before it can proceed, unlike the Family Courts. School treats everyone as an individual. Schools are built around treating pupils equally.

In the last chapter I argued – from my own experience and the shared experiences of other alienated parents – that the Family Court isn't fit for purpose in cases of Parental Alienation. In this chapter, I am going to argue the case that schools are fit for purpose and could play a transformative role in preventing the abuse of Parental Alienation – but due to a lack of training and policy leadership, they usually don't.

Schools need advice and training for divorce problems

In my case, it was the school that advised me to initiate a cooling-off period with my kids after our relationship ending argument (which I didn't realise was so serious at the time). This was the break in contact I agreed to after I had referred myself into counselling to deal with the profound loss I experienced after my fiancée Elle had drained our joint bank account and fled the country, assisted in part by my ex-wife. I referred myself to therapy in October, I finished the intensive sessions in December. At the end of January we argued and the split happened. After that, the school suggested a cooling-off break – which I agreed to as it seemed very sensible at the time – and engaged the services of a local child charity to begin counselling with my kids. This was agreed between us and seemed like a logical, practical next step to resolve the chaos that enveloped our world.

I am using the word 'seemed' there for a reason. The break *seemed* like a good idea. Cool off, take some time to think it through and calm down, who could argue with that? It *seemed* like a logical and practical approach to a relationship problem. However, in my case and in cases of acrimonious litigation between parents, taking a break also presents a real risk of damaging the relationship further through non-contact for a prolonged period of time. If one parent is an abusive resident parent who wants to alienate the other, the cooling-off period is an opportunity to create a rift that can never be healed. In my case, that is exactly what happened.

Also, if the counselling that takes place during that break isn't of a high quality with a specially trained child counsellor – and in my children's case it wasn't, it was an ex-social worker nearing retirement – the combination of a break and bad counselling just worsens the rift between you. This is what happened between me and my kids. Again, this is another one-size-fits-all problem. Cases of alienation or developing alienation need different handling from cases where there's a relationship breakdown but everyone wants to work it out. In my case, my ex-wife never wanted us to reconcile, and so the counselling was doomed before it began. If someone at the school had warned me of the risks of a break and bad counselling, that if it was handled badly it could make things worse, I wouldn't have agreed to it. There is a degree of risk management that applies to all therapy and counselling, and it's vital to remember if it is done badly it causes more harm than good.

Worse still was the obvious fact I should never have agreed to the break. At the time, nobody explained the risk of what that might look like in front of the court and Cafcass. The risk is simple – if you agree to a break, you are effectively the one who is responsible for losing contact with your kids. Agreeing to the break would go against me in later court hearings, which it did. The break was cited as the central reason why the courts would not make a contact order to restore my relationship with the children. In the final judgement, the judge made it clear that I was the one who broke off contact, and therefore, I had alienated myself. The fact I was advised it was a solution was irrelevant, if I had never agreed to the break my claim of Parental Alienation would have been significantly stronger.

Despite all other evidence that the children had been exposed repeatedly to information that was wholly inappropriate and a huge violation of my privacy by my ex-wife, the break was my doing and so the breakdown in our relationship was ultimately my fault. Despite the unarguable fact that the major reasons my children gave for not wanting to see me changed over the years of my Family Court struggle to reflect the things they had learned from being exposed to that information by my ex-wife, as far as the Courts were concerned, that cooling-off break period was my choice and therefore, I was the one who lost my kids. Nobody else was to blame.

I took the advice of the school in good faith, at a time when I was at an emotional low-point in my life. It was the worst thing I could have done, in retrospect. It was a disaster. If I hadn't taken a break, who knows what would have happened to us. For sure, there was no way my ex-wife could have used that break to do the one simple thing an abuser resident parent needs to alienate the other – and that is refuse to re-establish contact. I think the school was acting in good faith, but ultimately they were out of their depth. Their good faith attempt at a solution only served to make a bad situation worse.

I am also slightly concerned that the cooling-off period wasn't their idea either. One thing that became apparent in all my dealings with the school was the staff would discuss everything with my ex-wife. They would keep her informed of things when they happened, but I only found out about them after the fact. That included online grooming by a predator (and a subsequent police investigation) and self-harm. These were major breaches of the trust that should exist between a parent and school. I had to chase them for information which they freely shared with my ex-wife. My ex-wife was also in frequent contact with the senior staff at the school, as an active member of the Parent-Teacher Association. So the cooling-off break was most likely discussed with her before they discussed it with me. Given our increasingly acrimonious relationship – my ex-wife's grievances over money and also her refusal to comply with our contact arrangements – suggesting a cooling-off period was exactly what she needed to begin the full-blown alienation I experienced from that point onwards.

I cannot be sure, of course, but given how the school became instrumental in my alienation, I feel it is highly likely she pushed for that cooling-off break as a solution. Parental Alienation makes you paranoid at times, I know, but if that break had never happened I might not have lost my kids. It feels too much of a coincidence for me to ignore it.

I had informed the school that I believed my ex-wife was trying to cut me off from my kids. Their course of counselling came to an end, and the next recommended steps were to restart contact. My ex-wife agreed for the children to send me a text message. They did. I was delighted. However, then she reported to the counsellor that it was so distressing for them they never wanted to contact me again. This didn't make sense to me. We had been in contact before, we had exchanged text messages over a skiing holiday I had booked for February that was cancelled because of the difficulties. I exchanged those texts with one of the kids, who signed it off 'I love you Daddy'. Yet according to my ex-wife, just months later they were traumatised by sending me a text message? That didn't make sense.

At this point, I informed the school that I feared my ex-wife was alienating me from my kids. I also informed them that children in cases of Parental Alienation were vulnerable. I told them what to watch out for in terms of my children exhibiting behavioural problems, self-harm, inappropriate sexual behaviours, academic drop-off and so on. It was clear they had no knowledge or experience of Parental Alienation. It also became clear they weren't competent to deal with it.

As my worst fears over my vulnerable children were realised, it was obvious that I had put my faith in people who were neither trained nor capable of dealing with the problems my kids experienced. One of my kids' grades crashed. One of them was involved in online sexual abuse. One of them was self-harming. None of these things were raised with me at my monthly academic report meetings. I had to find out for myself by repeatedly asking questions. My ex-wife on the other hand was kept fully informed. I know this because it was only through back and forth of letters with my lawyers and hers that the full details emerged, and a court order for the school to share safeguarding reports with me. It turned out that all along, the school had kept my ex-wife fully informed of everything at the time, whereas I was informed after the fact in some cases, and not at all in others. This was a clear breach of my legal rights as a responsible parent. I was shocked.

I put my faith in the school, in their advice and in their selection of a partner organisation – a local children's charity – that could help us work out our problems. It was a mistake from which the relationship between my kids and me would never recover. It also revealed a much more destructive side to a badly managed school intervention than I could have imagined was possible. They had neither training nor expertise, and in effect they became an unwitting ally to my ex-wife in her abuse. The first counsellor they used with my kids wasn't a trained child counsellor at all but a former social worker, and my children didn't like her. It actively made them disengage from the counselling process. When kids resent the child counselling process it makes the breakdown between children and parent harder to overcome, not easier. That intervention was damaging to our chances of reconciliation, it didn't help it.

Did the school enable my alienation through a badly managed intervention?

If I think back to how the break-up with my kids happened, the school played a central role in it. In fact, arguably they facilitated it, although not intentionally. Whether they realised it or not the school that acted as the catalyst in the argument that split me from my kids, and the school that suggested we take a break – a suggestion that showed a lack of understanding of how a cooling-off period could damage my relationship with my kids and damage my own case before the Family Court, which it did.

The events are concerning because they feel contrived. They feel stage managed, but I accept this could be judgement of hindsight. What I know for sure is the sequence of events. At the end of January 2015, my children came for their usual contact weekend and one of them seemed upset. There were tears and one of them wanted to go home early. That same day I received a call from the school, asking me to go in for an urgent meeting on the Monday. This set me on edge and made the evening so tense it erupted into the argument that I have cited before in this book, that led to the breakdown of my relationship with my kids.

The children wouldn't tell me what it was about. Neither would the school. They said that they couldn't discuss it over the phone with me because the line 'wasn't secure' and they had to speak to me in person. Those words sounded so ominous. What could it mean? Not secure? That's what they say in spy movies isn't it? Perhaps they were concerned that I might record the call and it could be used at some later date in court. Who knows? To this day, I am baffled by it.

I was also really shocked. Reeling. I was still emotionally in a mess and still devastated from discovering my fiancée had stolen huge amounts of money from me and fled the country, and my ex-wife had somehow been involved. Once I involved the police she returned the money, and I dropped the charges. However, up until that point, it was theft, and I was a victim of crime. Then I get this menacing call about something so serious they can't even discuss it? I was trying to deal with too many shocks at once, I suppose. It really sent me into a tailspin.

I asked my kids. They wouldn't talk about it. It drove me crazy. I lost it. We had an argument. One of them was crying and asked to go home to my ex-wife, I got my housekeeper to take them home the next morning after their sports club sessions. In retrospect I wish I hadn't, I truly wish we could have dealt with it differently. However, as I have stated time and again, you aren't prepared for alienation. At this point, I could barely accept my ex-wife had a grudge bad enough to help my fiancée drain my bank account and flee the country. I had no idea she was manipulating my kids to hate me. I thought it was just an argument. It all felt so overwhelming. My whole life had gone from being on the verge of beginning a new life with the woman of my dreams to falling apart, and the only bright light in all that darkness and gloom was my kids – and now this?

The meeting happened the next Monday and I learned that one of the kids was upset by a school assembly on bullying and told the school I was a bully. In effect, the school took this as a complaint against me. That hurt so badly, it's hard to even write it now. I wasn't a bully. The thought my own child would go to the school and ask for help because I was a bully was unthinkable. I had no idea how to deal with it. The idea was absurd. I loved my kids.

It's also important to note that it was only one of my kids who made the complaint. The other seemed to get swept up in it. They were very close in age, however one thread of alienation that runs throughout my experience was the unarguable fact that one child was very active in their anger and hostility towards me, the other was passive. They were treated by the courts, lawyers and Cafcass like a unit. I think this is a subtle sign of Parental Alienation in progress. It makes sense that two individuals will respond differently to being manipulated, as in life, some people dive in head first, others get dragged along by their peers.

I think a large part of it came from the tutoring I organised for them. My kids needed extra academic support at their last school. I could see they were obviously bright and capable of good results, but where I was keen to help them with homework – my ex-wife would let them watch TV and play on the internet. Under my wife's care, they struggled with homework and needed more help. I was very keen for my kids to get a good education and the best start in life, so my ex-wife and I agreed to a tutor for their Eleven-Plus exams, which they were clearly not going to pass without help. Their tutor was excellent, but she and my ex-wife didn't get along because when the tutor visited the house to work on Eleven-Plus lessons, she would end up helping my kids do their school homework which they were always struggling to complete.

My ex-wife's view was simple: I was rich, she was rich, my kids had a fat trust fund – why would they need to go to university or pursue a career that needed high qualifications? They could leave school and do anything. Like I did. I left school and worked my way up through a number of international financial institutions in the city. However, what my ex-wife never appreciated was the fact as soon as I got the chance I put myself through university because I missed out on so much life experience by working my way up from the bottom. And working damn hard too. Graduates get more chances to start their career higher up the ladder, get more choices of career as well. These days it's getting harder and harder to work your way up from the bottom. I wanted my kids to do better than me and a university education was key to my mind.

My ex-wife fired the tutor about four months before the kids took their Eleven-Plus. She claimed it was too much stress for them. In fact my ex-wife, her mother, her sister and her best friend in their subsequent statements to the court said that the one-hour per day of tutoring was ruining their childhoods. They described the kids like slaves, trapped in their rooms, constantly studying. So my wife fired the tutor and my kids failed their Eleven-Plus.

You won't be surprised to learn – given how much the tutoring was blamed for my kids' hostility toward me – that even the judge in the final ruling three years later went on for pages about the pressure tutoring had put upon them. He cited it as one of the major causes of our break-up, when they were aged just 11. What will probably surprise you is when he wrote that, my ex-wife was sending me regular bills from tutors for the kids. They were both receiving weekly tutoring at that point, organised by my ex-wife to support their academic struggles. The same academic struggles I had raised with the court as a problem, the same academic struggles my wife denied and the judge dismissed in his final ruling. The sheer circularity of that is mind-bending. The fact I had insisted on tutoring kids who didn't need it became a major part of my ex-wife's case against my claims of alienation, and when the judge ruled in support of that view, she was having the kids tutored because they needed it. It was absurd.

Those bills for tutoring never stopped. My kids continued seeing tutors, I continued paying for it, however I have to assume it didn't ruin their lives as they, my ex-wife and her supporting witness statements said so convincingly before the court.

I did my best after they failed their Eleven-Plus to help them when they were with me. I facilitated extra school work so that they could pass the challenging entrance exams to their new school which was highly selective. I arranged a backstage tour of a famous theatre where they met and interviewed a celebrity and took them to meet a famous designer for their entrance exam report. They passed with flying colours and gained access to an exclusive private school. I felt so proud of them, and I was reassured they were fulfilling their potential.

I was not a bully. I was firm but fair about school work. But all work and no play was never an issue. My kids went on trips, treats, had TV and mobiles, games and all the normal things children want. The difference between me – the bully – and their mother – the ally – was I made them do their homework and arranged support where they were failing at subjects. She didn't do that, she was content to let them coast through with bad grades because they were rich.

I was not a bully, but I had been through a very traumatic relationship experience and couldn't deal with the accusation of bullying. There were no specific instances or examples given at the meeting. I hadn't done anything in particular, I was just a bully. I was controlling, too, apparently. That sounded odd. Controlling? It didn't sound like the thing an 11 year old would say after watching an assembly on bullying.

The previous contact weekend before this had happened, I argued with one of my kids who said I was mean to my ex-wife and mean to Elle. It triggered me. We rowed and I asked how they could defend their mother or Elle when one had stolen over £300,000 from me and broken my heart, and the other one had helped? By that point, the police had informed me – off the record – that my ex-wife was involved, something she later admitted in court papers. Elle, in later communications, elaborated on it. I should never have lost my temper or told my kids about their mother's involvement with Elle. I admit that. It came back to haunt me time and again as the main example of me talking negatively about my ex-wife in front of the kids. It meant all my protestations about my ex-wife sharing damaging information with my kids was dismissed as six of one and half a dozen of the other.

This is a matter of proportionality. Again, as with the tutoring issue, the courts don't have a sense of fairness or irony. They weighed my angry outburst over my ex-wife and her role in a serious crime against me as equal to my ex-wife systematically sharing private information about me and the court process with my kids – through negligence. It was tit for tat, in their eyes and in the eyes of Cafcass, and one of the therapists involved. However, these were not the same thing. Mine was emotional anguish that was as much about my pain as my ex-wife and fiancée stealing from me. We can all relate to losing our tempers. However, leaving private information lying around for someone's kids to find, information so damaging it will make them hate that person? That's a completely different act. To counter one with the other lacks any sort of proportion.

My ex-wife spent years turning my kids against me. I lost my rag and mouthed-off about her a few times but somehow, those things became equal in the eyes of the court. One cancelled out the other in the final judgement, even though one of them was an angry man in distress and the other was years of systematically exposing the children to personal information and court papers that in the end, were the main reasons they gave for never wanting to see me again. What my ex-wife did was not commensurate with what I had done, but it was taken as though one cancelled out the other. It was like comparing a mountain to a molehill.

After that argument, the next contact visit was the last. Suddenly I was facing accusations of bullying that I couldn't possibly defend because there were no incidents mentioned, nothing specific, just general bullying. Just generally being controlling. Something about the allegation without any specific examples didn't ring true. I suspected my ex-wife was putting ideas in their heads. My ex-wife had already told my kids that the woman I took the school Christmas ball was a prostitute, so I knew she was spreading malicious gossip at this point. I felt the need to explain to the school in that meeting who the woman was. She was an ex-girlfriend, it was a casual thing because I didn't want to attend the ball alone. I needed a date, she was a friend. The kids also met her. The thought I had introduced my children to an escort? That sounded like my wife. She had accused me of all sorts. It had to be hookers, it couldn't be anything to do with her or our failing marriage. In retrospect, I'm surprised I wasn't accused of being a drug-fuelled alcoholic because that's what every hardworking London businessman does at night – right?

My child made the complaint about me. My ex-wife claimed she knew nothing about the complaint, or the school's involvement. I couldn't believe that. My child went to the school to make a complaint against me, rather than speak to their own mother? The whole situation just felt wrong, somehow. It was more of my ex-wife claiming none of this was coming from her. She distanced herself from my kids and their hostility toward me from day one.

The upshot of the meeting was the school suggested engaging a counsellor from a local children's charity they worked with. They also suggested a cooling-off period between me and the children until there was some resolution of the problem.

That week I was due to attend the Parents' Evening. My ex-wife and I attended the event in two separate sessions with the kids, not together. My children were fine with me. They weren't scared of me. They didn't panic. It was just like we'd had a big row and things were a bit muted. Distant perhaps, a bit edgy, but it didn't feel like they would never want to see me again. It didn't feel like that cooling-off break would be the end of our relationship. I had no idea what was coming.

The realisation of my worst fears

When I tried to restart the relationship with my children, I was told they didn't want to talk to me, by my ex-wife. They were very hurt and angry I had broken off contact with them. But it was the school's idea! For the rest of my Family Court battle for the next three years, this came back on me time and again. My kids didn't break off contact, my ex-wife didn't break off contact, I did. The circumstances – a complaint to the school, the involvement of a counsellor from a local children's charity and a break that appeared to be initiated by me – made me look bad in every report that came since.

This is the terrible dilemma that hangs over you in Parental Alienation. You can't understand the complexity of the problem until it's too late. You can't know if you are taking good advice or making the right choice until it's too late. I sat in a room with two experienced teachers at a top private school who suggested I take a break and allow their trusted counselling partners – a charity – to bring about a resolution to an argument with my children. Like most people, I thought they must know best. They were completely wrong and arguably helped to destroy any hope I had of ever seeing my kids again.

They put me in touch with the charity. The charity wouldn't discuss it with me, but gave me the number of the counsellor. The counsellor wasn't a child estrangement or family specialist and after a lengthy conversation it became clear that my kids were not engaging with her and no progress had been made in the previous three months of sessions. My kids still didn't want to see me, and that was that. It was an impasse.

We agreed to work on a new approach. The social worker was nearing retirement, and so the charity's head of professional services offered to take over my case. She undertook wishes and feelings work with my children, and visited my ex-wife at home. She was very supportive of my situation, fairly noting that although there had been difficulties there was no reason to delay restarting contact via letters or text messages to warm us up a bit and take it slow, with a view to phone calls and then face-to-face meetings in due course.

My ex-wife agreed, but deferred any contact until after the children's end of academic year exams so as not to disrupt them. She then took them away to the holiday villa in Spain I had built, the week before their exams. They sent me a text message from the holiday home. I was delighted. I thought it was the sign we were turning a corner, but in fact, it was the reverse.

In the final report by the charity, the head of professional services wrote that sending the text message was reportedly distressing for the children, who wanted nothing to do with me. My ex-wife reported it made them angry with her for making them send it, and she didn't think they should be in a relationship with me because it was emotionally unhealthy for them. The counsellor asked why, and although there were no safeguarding reasons or any specific reasons, my ex-wife insisted they didn't want anything to do with me and although she thought this was a shame, she would support them.

The final report of the charity was quite clear, it stated that my ex-wife might be influencing the children's decisions – *'by omission rather than commission'*. That phrase was echoed in the sentiments of subsequent reports. The consultant child psychiatrist who described my ex-wife as *'passive'* and saying *'she won't promote contact'*. The family therapist says my ex-wife *'engages in criticism'* of me by affirming my kids' criticisms of me, saying *'he is like that'*. Even the heavily biased Cafcass report says, *'I wonder whether Mrs XXXX realises that her comments are the negative reinforcing comments that have been referred to and for which she has been criticised.'*

All my court interventions echoed that initial report from the children's charity. The same sentiments repeated over and over. I wanted contact, but my ex-wife wouldn't promote it. My ex-wife thinks a relationship with me is bad for my kids, and so she has distanced me from them and continued to do so.

The school for whatever reason created even greater distance by refusing to share vital information about my children with me, whilst simultaneously sharing it with my ex-wife. In effect, she had my kids and held all the cards as far as my relationship with them was concerned. I couldn't see them or keep track of their welfare, and through a lack of governance, the school played a central role – through incompetence more than malice – in helping her do that.

Schools and alienated parents: A complete lack of trust or transparency

Over the period of my Family Court interventions my ex-wife was elected Chair of the Parent-Teacher Association without anybody so much as raising an eyebrow. When I raised this issue in a formal complaint to the school governors, they resisted my claim of a conflict of interest. Which was absurd. I had already alleged my ex-wife was alienating me, and the school was well aware that we were locked in an acrimonious court battle. They had access to the report of a court-appointed expert regarding my children's diagnosis of anxiety and depression. They knew my kids were vulnerable and there were huge issues between me and my ex-wife. Yet they allowed someone who was part of that sort of messy battle over contact to chair the PTA.

At this point in time, my kids were 13 and I was constantly having to contact the school for information about serious issues affecting them, but meanwhile my ex-wife was working closely with school staff. Surely that's poor governance. The same staff I would eventually have to force into sharing information with me via court order were working side by side with my ex-wife. That was barely believable.

However, what it does is illustrate the struggle alienated parents face when it comes to being treated equally before the law, and before institutions like schools. Alienated parents are constantly fighting against battles against murky, badly governed bureaucracy and opaque, antiquated processes. Each responsible parent has a right to information concerning their child.

When it comes to schools, the fight for information is

always for one simple reason, to discover how the kids are doing. That's all. Divorced parents aren't trying to get the school involved in litigation, they just want to know how their kids are getting on. The problem is schools are only obliged to share academic reports, but not anything else *specifically*. Some things might be detailed, others not. They have to share admission decisions, parent meetings details, school events, school newsletters and peripheral stuff. They have to give access to copies of school photos, information about trips and decisions about suspensions and exclusions. However, what that amounts to is not much. Not really. It's lip service, nothing more. In reality, if your kids are in poor mental health or victims of online sexual abuse, the school isn't obliged to tell you anything if you're a divorced parent.

Again, in the same way that I argued the Family Court needs some sort of red-flag checklist where Parental Alienation is alleged by one side, so there should be some sort of red-flag checklist for schools to prevent the domestic abuse of Parental Alienation taking place via their staff and bad governance. Right now, there is no formal requirement for the school to monitor other problems in regulated ways or share specific information with both parents. Some schools are well run and governed, others like my kids' school, are hit and miss.

Some – in the state system – avoid getting involved because of Ofsted regulations or stricter guidelines on what they can and can't do in non-academic areas of school life. In the private school system it's generally better because they fear losing the income from a disgruntled parent, however private schools are not regulated in the same way and what support you can expect is highly variable. It's like pot luck and a postcode lottery all rolled into one.

Academic results aren't all that a school is, schools should be obliged to share appropriate information in cases where children are seeing school supervised counsellors, or experiencing school-related issues like social media abuse or bullying. They should all be obliged to record information where there are child welfare issues like self-harm or online abuse, in a format that is consistent. It should be no different from sharing academic results with consistent grades, or recording health stats consistently. There should be a basic set of safeguarding information, and it is a public scandal that your kids could be cutting their arms or flashing their bodies to strangers online and the school is not obliged to inform both parents, or record it in a formal way that is the same for every school.

Every teacher must have a DBS check before the law allows them to work with kids, but every school doesn't have to inform both legally responsible parents if they have a self-harming child or if the police are investigating an online child abuser that has targeted their 13 year old. That seems to be a glaring omission.

In my case, the worse my children's lives became, the harder it became to get my ex-wife and their school to share information with me. The one thing the school cannot do, is restrict information given to one parent at the request of another, however if the children request information is not shared, the school can retreat behind the Information Commissioner's Office code of practice, based on the Data Protection Act of 2018. This is another one of those examples where in a case of alienation, the game is rigged against you. Why would your children refuse to give express written consent for you to see their records? Think about that for a moment. If it reaches a point where your own kids refuse to let you see their records when they freely allow them to be shared by the other parent, that should raise a red flag in itself.

Imagine my horror when I learned of the online abuse one of my kids had experienced. I only learned the full details after the school had informed the police. I was called on the phone and the teacher downplayed it, saying that there had been some inappropriate use of social media and it was *'what kids of that age do'.* The school reassured me that they had given the children tips about online safety and it was all fine. I received nothing in writing. It didn't make sense to me, so I asked more questions. They were vague. In the end, it took legal letters to my wife's solicitors to reveal the details. Without going into distressing details, it involved the sending of nude selfies by a couple of 13 year olds – one of them my child – to an adult abuser. The abuser subsequently blackmailed them for more pictures. It made me sick. My baby was being harmed like that, and I didn't even know? It's truly the stuff of nightmares.

Imagine my horror when I discovered I had not been informed of my other child's self-harm, even though I spoke to someone at the school who knew about it. That staff member misled me to the point of lying. Again, I had to resort to legal letters to have the information disclosed to me by my ex-wife's lawyers. It emerged that on the day I called the school for an update on one of my kid's counselling sessions – when I was assured my self-harming child was doing just fine – but the records show that same staff member called my ex-wife that same day to inform her my child was self-harming. That was a complete breach of trust, and a breach of her responsibilities to me as a parent.

When I did discover the self-harm, I went to see the school counsellor and saw my ex-wife at school. She was there to meet with the counsellor over the self-harming issues. What my ex-wife had described through her lawyers as mild and something lots of kids do, the counsellor was very concerned about. My child had cut their arm over 40 times with a razor and cut the words *'allegedly a toy'* into their thigh. I was horrified. Another nightmare scenario, where your child desperately needs protecting and you aren't allowed to help.

I was shocked to learn there was no formal risk assessment procedure at the school regarding issues like self-harm. I asked to see it, they refused. When I finally got a court order to see their safeguarding files I discovered there was never a formal safeguarding policy or risk assessment for any of the problems my kids had experienced. It was amateurish, ad hoc policy at best. Proper policies, guidance and assessment procedures are essential for one reason, they reduce the risk of inconsistency or manipulation of a situation by individuals involved in the situation to which the policies and procedures apply. As a finance guy, my working life is ruled by compliance, reporting and oversight. It's the law. It prevents abuse, and reduces errors. How can there be less oversight of children at a school than the law demands for money in a bank?

At that point as well, the teacher and my ex-wife had colluded to keep that information from me. I was very upset with the school staff member who simply refused to accept she had done anything wrong by informing my wife but keeping it from me. It was, she insisted, for reasons of data protection. This was justified based on the simple premise that my child had asked the counsellor to keep it from me, but it was okay to inform my ex-wife. That is precisely what you would expect a child to say if they have been manipulated by one parent to be hostile towards the other. Again, in alienation cases, that is a warning sign from a child, not a sign of their competence over their own data privacy.

In the school's glossy brochure it says:

'We want to work in partnership with you and will keep you informed about your child's progress, academically and socially, and about the life of the School'

But when I wrote to them demanding to know why they hadn't informed me about internet grooming and abuse of a 13 year old and the subsequent police investigation, their tone was markedly different.

'Whilst we acknowledge a duty of care for our students from a safeguarding perspective, we would not normally act as intermediaries between two parents regarding an issue that had occurred in the family home.'

Again, this completely misrepresents the situation. I wanted to be kept informed, they had not done so. I did not ask them to act as intermediaries between two parents in the family home. In fact, that was not the family home but just one of the parent's home. I also had a home, and an established routine of contact on alternate weekends plus midweek sleepovers. They had bedrooms and clothes and toys there. They still do. That, my home, was the family home as far as I was concerned and there had been no incidents there. However, there was a risk, clearly, in the modern world of social media, tablets and smartphones, that there could have been safeguarding issues in my home too. The school's safeguarding responsibility was clearly to keep both parents informed so that the children could be properly safeguarded in *both* of their responsible parent's homes, not just one of them. What happened, instead, was they kept my ex-wife informed and excluded me. They completely failed to inform me until after the damage to both children was done through bad judgement and poor governance. Data protection was an excuse to avoid admitting their faults.

That gap, between the school's glossy marketing and the reality of their response to my complaints sums up the experience of an alienated parent. The school says it wants to work in partnership with you, and keep you informed, but in reality that only applies if you aren't divorced and your ex-partner isn't chair of the PTA. If that sounds cynical, how about this – they want to work in partnership with you and keep you informed provided it doesn't involve online perverts abusing your kids, self-harm or a police investigation? That was equally true in my case. The school will hide behind absurd ideas like the things kids do with their classmates don't count if they happen partially outside the classroom. They hide behind notions of there existing only one family home, when in divorce cases there are two family homes.

They hide behind arguments over acting as intermediaries when they were never asked to act as intermediaries between my ex-wife and I. They informed her, they did not inform me. There is no intermediary, there are simply two people with an equal right to be informed.

This brings me back to my original point about the role of schools in Parental Alienation cases – there has to be reform of the way schools are obliged to conduct themselves in acrimonious divorces and child arrangement cases. Without proper guidelines, without proper training and competence, there is real danger that school might act with the best of intentions but their impact on the fragile relationship between a divorced parent and his/her children could be harmful. In cases where Parental Alienation is alleged, a badly managed school intervention can make the alienation much worse.

In my case, this was demonstrated by the school suggesting a cooling-off break that was the end of contact between me and my kids.

It was also demonstrated when the school allowed a child who is self-harming to keep it a secret from one of their parents.

It was also demonstrated when there was online sexual abuse of children taking place with friends in the same class, and the school informs the police before they inform one of the children's parents who is visiting the school for monthly progress reports.

In my case, when I pressed the school for information, the answer was to hide behind the Data Protection Act of 2018. They insisted that without the express written consent of my children, they were not allowed to share information with me. Data protection is a civil right. A right to privacy. In this case, whose privacy were they protecting and from whom?

They were protecting the privacy of two 13 year old children from their desperately concerned father with legal parental responsibility? Over what? Over sending nude selfies to a pervert and self-harm that had occurred while they were in the care of the mother. These aren't privacy issues, they are serious threats to the physical and mental health of children. They raise serious safeguarding concerns about their safety in my ex-wife's home. In both cases it affected multiple children at that school. They had a duty to inform me, and all the parents of the kids involved. You can't help but wonder whose privacy they were concerned about, the children's or their own if word got out that their safeguarding was seriously lacking.

Imagine my horror when I took this to the top of the school and the response from the head was to suggest I take my kids away and send them to another school. This was the same head teacher who refused to give me access to my kids' records without their consent. How could I take them away from school if our relationship was so bad and my wife – who was chair of the PTA and in regular contact with the same head teacher – would clearly not agree to changing schools?

That was the last straw. The head teacher knew that I couldn't force my kids to change school, nor force my ex-wife to agree to it. So why write that in a formal letter to me? I felt so angry. It read like a deliberate, high-handed dismissal of my complaint over their handling of my kids' problems,

problems I had warned them about over a year before when I learned of the problems and dangers children of alienated parents encounter.

In the end I was forced to take the matter to court. And a year later, the judge issued a court order to the school, to release all my children's safeguarding records relating to the abuse and the self-harm, and anything else they had kept from me but shared with their mother. Of course, by then, the damage was done. The abuse had been suffered. The cuts had scarred. And my kids had been diagnosed with anxiety and depression and were receiving therapy in a private clinic.

When the parental alienation hurricane hits you, you can't see the big picture or tell the story of A leading to B and then C leading to D. Instead, you take people on trust. You take institutions you have no reason to doubt, like the Family Courts, like Cafcass, like therapists and schools, on trust. You put your faith in things everyone is taught to take for granted in our free, democratic society, like justice. And of course, you take on trust the idea that schools have only got your kids' best interests at heart. You assume that dedicated school professionals whose entire reason for existing is to teach and help your children will help you. You assume they will put the welfare of your children first, and you assume they have all the training and skills required to do it in the same way you assume an accountant can do maths and a surgeon knows the difference between a vein and an artery.

I assumed teachers know what is best for kids. I assumed the exclusive, expensive private school I sent my kids to was – as its brochure suggested – offering my kids an education and a standard of care at the very highest level.

I assumed wrong.

Just like the Family Court isn't capable of dealing with alienation, schools appear unable to do so either. The difference is, where Family Law requires change at a national statutory level, schools could adopt a code of practice and better safeguarding procedures right now if they wanted to. It is profoundly in the public interest that they do, and most alienated parents groups and divorced parent charities and campaign groups are campaigning for it.

Without reform, the danger remains that schools can unwittingly become part of the domestic abuse of alienated parents and their children. As it was in my case, and countless others, and remains so.

The idea of a school becoming a mechanism that enables domestic abuse should be unthinkable, but without clear guidelines and proper oversight over the issues that apply in contact cases and Parental Alienation, the shocking truth is they can and they do.

Chapter 7:
The unintended consequences of trying to start over

Parental Alienation is life changing. That term – *life changing* – is a cliché. It gets used a lot in marketing and it's rarely accurate. The *life changing* magic of toothpaste or low fat spread or that new car you always wanted is a well-worn trope of modern day advertising. But for Parental Alienation, *life changing* is the only way to describe it. Parental Alienation quite literally changes everything from your day-to-day experiences through to your feelings. It bears similarities to post-traumatic stress disorder in the way it comes and goes, and the way events taking place around you can trigger the sudden onset of intense memories and feelings you aren't always prepared for.

Worse still, Parental Alienation makes you look back at events and memories and re-evaluate them. You spend hours reliving conversations and second-guessing yourself. You spend hours wondering if other people knew more than they let on, or were dishonest with you, or had motivations that weren't as innocent as you assumed at the time.

Parental Alienation doesn't just change your life now and in the future, but it even changes your past and your memories in completely unexpected and disturbing ways. I have spoken to many alienated parents and many of us share the experience of waking up one day and feeling like we're living the plot of a movie. Everything feels strangely ominous, or sinister. It is hard to know who you can really trust, and who is – or was – really on your side.

Alienated parents will often report a rollercoaster of emotions – you wake up angry, you wake up hopeful, you wake up every feeling both at once. The thing you have to avoid is completely losing perspective and losing touch with the life you lived before. Your memories are tainted by your current situation but they weren't all bad. You have to make a huge effort to preserve and cherish the good times, rather than let everything become a sad reminder of what you have lost. You had love, you had closeness, you were happy. It was real and it was wonderful and you can have it again. You can't afford to lose hope.

You can't afford to lose the natural, free-flowing happiness of parenting that you enjoyed before you lost your kids. You can't forget giggles of blowing raspberries on your kid's bum cheeks when you were drying them after bath time, and the belly laughs when you watched that funny movie or had a snowball fight. It was good. It was great. You were happy together and you loved each other. That is why it hurts so badly now you are lost to each other.

Alienated parents have good days and bad days. For me, I hit milestones like Father's Day, my 50th Birthday or graduating from my executive MBA and they turned into something to endure more than something to celebrate. I have days where my heart breaks for my kids, others where I feel angry with them for being a part of the pain I feel and the abuse inflicted upon me. I have to remind myself it's not their fault, that we are both the victims of domestic abuse. It's torture some days.

But then I remember how those two, wonderful children responded when my fiancée left us in such a mess. Not the argument that came months later, but when it was raw. When I was hurting. They saw me, in pain, and they supported me. They were protective of their dad. They helped me get through an exceptionally dark time. They were kind. They made me laugh. They hugged me when I cried. They asked me what was wrong. And they were angry with her and said she must never come back into our lives after what she did.

If I let the pain of the alienation win, or the bad days overtake the good days, I would risk forgetting that my kids and I were close and loving before this happened. Losing those memories would be worse than carrying the pain of Parental Alienation. One day, we might reconnect. One day we might reconcile. And when we do, remembering what we used to mean to each other and sharing memories of the good times will be a vital part of healing the rift between us and moving on with our lives.

The reason I raise the second-guessing and tainting of memories before the alienation is simple, because it can also be useful, in a way. Re-evaluating memories helps you look back and see things you couldn't see at the time. In my case, I think there were many events that were mostly the warning signs my ex-wife was trying to alienate me from my kids. However, I can also look back on the terrible way my fiancée Elle betrayed me and shook my world to its core and see all the things I missed because I saw her through rose-coloured glasses. I was head over heels in love and it made me blind to the reality of my situation. That reality was falling head over heels with someone that had serious mental health issues, who was capable of wrecking the lives of the people around her.

For the rest of this chapter, I want to tell that story with one overriding goal in mind, it's not to relive painful memories, but to explore the issues it raised that became central to my alienation from my kids. The break-up of my relationship with Elle shows how a bad relationship after a divorce can make a contact situation much worse. In my case, the damage our break-up did to me and my kids was the catalyst that turned my deteriorating relationship with my ex-wife into full blown Parental Alienation.

How I fell in love with Elle, and how much it made my ex-wife hate me

Elle was about 14 years younger than me, a slim, beautiful blonde. She looked like a model, and people often remarked on it. I saw her sitting alone at the bar in Harvey Nichols. I had been meeting a friend for lunch that day, I stayed on to have a drink at the bar before I went home. I saw her, a very striking beauty to my eyes, drinking alone at the bar. Something made me sit down next to her and strike up a conversation. The chemistry between us was instant. We just clicked. It had that love at first sight feel to it, which sounds gushy and silly when I write it down, but that was how it felt.

I had just emerged from a very trying few months. This was the period in 2012 when my ex-wife took me to the High Court for an additional cash payout of around £700,000, plus forced my children's trust fund to pay her an additional £200,000 which she originally wanted me to pay to her parents rather than put it in trust for my kids for some unknown reason. It was also the same period where my company was involved in a very high profile merger, and my ex-wife had begun to refuse to honour our contact agreements, and so I had been forced to get a court order to address it. I was also in the middle of the claim from my previous girlfriend who was pregnant, and demanded a large sum for a baby I didn't even know about until our relationship was over. When I read that written down, it sounds like something out of a TV soap opera. It had been an exhausting couple of years.

My kids had started with a tutor for their Eleven-Plus exams and entrance exams for the highly selective school I wrote about in the previous chapter. This had caused some tensions because my wife was not supportive of it, both the tutoring and doing homework. My ex-wife was using that against me, slowly turning me into the caricature of a strict Victorian father, the homework-obsessed disciplinarian she and my kids would later describe in court. She would 'support' them by presenting me as a boring parent who wanted them to do extra lessons and visit art galleries, while she would present herself as the easy-going one who would let them skip their homework and snuggle on the sofa watching the TV. Anyway, without support from my ex-wife, the tutoring was becoming an issue. My kids would come to my place, have their tutor session then dinner and a weekend of fun. It was just an hour every few days, and sometimes on weekends too. They made it sound like a prison work camp.

My ex-wife was very envious of Elle, a much younger woman who looked like she could be on the cover of *Vogue* or walking down a Paris catwalk. I don't think the envy was just over her looks though, it was over the way we were as a couple. Our relationship represented something very different from the relationship between my ex-wife and I, not just before our divorce, but even before we had got married. My ex-wife and I had become romantically involved under very different circumstances, I had known her at school from when I was 14, we had grown up together. My ex-wife and I were from a small working class community in a small town. It was a boy-girl-next-door sort of story. We went straight from romance to marriage and kids, work and the school run. Her parents were always around. Our friends and the things we did were the same year in, year out. It all went a bit flat. It wasn't anybody's fault, it was just the daily grind and being stuck in a bit of a rut.

Elle and I were different. I was different with her. She was different with me. I'd become a very successful businessman. I'd become a more travelled, educated and cultured man than the small town teenager I was when I met my ex-wife. Elle was a glamorous American and claimed to be a successful professional in her own right, with a sense of style and elegance that made her stand out from the crowd. We met in a bar frequented by celebs and jet-setters. We travelled in style and lived the high life. I think my ex-wife saw that and it made her more bitter. Her boyfriends were always the same, middle-aged men from the small town where she lived via dating apps. Mostly loafing about on her sofa and living off her obvious wealth while they themselves were employed in low-paid jobs.

My ex-wife's life after our divorce, despite her considerable personal wealth, didn't really change much from how it was before. It was more of the same-old-same-old that killed our marriage. She drank too much. I believed she was an alcoholic – something the kids would often complain about – functioning, but all the same, I worried. She lived in the same place, went to the same pubs and restaurants, watched the same shows on TV, and did all the same things she did before we split. I, on the other hand, moved to the heart of London, and Elle moved in with me a few years later. Elle and I went travelling, we went to concerts, we ate out at celebrity chef restaurants and took boxes at the opera and the races. I think to my ex-wife, my life and my new girlfriend made the grass look much greener on my side of the fence than hers, and that made her envious and bitter.

I believe it played a huge part in motivating her to step up her campaign to alienate me. But there was one critical factor yet to emerge.

Me, Elle and my kids

Elle and I began dating, and it felt so natural and relaxed that I knew I would introduce her to my kids. By now, I had learned the hard way and been in a relationship with a woman my kids didn't like – Polly who broke up with me over the mention of a prenuptial contract, and another with the 'accidental' pregnancy and claim for money. I had been on a few other dates but not met anyone I would introduce to my kids. Those events and my children's sensitivity to a new potential member of our family weighed heavily in my mind as I think they do with most divorcees in a similar position. I was determined not to bring anyone into my children's life until I felt sure there was something serious there. For me, the kids and their feelings came first. I would rather be single than risk upsetting my kids.

Over an intense few weeks – a whirlwind romance, I suppose – I became sure that Elle was the one for me and strangely she moved in by stealth. She had told me that she was in a difficult accommodation situation because she had been relocated to the UK from America to take on a new position at her company's UK division. Once she had moved, the company had decided not to continue with the plan and withdrawn the offer, they had fallen out over it and Elle was now stuck in the UK. She said she was working at a company on Bond Street while she worked it out. In retrospect, I should have been more critical of that. It didn't quite add-up. However, at the time I was seeing the world through rose-coloured glasses and soon we lived together in Regent's Park with my personal assistant Pete.

There were early signs something was wrong. When we were first dating, I sent Pete to pick her up from her office on Bond Street. Pete was ex-military and a former close protection bodyguard. As a result, he would usually arrive everywhere early to scope the place out a bit – old habits die hard, and all that. He arrived early and was surprised to see Elle arrive, not leaving the office building through the front door, but coming up a side alleyway. He mentioned this to me. He said he thought it was odd, and possibly a sign she wasn't really working there at all. I ignored it. She said she left the job later on, so the issue never came up. Pete's job was to be suspicious and to look out for me, I put his suspicions down to that.

I introduced Elle to my kids one Saturday afternoon as we all went to see a show together. They were as smitten with her as I was. Elle was a lot of fun. She had a youthful, energetic sparkle about her that children loved. She looked a bit like a Disney princess character, she was warm and kind, my kids thought she was fab. This made me love her even more, naturally, because when your kids like someone and that person is kind to your children, you naturally grow fonder of them. The way she was with my kids reminded them of a big elder sister, I suppose. They described her in those terms, and of course, when the split happened that made the anguish and the loss my kids experienced even worse.

Throughout our relationship, Elle tried very hard to engage with my children and their lives, including making the most of the arrangements with my ex-wife over travel and weekends. She took this on to keep the peace and to be honest I was happy to be removed, and I thought my ex-wife might get on better with Elle, another woman, than she did with me. Actually, in hindsight again, I realise this worked against me in the long run and led to my ex-wife influencing events that would ruin my happy home and all the plans I was making.

I think the early warning signs were there and I didn't see them, or chose not to. As I wrote earlier, Parental Alienation makes you second guess everything. But nevertheless, I was very busy with my retirement plans, I was also consulting for various high-profile clients and often in London. This left Elle alone with Pete a lot which was a source of tension. Especially after we moved from my London home to the farm in the country to be near my kids and their school.

Pete was in charge of the move. Elle kept offering to help, Pete was reluctant to let her because he was suspicious of her. In the end, he caught her packing up the items in my bedside cabinet, and they had a disagreement over it. After we moved to the farm, Pete and Elle would clash over organising the builders, those sorts of domestic arrangements. It made the place feel tense, and it made things difficult between Pete and I. Pete had been a very loyal companion and ran the house well. Suddenly, he and Elle were clashing over surveys or building quotes. It was very tiresome.

A rot set in for the three of us. Pete had told me, a few times, that we kept receiving wrong number telephone calls from America. He was suspicious of these calls that because Elle was an American, it was potentially some sort of scam. Possibly a burglary plot? I dismissed his concerns. I was in love with Elle, I couldn't believe it.

Then Elle began insinuating, subtly, that Pete had been flirting with her. Or had been spending too much time in the same parts of the house. Or he'd said something, or looked at her in a strange way. It was a very subtle drip-drip-drip at first, I dismissed it at first too. Pete was a decent, loyal friend and he loved the kids and had helped to keep my home together. Pete, meanwhile, told me that Elle had dropped her underwear on the stairs and then called down to him, asking him to pick it up and bring it to her in our bedroom. That sounded unbelievable. It sounded like he was making things up to get rid of her because they kept arguing over the house and the builders.

Pete was so suspicious that he even told Elle that he had killed a horse on my instructions, to intimidate an old acquaintance who kept horses up north. He did it, he later told me, to test her loyalty. His theory was simple – if Elle was genuine, she would raise it with me or keep it to herself. If she was a fake, she would tell people I had arranged to have a horse killed and we'd know she couldn't be trusted. It was a stupid trick to my mind. It didn't make me listen to him, it made him sound overly suspicious. I had completely forgotten about it until my ex-wife told one of the court assessments that I had a horse killed to intimidate someone – I couldn't believe it. Or in other words, Pete was right and Elle was a lot more deeply involved with my ex-wife than I knew.

However, the tension at home eroded the relationship between Pete and me. Worse than I realised. In the end, it made me resent Pete for coming between me – his employer and Elle – my girlfriend. I wanted to marry her. I was planning it. When I proposed to her – in the Spring of 2014 – with a £60,000 engagement ring I had designed by the Queen's jeweller, she said yes. I arranged it as a surprise. We got engaged in the local park. I had the ring, we went for a walk, and I had arranged for a photographer to hide in the bushes at a certain spot. So I proposed, on one knee, she accepted and then suddenly he leapt out and started snapping. It might sound a little odd to you, but she loved it. It made her feel like a celeb, she loved that kind of thing.

And then dropped this terrible bombshell that Pete had told her in advance that I was going to propose. I was gutted about that. It wasn't true. Pete didn't know I was planning it, and to this day he insists it was a surprise to him. However, it soured things between us for a while.

In the end, the rising tensions between Elle and Pete, and our strained relationship drove him to resign. I don't blame him for it. I felt conflicted, but I had no reason to doubt Elle. I would, however, in time, come to realise she had serious mental health issues. She was a compulsive liar and lived in a fantasy world.

I think, looking back, I was also wary of Elle in some ways. She very quickly adored my kids and they adored her back. They liked Pete too, and he was great with them, but Elle and my kids were like instant family. All the same, in the back of my mind – perhaps because of the odd story she had given me about her job, or something not ringing true about Pete's alleged flirting with her – I was always cautious about leaving her alone with the kids. She had a slight edginess about her that would manifest sometimes. You could say she was a little highly strung perhaps. Nothing major. She was all sweetness and light most of the time, but when nobody was looking, she could look troubled. She would sometimes be snappy and irritable over nothing. Sometimes she would talk to me about the things we were doing, or the places we went, that bore no relation to my experience of them. Her perspective on life was very different from mine, I think. I wanted to make sure I didn't make any mistakes with the kids, and especially with Pete leaving, that meant I would need to take even more care over how they were looked after. To that end, I spent more time with the kids.

Overall, Pete's departure was a shame but otherwise it

felt like everything was on the up for us, as a family. Elle and I were blissfully happy most of the time. The kids were happy too. They had a new home with big bedrooms and all the land they could want to run around in. They had a new big-sister character, they had their dad with them every week, without having to schlep into London. It was as close as I could get to living with them, and it made me very happy. We were getting married, my kids were super excited. What could go wrong?

My concerns over Elle began to grow

The farm needed a lot of work, renovating and extending the farmhouse and buildings. I wanted to make it into an ideal family home, and so spared no expense or time in making that my primary focus. Elle and I seemed to be going from strength to strength, and even my ex-wife who clearly didn't like Elle, seemed to settle into a routine without complaints or constantly calling the kids when they were at my place like they did when they stayed with me in London. Elle dealt with making arrangements, so that became less stressful too, plus being so near meant the contact issues had resolved themselves as transport was no longer an issue.

Looking back now, I can remember a lot of things that seemed out of whack. When Elle's birthday was approaching in June 2013, I planned to surprise her with a helicopter ride to a romantic weekend away. We were due to fly back from there and straight on to Royal Ascot for the spectacle and pageantry of the world famous races. It was going to be a wonderful few days. At the last moment, Elle came to me and was very upset. Elle told me a friend of hers from

LA had *'hand cancer'* and she was going to be nearby at a film festival in Spain. Elle said she couldn't miss seeing her, and would have to drop everything and go straight away. I couldn't argue with it. She went off to see her friend, and I invited some friends over to the farm for a bit of a lad's weekend. Beers, pizza, football. I was making the best of it.

Out of the blue, on the Sunday morning, Elle appeared. She said she had come back to surprise me. It was 8.30 am. How did she get to the farm from Spain at 8.30 am? That would mean catching a 4 am flight out of Madrid. There are no flights at that time from Madrid to London. It didn't make sense, I checked the arrivals to be sure. Nothing had landed to get her to my place at that time that morning. She seemed so bright and breezy, I put it to the back of my mind, but I knew something wasn't right. After she had stolen money and broken my heart, Elle claimed she had actually used this weekend to go to London and have a secret abortion on her birthday. I don't believe that either. It made no sense that she would do something so drastic in secret on her birthday but that is just a flavour of her crazy world.

However, unaware of that, our life carried on as normal, we didn't mention the strange weekend again. We had – as all couples do – some arguments, but generally speaking we were still very happy, the kids were happy, and all went well.

There was an unfortunate incident where one of my kids got locked out of their Apple account and asked to borrow my iTunes account log-in to download some games. That meant the iPad uploaded my pictures, including a few of Elle topless. That was a bit awkward, in fact, it came back to haunt me in the Family Court that I had let my kids see inappropriate material. It was innocent enough, Elle was sunbathing, I snapped some pics of her, joking around and pretending to be a paparazzo. It wasn't porn. It was just poor judgement I guess to let my kid use my iCloud account without thinking those pics were linked to my account. As you can imagine my ex-wife and her lawyers turned this into a crime of horrific proportions although when I spoke to my kids about this they said they hadn't seen anything and were slightly confused.

Elle and I did have one very concerning argument though. We were out in London at Ronnie Scott's jazz club. We went with some friends – one of whom was a well-known celebrity socialite – and we had a lot of fun. Except Elle took exception to the celeb, or something like that. She became moody. Angry. It was embarrassing.

I went to the bar, came back and she'd gone. And so had my keys. We hadn't argued, but I was worried. She wasn't picking up the phone. She just vanished. I assumed she had only one place to go, home, and so I made my excuses and left. I got back to the station and my car was missing. Elle must have taken it. She was clearly over the drink drive limit, and this chilled me to the bone. Was she dead in a ditch somewhere? Was that the reason she wasn't answering her phone?

I raced home to the farm. I was all locked up. I couldn't see my car. I had to climb over the gates in the rain, unsure what I would find. I was terrified. And there was Elle. In the house. Packing her stuff. She said I hadn't paid her enough attention, that I'd been ignoring her. That I was flirting with the glamorous celeb. We argued. Shouted. I offered to help her pack because she was throwing a tantrum. It was very embarrassing. However, we made up soon enough, that night. I thought it was just a lovers' tiff as they call it. Passions spilling over, too much to drink, all the usual excuses. After all the emotional turmoil I'd lived through with the divorce and with previous relationships, I didn't think it was anything more serious than that. We were soon back to normal.

There was another strange event. I had arranged a blind date for a friend of mine – a work colleague who was a prince from a European royal family, and my dear friend Maxine who had been a good, close friend for years. I thought they would hit it off, and so I arranged a double date with them, Elle and me. Elle knew this was the plan, and seemed fine with it. However, the moment I saw Maxine and kissed her – same as I always did – Elle became furious. She spent the whole meal making curt remarks to Maxine. She seemed hugely jealous. It was so awkward. When we left, leaving a very strained atmosphere behind, she was furious about the way I had greeted my old friend. I couldn't believe it, I had set up a blind date, I wasn't dating! After that, Elle made it quite clear that she didn't want me seeing Maxine anymore, friend or not. It made things difficult but me and Maxine were okay. It wasn't like we saw each other that much anyway. But Elle's temper and her sudden jealousy was again, a warning sign I should have picked up on. She even logged into my Facebook page to unfriend Maxine which I only realised many months later.

Life after that was good. Christmas came and went and we had a lovely time with the kids, trips to London to see *The Nutcracker*, a visit to the Winter Wonderland theme experience, we played games and I got on with renovations and building work at the farm. Elle was happy. The kids were happy. In March I commissioned the Queen's jeweller to make her an engagement ring. It was January 2014.

I am a very traditional person in many respects, I suppose and I wanted to do it properly. So I arranged for us to visit America, and to see her father and family so I could formally ask for her hand in marriage before I popped the question. We went to her hometown. We met her parents and I got their blessing to get married. They seemed very nice and welcoming, but there was something odd about it. Here were small-town farming folk with this glamorous international jet-setter for a daughter. They didn't quite match-up. Then again, here was I, with a Ferrari and 13 acres of farm estate, and I grew up in a small working-class town. People can change and move on.

From her hometown we went to the city to stay with her cousins. Again, they were very warm and welcoming, more urban like Elle than her folks. However, Elle's aunt wasn't around, she was in a psychiatric institution with paranoid schizophrenia. I didn't think too much of it at the time, however, it must have struck a chord with me somewhere. Slowly things were starting to take shape in the back of my mind.

Elle's strange job situation, her mysterious trip to Madrid, the mood swings and the storming out of Ronnie Scott's. The sense of caution I felt about leaving her alone with my kids. The escalating tensions and accusations between her and Pete. The strange wrong number calls. The furious reaction to Maxine and me. Now, I meet her family and find her parents seem a little distant, and there's a history of mental illness in the family. I had no idea, of course, that the police would contact her father after the theft occurred to discover Elle too had a diagnosis of schizophrenia.

We returned home and in March, I popped the question, and she said yes. It was a fairy tale coming true. Pete left, which was sad for everyone but we were carried through it by the excitement of planning the wedding. My children were especially delighted. Elle and I told them we wanted to get married, and we told them we were going to start a family. My kids were ten years old, and the prospect of a wedding and a huge party, and a new baby brother or sister was very exciting for them. It made us all very excited and I can't describe how happy we were.

And then it all crashed down. It was the thought of me having another child that sent my ex-wife over the edge.

The day my world span off its axis

It was 8 July, I was in London that night. I watched the Brazil–Germany World Cup semi-final that saw Germany hammer Brazil 7-1. It was a great night out with the lads, and I stayed over in London. Elle knew I would be watching the footy with my mates and staying over. I arrived home the next day and she was gone.

At that time I had a crew of builders at the farm. They had seen her the day before. My friend Dave, the project manager who was managing the build seemed concerned, he could see how worried I was.

Then I got a text. It was from Elle. She called me darling. She said she was sorry. She had gone home to America and that she would always love me.

I was in shock. It was payday for my builders. I asked Dave

to pay them in cash, which I always did. I kept the cash in my safe.

Dave called me to my office. The safe was empty. £25k in cash was missing.

At that moment, it was like the world was crashing around my ears. I couldn't believe what was happening. All I could think was I had to go after her. She was having some sort of crisis, she needed help, I loved her, we were engaged. We had been engaged for only three months. My whole life was revolving around her and so were my kids.

So I tried booking a ticket to America only to realise shortly after she had taken my passport too. That's when I discovered £306,000 had been transferred out of our joint account into hers. That was exactly 50 per cent of the balance. I couldn't understand it. We had an agreement with my personal banker that Elle couldn't make any large purchases without my approval. I don't know how she managed it, however she was smart about it. Half the account in a joint account belongs to one of the co-signers. Technically, Elle had done nothing wrong in the bank's eyes. My personal banker had missed the transfer to Elle's account – after all, it wasn't a purchase. The money had even been converted into US dollars and sent to another account.

Suddenly the cold hard reality of it began to sink in. Elle wasn't grabbing the cash and running away in a fit of nerves. She was robbing me. She was a con artist. A mentally ill con artist, perhaps, or perhaps a sinister criminal mind. The thing was, I knew in my gut it had to be more complex than that – who else was involved? You can't just leave the country with £25k in cash. Most countries limit the cash amounts you can take on a plane to less than half that to avoid money laundering. Could someone else have the money? Was this some kind of elaborate sting? I was reeling. And I couldn't reach Elle. Day after day, I couldn't reach her. Five days, was it six? It all blurred. Nothing made sense.

I called the police.

The local police weren't used to that kind of call. They were sceptical. Here I was, some guy claiming to have a safe full of cash and a girlfriend who'd done a runner with that and half the joint account. She had access to the joint account, and so that wasn't exactly a criminal act, but the theft from the safe was. They issued me a crime reference number and eventually sent someone round to update me on their investigation, but it was underwhelming to say the least. Their investigations included a call with Elle's father, who explained in mitigation that she had suffered from a devastating and life limiting bout of mental illness that meant she was prone to being a fantasist.

Suddenly, it all started to fall into place.

She was sitting at that bar in Harvey Nichols, waiting to meet a rich man.

She never had a job to come to. She wasn't working on Bond Street.

She had no friend in Spain.

Her moods and the strange vibes that made me cautious about leaving her with my kids were down to her issues. Mood swings.

In later testimony from my ex-wife to the Family Courts, the story emerged that Pete had tested Elle with a year before – that I had him kill a horse. It proved one thing to me – that my ex-wife and Elle were clearly a lot closer than I thought.

Elle had also told my ex-wife that I had imprisoned her in the gym at the farm without water. Apparently my kids let her out, and she cried and told them I'd locked her up as well. This was all, of course, more paranoid fantasy. I was shocked that even my ex-wife could believe a story like that – she had seen the gym, she knew it didn't have a lock on the door and floor to ceiling windows, that opened from the inside, on the ground floor.

Of course, I didn't know then that my ex-wife had been fuelling these fantasies in some way, and had agreed to take a suitcase for Elle in safe keeping, in case she needed to escape. Apparently – as my ex-wife also told the courts – Elle had asked for her help because I had threatened to burn her suitcase. Which was bizarre. Here was a woman who ran off with over £300,000 and a £60,000 diamond engagement ring, hiding suitcases? Of what? It was like living in a delusion.

Worse than the fantasies were the reality of what happened to the £25k. Elle had given it to a friend of hers, who worked at a very famous international bank. I hate to think what shocking fantasies she must have told them to make them assist her by holding onto a stolen £25k.

Eventually I wrote to Elle's family and said the police were now involved. Elle called me that day.

She sounded strange. She was thought-disordered, and clearly having a mental breakdown – I was in shock.

She told me that she never went to Spain, that instead she had gone to have an abortion on her birthday because she didn't know what to do. She told me that she'd given the money to a friend, to hold onto. She couldn't explain why.

She didn't mention the suitcase or my ex-wife. She never mentioned Pete's story about the dead horse either. At this point, I was hurt and in shock, and in a way my heart went out to Elle and her obvious distress. However, the friends who'd taken my money were about to get the fright of their life. I didn't have their numbers.

I asked for them.

She wouldn't let me have them.

At this point I told her that I knew their bosses well, two of the largest investment banks in the world. I said I would have to inform them, the regulator and the police, and it would inevitably become newsworthy. It would be a press feeding frenzy, they would also almost certainly go to jail, and even if they didn't, their careers would be over.

They had £25k of my stolen money, and no way were they getting away with it.

She sent me the numbers. I called them. I said I knew everything and I wanted the money back. Now. They said they couldn't get it, and they were at a Sunday afternoon barbeque.

Imagine that. Imagine taking £25k in stolen cash from a woman having a full-blown psychotic breakdown and when the owner of the cash calls, you say your barbeque comes first! I couldn't believe it. I said they could leave the barbeque and get the money, and bring it to me, or they could wait for the police to arrive and arrest them, then the police could give me the money back.

They agreed to meet me and returned the money. I felt disgusted. Suddenly, as my world is falling apart and my heart is breaking, I am forced to stand in a train station car park and take a carrier bag full of banknotes like some sort of gangster? I can't describe how much that damaged my trust or how shocked I was.

Meanwhile, I helped Elle arrange a flight back to London. She had a weird hold over me even after a criminal act, which even now I can't quite explain. I didn't know what to expect, but I was willing, even after all that, to work it out if we could. It was desperate. A terrible decision on reflection.

The end of the engagement, and the breaking of my heart and my kids

When Elle came back, she had arranged for the money to be repaid into what was our joint account – she had been removed. My lawyers advised me not to take any legal action against her accomplices on the grounds the news would leak out into the press and undoubtedly be embarrassing for all concerned, including my kids. I didn't want that. They were distraught enough when they found out Elle had gone. I think they were very hurt by it all and when I said she was coming back to work things out, I think they felt as angry and confused as I did. I can only imagine the conversations with their mother at that time.

We spent a month trying to work it out. It felt difficult, but possible. I loved her. I believed she still loved me. Sure, she had problems to work out but I felt we could. Things weren't easy with the kids, they we re very wary of her now, but like me I believed they wanted it all to work out. We tried to get back to normal but we didn't. It's hard to come back from that kind of upheaval. It was like sleeping with the enemy.

It finally ended as suddenly and unexpectedly as it began. We went out with some friends, Elle came home early. I was worried. To be honest, I feared another shock waiting for me when I got home. As I ran through the many things that had happened with Elle, they took on a sinister quality. She had, whether she realised it or not, isolated me from my closest friends and help. She had distanced me from one of my oldest friends, Maxine. She had driven a wedge between me and Peter, to the point whereby he resigned. She had involved people I knew socially in the theft of money from my safe. She had isolated me from the people in my social circle before she came on the scene. And there was still this sense that it was just the tip of the iceberg. Were the phone calls – the wrong numbers – from America for her? Was the man who kept calling involved?

That night I had a curry in town with one of my oldest friends, Toph. He saw I was worried about what I might find back home when I got there. We even joked – gallows humour – that we'd arrive home and she'd be waiting with some American guy to murder me. Or she'd fake her own death in order to rob me, like in some Hollywood crime thriller. Toph said he'd come back with me, as much for moral support as genuinely in case something dreadful were about to happen. He was worried about what we might find, and insisted I called the police and warned them that we were worried. Just in case she threw herself down the stairs and claimed I'd beaten her up, or she had an accomplice waiting to kill me.

But Elle was fine. It was all fine. She picked us up from the local Indian restaurant.

Toph stayed and had a nightcap. Elle was more than fine. She seemed so happy. She talked at length about how glad she was that we had reconciled after the split, and spoke at length about our wedding plans. I was completely taken in by it, as was Toph. We said goodnight, and he said he was so pleased for me, for us. He was genuinely looking forward to our wedding.

The next morning I drove Toph to the station but when I returned there was a buzz at the gate. It was a removal van with a police escort. I opened the door and the policeman barged in, demanding to see Elle. I said she was upstairs. He was acting like she was in danger. He called for her. And when she appeared asked her if she was okay, in the way policemen ask abused wives when they are called out to a domestic incident on a TV show.

She said she was okay.

The policeman looked at me like I was the scum of the earth.

Elle stated it's over. She was leaving. She had arranged a removal van to ship a container of furniture back to the USA, which she said I had bought for her and so therefore it was hers. It was most of our bedroom. I let it go. I could replace it easily enough. I didn't want to argue about it, especially with an angry policeman there waiting to arrest me.

It was dreadful. But it wasn't the devastating shock of before. It was just sad, as all break-ups are. To be honest about it, I knew it was over. I desperately wanted to relive the fairy tale, with the happy ending, the Disney Princess and me, the kids, a new family in our dream home farm. That must sound so naïve to you, but who wouldn't want that? The truth is, you can't put all the pieces of that jigsaw back together. I was in love with someone who was mentally ill. A fantasist, a criminal that did so much damage through the lies she told and the way she messed with our emotions.

I can't blame her completely because she was unwell, any more than you can blame someone with the flu for sneezing. But the upshot was she told my ex-wife lies about dead horses and being imprisoned in my gym that were regurgitated in Court and given to the Cafcass Guardian, who painted me to be some sort of gangster.

Worse, she broke my heart. Worse still, she broke my kids' hearts. They went from planning for the dream wedding of their daddy to someone who looked like Elsa from *Frozen* (which was a smash hit movie they loved) to seeing Daddy hit rock bottom. Elle betrayed them as much as me.

Worse, it meant when my ex-wife allowed them to discover about my estranged child, it pushed them over the edge. Elle and I were planning to start a family. My kids were excited at the prospect of a new baby brother or sister. Then it was all gone and they were devastated. Then my ex-wife tells them they already have one that I hadn't told them about, that they had a half-sibling all along and I'd kept it from them? It turned them against me. No doubt. Of course it did.

I never told them the full extent of Elle's problems. I couldn't expect a couple of 11 year olds to understand all the things that happened with Elle. The money, the mental illness, the lies. They thought I'd argued with her but what I didn't know at the time was my ex-wife was involved with Elle, with the theft, and was clearly part of this elaborate plot.

I resolved things had to end, so I made the policeman a cup of tea, and set to work helping the removal men load up the van. I thought to myself that the sooner it was done, the sooner the nightmare would end.

Elle left with the policeman. She left me loading the van with the removers. She called me, said she was at the local police station. I don't know why she was there or why she called me. I am not convinced she was at a police station. Who knows? We said goodbye and that was that. She left with a container of furniture and a £60,000 engagement ring. Dave, my project manager at the house, watched the whole thing in disbelief.

I told Toph she had gone. He couldn't believe it. He was a very smart guy, married, successful in finance, a man of the world. He was equally devastated, he said he was completely convinced by her the night before. He told me that someone who was capable of being that believable – talking about wedding plans – while they had actually already booked a removal van – was dangerous. Very dangerous.

The loss of a relationship like that, even without all the madness and drama, makes you grieve. This whole episode had been so shocking and traumatic, I was barely able to get through the day at some points. The theft and the lies were one thing, but that policeman left me feeling so violated. I am a regulated person and I am not a criminal but he turned up and barged past me like he was Rambo and I was about to murder someone with my bare hands. How dare he? I was the victim. I was a victim of theft. Of emotional manipulation. I was the victim of something I could barely piece together. Was she ever real? Was she just a cold-blooded gold digger, looking for a rich fool to rip off? I don't think she was. I think she had many different moods and personalities inside her, and she didn't know who she was.

Dave was a rock though this period. He was with me

almost every day and he literally picked me up off the floor. I can never thank him enough for helping me through the distorted reality my life had become. That year I bought him a watch from Patek Philippe to say thank you. He saved my life.

The aftermath

I decided that the policeman – barging in like that – had gone too far. I was an upstanding member of the community. I was an active fundraiser and donor for multiple charities. I had been the victim of crime. This guy – who may only be doing his job – ends up acting like a bodyguard to Elle? She needed a psychiatrist, not a police escort. If anyone needed the protection of the police, it was me. I was the victim in all this, not her.

I complained to the local police. An inspector from their neighbourhood policing scheme explained that Elle had made a number of false allegations about me, saying she feared for her life when she came to move out. I was, allegedly, a violent man who had a history of violence against her. It was a tissue of lies. I wasn't surprised, at this point, nothing she had said or done would have shocked me. Eventually, I met with the inspector and he began an investigation into my complaint, which I then made formally through my solicitors to ask them to expunge all the baseless, false allegations made by the mentally ill thief who had stolen almost £350,000 from me with accomplices.

I then referred myself into therapy with a psychiatrist who specialises in working with people who have suffered extreme shocks and personal problems. He came highly recommended because he also worked extensively with high net worth individuals and celebrities, so he was experienced with situations where a rich man or woman had been exploited for money by people like Elle.

The first thing he did was make me delete her number from my phone, and delete her from my contacts. He said she was toxic. He was right. Elle did contact me again, she talked about arranging the return of the furniture and us getting back together. I didn't believe it.

I did see Elle just six months later. She kept contacting me, asking for a chance to reconcile. I met her in Singapore and we planned to spend a week talking things through. I went seeking closure. I wanted her to admit what she had done, to admit what had really happened. I needed to know. She also claimed she had lost the engagement ring and wanted me to make an insurance claim for it. I didn't. I knew she had it when she left. First she claimed it was lost at the police station. The police were in contact with me to look for it in my house. I had my builders search the driveway and the grounds for it. The police couldn't find it. The insurance claim was just another scam. She told me, eventually, after I had gone to see her in Singapore that she had in fact sold it. Mental illness or not, I think she was a compulsive con-artist. She was effective at it too. Arguably, her mental issues came and went, but she was lucid and competent enough to be a damn good thief. I was a rich middle-aged mark, she had made plenty of money from exploiting me, I am sure she wouldn't hesitate to try again.

She kept contacting me. She still does to this day. Always some strange story, always some desperate situation she needs help with. I respond kindly, with a supportive message but I am under no illusions about just how ill she is, and how everything she says is pure fantasy. Now I have enough distance from the pain and shock of what happened, I feel sorry for her. She is sick. She needs help. That is the real tragedy in all of this, not just how badly she hurt me, and how much she damaged things with my kids, but the fact she is completely out of her mind.

Back then, when Christmas 2014 came, it was miserable. I was sad. The kids were sad. Christmas makes sad times even more acute. In the two months that preceded it, my relationship with the kids deteriorated. I was depressed. I was in therapy, which is hard. I was grieving. My trust in people was at an all-time low.

I found one of my kids crying under my desk. They had found a CD in the computer, left for me by Elle. I had no idea it was even there. It was a mix of songs – all the songs we used to listen to. And a message for me from Elle. She had recorded it and left it there before she left for the second time. It rammed home just how much damage she had done to us as a family.

'Darling I want you to have this CD as a memory of all the wonderful times we've had together, thank you so much for looking after me so beautifully, I will miss you so much … Meep. Okay, I love you darling.'

'Meep' was a family word that we used with the kids and meant 'be happy and kind'.

This was a recording from the same woman who arranged a police escort for protection when she left with a container of my furniture, and a small fortune in watches and jewellery? I played it to the police. They could hardly believe it. Clearly, they had been taken in by Elle, as I had.

I also worked out why Elle came back after the theft. It was never to make up, not really. She was afraid. She had cold feet, fearing the law would catch up with her and her accomplices. She came back to cover her tracks and destroy the evidence. I discovered she had been through all my records, in my office, my emails and my phone and deleted everything. Every mail I'd sent her. All records of what she had done, and my efforts to complain to the bank, and the police. All I had left were the key messages I had saved in a file and some that I forwarded to friends. I did that because I had nobody to talk to, and I thought my story was so far-fetched nobody would believe it. Those friends were my only witnesses to what I'd been through. Them, and my ex-wife of course. Who knew much more than I could ever imagine.

At that time I came to rely heavily on my new assistant and housekeeper – Kate – for support with the kids. I was a mess. Life wasn't great. Kate was great with them and very supportive. My kids were hurting and so was I. It felt like all our hopes had died, and we were mourning for them.

In January, the police inspector informed me he had completed his investigation and wanted to see me. All the allegations were removed from my records, due to the circumstances of Elle's theft and departure, and the fact she was clearly either a con-woman, mentally ill, or both. He apologised on behalf of the local police, and explained that the aggressive constable that barged in that day had acted inappropriately. We had a coffee together, and I felt comforted by it. Some closure, or so I thought.

What happened next pushed me over the edge, and was the seed of the row that split me from my kids forever.

As he was leaving, the inspector paused and gave me an ominous warning. He asked me if I knew of anyone else who might want to cause me trouble.

I didn't know what he meant.

He explained that during his investigation of the Elle incident, and the broader issues of the theft, he had discovered that someone else was involved. Someone I knew. Someone I obviously did not suspect, but someone who was clearly motivated to assist Elle in her theft and in her fantasy accusations against me.

I was stunned. I asked who. He said he couldn't give me a name. However, I deserved to know because I was vulnerable to abuse from this person as they were close to me. I had no idea who. I listed a few names of people who might have been involved, including the pair who had taken the cash from Elle – I'd kept their names out of it before.

He shook his head.

When I ran out of names, I said, off-hand 'Well the only person left is my ex-wife, but she'd never do something like that.'

He looked at me, eyes fixed on my own, and replied, 'I have never seen anything like this in my 24 years of service. I wouldn't rule it out, sir.'

I thought I was going crazy. Here was a police inspector, telling me informally with a nod and a remark like some sort of spy in a Cold War movie, that my ex-wife had been involved with Elle and the devastating events I had lived through. It was unthinkable. I was reeling from it. If my ex-wife was involved in that, what else could she have done? The shock was terrible. I was already close to rock bottom emotionally, I wasn't sure how much more I could take. It nearly drove me over the edge.

The events with Elle directly led to the arguments I had with my kids, which led to our separation. The discovery my ex-wife was involved led to me telling my kids about it in a lapse of judgement, which caused the split that broke us apart forever. While the responsibility for that argument and what I said was clearly mine, and I am sorry for it, I believe it would never have happened without my ex-wife helping Elle, and colluding with her. Let's face it, my ex-wife revealed in a subsequent court assessment just a year later that she had discussed the horse-assassination lie my assistant Peter told Elle to test her. That proves my ex-wife and Elle were a lot closer than they made out. And she also admitted helping Elle hide a suitcase from me, shortly before she emptied my safe and drained my bank account.

That person, my ex-wife, does she sound capable of psychological manipulation to you? I think so. She was involved with a mentally ill criminal who was my fiancée, who literally filled a bag with money, took the engagement ring, took furniture, broke my heart and wrecked my life.

Could someone like my ex-wife – who a police inspector warned me to be wary of – be capable of Parental Alienation?

Chapter 8:
My ex-wife

I can't really explain why my ex-wife did what she did, or what her motivations were. In a way, I wish I knew the reason for it, something I could argue against, something I could fight. Something I could use to explain the terrible hurt I believe she inflicted upon me and my kids. But the fact remains my kids hate me, I haven't seen them for years because of it, and they grew to hate me while we were supposed to be on a cooling-off break to repair our relationship. I think maybe that cooling-off break was my ex-wife's plan all along. A break of months, with no intention to restart it. In those months they grew to blame and judge me, for reasons that changed over time as they learned things about me while in the care of my ex-wife, things that were private and they weren't old enough to handle. That sounds like Parental Alienation, and my experience feels like it. Which means – if it's true and I am correct in my feelings – that my ex-wife was my abuser.

I know, from the police inspector and my ex-wife's own testimony in a court assessment by a leading consultant child psychiatrist that she was involved with Elle and her theft from me. I also know that she and Elle had talked about intimate details of my life, including repeating a test that Pete my ex-assistant had set for Elle, specifically to find out how loyal she was. My ex-wife repeated that lie in the court assessment, and Elle was the only person who could have told her as she was the only person who Peter had told. Even I didn't know about the 'Horse-gate' at the time, it was only when I told Peter that my ex-wife had claimed I'd had a horse killed that he told me what had happened.

So I can say with certainty that my ex-wife was an unpleasant influence in my life after we divorced, at best she was meddling in my relationship with Elle, at worst, she was trying to wreck my life. What happened with Elle, and my kids, is certainly as close to wrecking my life as anything else I could imagine.

The reality of the situation is I will probably never know why my ex-wife attacked me like this. Worse, I sometimes wonder if she did it without even knowing why herself. I am sure that she used access to my children to make my life harder. She told me she wouldn't do any travelling for my contact weekends which both stressed my time at work and reduced my time with them. And what I think happened next, was when the court ordered her to make access to my children easier for me, she set on a new path to torment me by using my children themselves to make my single life harder. As for the rest of the abuse I endured, who knows what drives someone to do that. I don't.

Parental Alienation often begins as a relatively minor issue. The resident abuser parent usually begins by making access a problem for the non-resident parent. I know first-hand from years of working alongside family lawyers that this is a common pattern in messy divorces. Access to the children is a lever that can be used to influence financial settlements, or whatever the dispute is really about. The children and arranging contact become a way for one parent to bully the other, in the same way that withholding maintenance can be a tactic used by one parent to bully another.

It can also be the beginning of Parental Alienation, and it can be very effective because when a resident parent – especially a mother – makes access hard it takes a court order to address it. Which takes time and money, and inevitably sets the parent who left the family home against the one with residency. The court usually finds in favour of resident parents.

However, when the court addresses access disputes in favour of the non-resident parent – as they did with me when my ex-wife refused to do any travelling for contact weekends – this forces an escalation for abusers. Their only option is to limit access through another route. In Parental Alienation, that route is the kids themselves. If the resident abuser parent can make the children reject the other parent, it's almost impossible for them or the court to do anything about it. In simple terms, if the court rules that you can't stop your kids from seeing your ex-partner, the fool-proof workaround is to stop your kids from wanting to see your ex-partner in the first place. Wishes and feelings are paramount in the Family Courts. If you can control your kids' wishes and feelings, you effectively control the outcome of your children case.

It's a perfectly wicked thing to do. I use those words deliberately. It's a perfect way to break the parent-child bond, and it is a truly wicked thing to do because it hurts the children and the parent to satisfy the abuser. It is sadistic. Unthinkable to most people. It takes determination and the capacity to watch other people – including your kids – suffer to get what you want. It is a shame – and shames many Family Law practitioners – that a whole industry of lawyers and experts exists to deal with these problems but despite the vast sums of money they earn in fees, they seldom do.

In fact, they might even become experts in making these problems worse. I am reminded of my own ex-wife's barrister. He never met my kids, he never met me outside a courtroom. He never saw me parenting. Or my ex-wife. He never saw anything but court papers and instructions to fight my claims. But he did his job, he argued passionately and convinced a judge that my kids were better off without me in their lives. To make that sort of impact on the lives of children you have never met – for money – belongs in the dark ages. Not the modern world. It's out of touch with the way we solve problems in so many other aspects of our lives and relationships through arbitration, tribunals and mediation. It's another reason why I believe the Family Court isn't fit for purpose.

I can understand why my ex-wife might want to hurt me, that's not unthinkable I suppose, even though I thought our divorce was amicable and we remained on good terms – in fact at one point Pete and I taught the kids to ride bikes in her back garden one afternoon. We all know that divorces can be messy, and that people can make it very personal and painful. It's not a surprise when you learn there was a dispute over contact or a mud-slinging campaign over money and so on.

But I cannot understand how my ex-wife could see my children be groomed on the internet, become anxious and depressed, act out and self-harm, and deny there was a problem.

Parental Alienation creates a loophole that completely destroys the possibility of joint contact and bypasses the Children Act legal imperative to preserve a relationship with both parents for the welfare of the child. The loophole exploits the fact that all Family Court judgements and recommendations are subordinated to the child's wishes and feelings. When the voice of the child is heard – if their wishes and feelings are to never see the alienated parent again – that overrides everything else. I am not denying the voice of the child, but as I have written about at length in this book, if their voice has been manipulated by the resident abuser, it's not really their voice at all. That's the loophole.

The court hears the child's voice, but the child is speaking the abuser's words. That mismatch of voice and words is the trump card that beats all other cards in the deck. Fighting against your own child's wishes and feelings makes you sound like the bad guy. It forces you into a position where you have to argue your kids have been manipulated and they don't mean what they are saying.

In effect, what everyone else hears is an angry divorcee saying their own kids don't deserve a voice in the proceedings, and their wishes and feelings don't matter. They hear you arguing your kids need psychiatric help. Your kids hear that too. You become the villain of the piece. You are labelled as the one who disregards your kids wishes and feelings, you are labelled as the one who undermines their self-esteem by arguing they need psychological help. You end up sounding like you're arguing a law suit against your own children, not supporting them. The wishes and feelings loophole closes around you, making your kids sound like victims and making you sound like a bastard.

The power of this loophole is unimaginable until you find yourself caught in it. Suicide rates among alienated parents – especially fathers – are reported to be significantly higher than average, even compared to high risk groups like sufferers of depression. I can understand it. I have told myself many times that I am no good to my kids if I'm dead. I never looked into that particular void because I knew I had to keep going for my children's sake. However, there comes a point when you realise you have lost – and lost everything – and I am not surprised that many people can't come back from that. Hope gets lost in the loophole, and sadly, lives are lost in it too.

Having endured all of that, it would be easy to turn it into a tirade of abuse directed at my abuser, my ex-wife. However, I am not going to do that. In this chapter, I will do two things. I will ask why, and will show how.

I will guess the first answer – why she did this to me – because it can only ever be a guess. And I would ask you to treat it as such and make no judgements about her from my supposition. That is because I have no evidence. No proof of the why. She has never told me why. She has never given me a reason. She has never even admitted alienating me. I suspect she was encouraged by her own family, who were very close to her. They closed ranks around her against me.

It is, as far as she has told the courts and the experts, my children's own spontaneous decision to cut off their loving father with whom they had a close relationship for reasons that at the time, didn't quite add up. All my ex-wife has admitted to time and again is supporting my kids in their desire to erase me completely from their lives. Except, of course, financially. They have never refused the school fees or lifestyle afforded by my maintenance payments or financial settlement. Nor would I expect them to. And neither would I withhold them, either. But apart from a purely financial connection, I am all but dead to them. Imagine that – my children don't want me but they accept my money. That isn't reflective of a healthy set of values, it is certainly not how I taught them to value people or money.

The second answer – how she did it to me – is something I can prove. Or rather, I can show you what she showed me through her testimony to the courts and court-ordered reports. She revealed a lot about herself in one report in particular, where she accidently revealed an involvement in my life, behind the scenes, which is nothing short of sinister. That involvement in my life began when we were first divorced and continued ever since. I will show three pieces of evidence, which came from her and her legal team via the courts, which expose her to be more than capable of manipulating my kids against me, because the evidence shows her manipulating other people against me.

Question 1: Did my ex-wife alienate me?

That question tortured me for a long while.

Here's my answer.

I think my ex-wife regretted our divorce. That might

sound odd to you, I accept that, after all she was the one who wanted it. But I wonder if her identity was mostly made up of being a wife as well as a mother. Giving up the wife part of that equation must have shaken her self-confidence a bit, like it does for most divorcees. It must have challenged her sense of identity, because divorce does that to everyone. Our sense of identity is held together through concepts like being married or single, child or adult, a teenager or a thirty-something, gay or straight, religious or atheist, parent, grandparent. Our personal identities – and the roles we play in our families and social networks – change over time, depending on our age and life experiences.

I think becoming single again was a bigger deal for my wife than it was for me. For me it was progress. We were stuck in a rut. I think she found it harder to come to terms with than I did. I wonder if she was hurting or angry with herself for choosing divorce instead of trying to work it out. She never wanted marriage guidance. She never wanted us to work out why we lived more like brother and sister sharing a house than husband and wife sharing a bed. Would I have given us another go at the end? No. I would have at one point though. I had asked for us to go to marriage counselling a couple of years before but she completely dismissed it out of hand. She insisted we were fine, and I was just being dramatic. At this point, we hadn't been physically intimate for about a year, which she didn't seem to mind for some reason. I don't know why, perhaps she was depressed after the kids were born and that was how it came out.

What I can say for sure about my ex-wife, is she was heavily influenced by the opinion of her family and peers, especially the women in that network. The community we came from is a stereotypical London commuter lifestyle. The man takes the train into the city, the wife stays home and does the school run. The man makes a lot of money, the wife spends it. The men play golf at weekends, the women all meet up and moan about their husbands spending too much time at work and playing golf. And so on. It's a cliché but it is rooted in a degree of fact as well. My ex-wife was one of a group of wealthy housewives, with top of the line luxury SUVs and holiday villas in Spain. They didn't work, they had fake tans and blonde hair, they dressed in designer labels. They all had kids at private school and they all lived in big houses with pools.

Within that group, there was considerable pressure to conform. Getting divorced put membership of that group at risk – because if you lost the money and the house, you would lose touch with your friends. In my ex-wife's case she made millions in the divorce and bought a huge house. She was still very much part of the set – I was wealthy, so it made her the richest divorcee. But somehow her status was damaged.

When my life took an upturn, and I suddenly made huge profits from the sale of my company, she sued me for more money. We settled out of court but it was an expensive and damaging process – the details of which I never shared with my kids. However, then I met Elle and moved back into her social world by living nearby. Suddenly, I was competing, not just with my beautiful younger fiancée, but with a bigger house and more money. Worse, I was planning a new family and I think my kids wanted very much to spend more time with me as a result. I think my ex-wife genuinely feared the kids would want to live with me, it made her press the alienation accelerator. There was a constant underlying drive to create alienation, but this was now turbocharged.

My wife was financially independent from me. She didn't need to keep on good terms with me. She could afford to cut me out of her life, knowing I would keep paying the school fees. And if I didn't, she could afford to sue me again. She was in a powerful position. She was also surrounded by people who supported her against me. Her parents, her sister, my sister, her best friend – they closed ranks around her. She even claimed money to support her parents and so on. I am quite sure her supporters were living off her and remained close to her because of her wealth. Money can be toxic. It makes people greedy. It makes them envious of others. It becomes an obsession for some people. I think my ex-wife had an unhealthy relationship with money because she never earned it for herself. Her goal in life was to marry a rich man. She made it. Her goal in life then became to get a huge divorce settlement from a rich man, she made that too. After that, she had no goals, I suppose. Except to preserve her status – and ensuring the kids never wanted to live with me instead of her became a major part of that.

I think partially the problem was how my ex-and I got together. I'd known her since I was 14. We were at school together, knew each other reasonably well. We were friends. Never romantic. We didn't get together until a couple of weeks before I was due to marry someone else. It came as a bolt from the blue. I was 25, I was doing well in the bank, making good money and everything was on the up. A couple of weeks before the big day, I called my ex-wife up and asked her for a drink – as an old mate – to celebrate. We met up and went out clubbing, as our group of mates had done a hundred times before. It wasn't unusual, lots of people from school and friends wanted to meet up and have drink when they found out I was getting married, just like I had gone out for drinks with them when they got married.

But then, that night as the evening wore on and the drinks went down the unthinkable happened. We kissed. It was passionate and it completely blew my mind. I was supposed to be getting married in a couple of weeks, what the hell was I doing? I suddenly felt this surge of emotions for my ex. It seemed like a Jackie Collins romance novel or something. Unrequited love of a boy and girl from the small town who met at the wrong time. It sounds so cliched but it's what happened.

I couldn't go ahead with the marriage. I was suddenly in love with someone else, and I had no idea what to do about it. It made me panic with the thought I was making a terrible mistake. I told my parents. I told my best man. They all said the same thing. It was just jitters. It was last minute nerves. Everyone does it, has a last minute wobble and does something silly. It was that 'What happens in Vegas, stays in Vegas' kind of thing. At that point, I realised something for the first time. People, even family, are often too focused on appearances or their own personal preferences than other people's. In my case, everyone seemed more concerned about the embarrassment of cancelling the wedding reception and the social awkwardness of telling people the wedding was off than my feelings or worse, me and my bride-to-be making a terrible mistake.

So I told my fiancée that the wedding was off. She hit the roof. She couldn't take the shame of getting jilted, so to speak. She insisted we got married and went on honeymoon. She wrote me a suicide note. I didn't know what do to. She begged me to get married, said that if we couldn't work it out, then we could come back and get a quickie divorce. However, the wedding was going ahead. And that was that. We got married. We went on honeymoon. We came back and got a quickie divorce. My ex-wife and I got together pretty much straight away and got married three years later. My kids were born five years after that. Five years later, my ex-wife told me she considered our marriage was over, just before I turned 40.

I wonder now, in retrospect, if my ex-wife was motivated to win me as a husband because she feared falling behind her social set even back then. Her friends were getting married to men with jobs in the city, same as me. She wanted to keep up, same as she did in later life with a pool and a fancy car. I wonder if it was possible that as all the eligible bachelors from our little corner of the home counties got married and moved on that she felt she was missing the boat.

It's fair to say that within our group of friends, I was doing well career-wise. I was rising through the ranks fast, with money to spare and great prospects. Did that influence her to get romantically involved with me, when I was two weeks away from getting married? Did she see a rich bachelor about to slip away and decided she wanted me? That sounds unbelievable, doesn't it? How cynical and mercenary it makes her sound. Then again, if you told me then that one day she would drive a massive rift between me and my children and do nothing to help us heal it, I wouldn't have believed that either.

I do know for certain that she never complained about marrying a banker, with all the long hours and hard work that comes with it. She knew what she was getting into, and she never minded the money, the cars, the houses and all the things that came with my career success.

My friend Toph felt convinced that she was spiralling down after the divorce. He knew us both before we got married. He said she was like her circle of friends, a very materialistic woman. He joked with me that they all spent their money on white leather sofas and Pinot Grigio, so they could sit on each other's white leather sofas and drink Pinot Grigio while they moaned about their husbands who spent too much time working and playing golf. Toph believed that she feared losing the kids, which were a source of income to her. She didn't work, she lived in a seven-bedroom house, she had expensive tastes and a lifestyle to support. She last worked a decade before, in 1999, earning £29,000 as an office administrator. Hardly the career she needed to afford the life she became accustomed to. If the kids had come to live with me, she would have lost out financially. Was that possible? Toph also said that the stigma of losing her social status as the wife of the richest man in their social set would have made her bitter. I can't be sure of any of that.

What I do know is she was very closed off to me after the divorce. I remember when I made my new will, after I moved to London. I called her and asked if she would be an executor of my will. This was important. I wanted my kids to inherit my wealth but not all at once, and not at a young age. That much money could ruin a kid's life. They would never have to work again, they could do whatever they wanted.

I feared them becoming junkies and wasters. I wanted my kids to have a work ethic and an education, not live like the idle rich. My ex-wife refused to be my executor. I asked her why, and she wouldn't say. She simply said she wouldn't do it. I tried to explain why and she wouldn't hear of it. She behaved like it was some sort of trick.

What I do know is regardless of how she felt after our divorce, I moved on in a very obvious and tangible sense. I moved to London. My business moved up a gear. My life options multiplied. I was enjoying a new life in the heart of the capital, with all the culture and social life that comes with it. She stayed in the same town, literally a few hundred yards away from our old house. She was still a stay-at-home mum, still spending the days seeing the same friends, on a white leather sofa, drinking white wine or vodka and diet coke, going to the same places, doing the same things. She still lived in a big house, with the kids at school all day.

When the dust of the divorce settled, I was busy. I was working, I had a thousand things to occupy my time. For her, it was the same-old-same-old, I suppose. I thought that was what she wanted. When I wanted to change our lives, she always wanted things to stay the same. I think that was partly the root of our intimacy issues. We could go for months – over a year – without sex. She seemed fine with it. I wanted to change that, she reacted badly to it. She was rather narrow-minded about sex in general, it felt like what went on between a husband and wife in the bedroom was very much about making babies, not the modern sense of a healthy romantic sex life.

I also wonder if she was depressed in some way. I think the boredom or lack of direction she must have experienced after the divorce – which keeps you occupied and motivated while still ongoing – made her focus on her negative feelings about how I was moving on and she wasn't. It sounds like a cliché but I felt my divorce freed me from a rut I was well and truly stuck in for the last few years of our marriage. I think she resented that. I can understand it, to a point. I left and began to thrive without her. She had new men in her life, but it never seemed that serious looking from the outside in. I can't say if it was or not. My kids would talk about them, of course. The first one, the father of the local thug shouted at my kids and scared them once. The next guy they really liked, but it broke up because my ex-wife found him to be possessive and controlling. The last one, according to my ex-wife, wasn't interested in kids. My kids said he'd come over with his mates to watch the football while my ex-wife served them drinks and snacks like a waitress. They didn't like that.

That's all I know. My view was shaped by the fact my ex-wife was still mostly in the house, all day, waiting for the school run. And in the house all night, watching the TV with a drink or two. I think she was bored. That's not healthy in the long run. But I can only speculate on all of that, and to be honest, I don't think I really have any right to put any more speculation than that down in this book.

What happened to my ex-wife is her story, not my story.

My story I know to be true because I have lived it. I am living it now. At the outset of this book project, my goal was to avoid a he-said-she-said rant or throw insults or accusations at someone with no right to reply. This is why I have worked with a writer to ensure nothing I have put in the pages of this book can't be supported by an email, letter or court paper.

I have set a standard for this book that means I have left out many things that were just suspicions or conclusions I have drawn for myself without evidence to back it up. That sort of thing would undermine my story, and it has been such a dreadful lived experience of abuse the only thing that makes it worth telling is the fact it is true. Nobody can dismiss me as a disgruntled ex-husband with an axe to grind. I have that at least to hold on to and remind myself that I am not losing my mind, this terrible thing really did happen to me.

So before I say anything about my ex-wife, I have to say this. I don't know why she alienated me from my kids because I can't prove it. Acrimony in divorce is often caused by one partner moving on and the other getting stuck in the past, and the fact the resident parent chooses to act against the other parent through limiting access to the children isn't that unusual. The first report – from the children's charity when my kids and I first took the school cooling-off period – said my ex-wife still felt considerable pain and hurt towards me and suggested that was influencing her reluctance to support my efforts to restart contact with my children. That seems to be the why, or as close as I will ever get to understanding it.

I believed my ex-wife was a good mother. I said that in my very first court assessment. It was held against me by Cafcass, because they claimed it was self-contradictory. How could I claim she was a good mother while simultaneously claiming she was alienating me? At the time, I could separate the two things out mostly because I had no idea just how dark and sinister things really were. I said it during the first assessment with the consultant child psychiatrist, before I fully realised she was both targeting and alienating me. Before I had the chance to read the report from her and my kids – that was a game changer. I believe that the children – and her standing in our circle of friends as a devoted mum – became so central to her life that when she became angry and bitter towards me after our divorce, the kids were always going to become a part of it. She built her life around the kids in a way that meant they became the reason for everything.

Our divorce settlement was dominated – fairly – by the fact she was a stay-at-home mum and I was a high earner, so I should provide for her. I accept that without argument and I settled generously because I believed then – and still do – that a husband and father should look after his wife and kids financially if that's their situation. Supporting the kids' school fees and maintenance was never challenged, I was happy to settle and move on.

The kids and her family became a way of relating to me. Arrangements and decisions about the children made them a channel that connected us beyond the clean break of the divorce. More than that, her reasons for not encouraging contact or helping me resolve the issues with my children was – as she claimed – to support my kids. She didn't have to make out I was a safeguarding risk to them, because once they decided they never wanted to see me again, all she ever had to do was be a good mother and support their wishes and feelings. As I wrote earlier, this is the loophole. It's a clever self-referencing paradox where the abuser parent never directly abuses the other parent, they simply support their kids and make them a proxy by which the abuse takes place.

This is something you will encounter time and again in

stories of alienation. It is the fundamental nature of it, in fact. Children are exposed to a negative reaction when it comes to the other parent by the resident abuser parent. It might be through the things they say, or it could be more subtle like they get annoyed or upset when the child mentions the other parent. There could be a lot of different influences that psychologically condition the child over a period of years to avoid mentioning the other parent, then avoid seeing them. And of course, when we are trying to avoid something we invent reasons why it's justified. Like kids can always find a good reason why they hate broccoli or don't want to go to school, even when there is no good reason for it at all.

If she did alienate me, how did she do it?

Any experienced family lawyer will tell you that the courts take personal attacks and remarks with a pinch of salt. They will tell you that in family law, people often display a tendency to make up wild accusations or attempt to assassinate the character of the other side. They will tell you that judges and court-appointed experts are well aware of this and ignore it. In my case, my own solicitors – and I had a few during my Family Court journey – told me to ignore what my ex-wife said about me in reports, and not to respond to her wild accusations for this reason. They told me the judges don't take any notice. They told me to focus solely on my kids and their welfare, and let her throw insults and accusations all she wanted because it wouldn't make any difference to the outcome.

Except, of course, that's not the whole story.

Perhaps the judges don't take much notice. In my case,

I had six different judges, most of whom seemed to have barely even bothered to read my papers. Did they take any notice? I can't say they did. Particularly the Deputy District Judge who gave my final ruling, mentioned quite a few things that were irrelevant and had nothing to do with my ability to parent my kids. The judge, in fairness, did say as much. However, the fact they mentioned these untruths meant they had figured large enough in the decision-making process to be considered and dismissed. That is not the same thing as ignoring them or taking them with a pinch of salt.

What I find more problematic about the wild accusations and slurs my ex-wife made was the fact they were recorded in the court-ordered assessments by experts. This is normal, the experts interview all parties and note down testimony. They include it in their reports, verbatim and unchallenged. You could claim your ex-partner was a vampire and they would write it down. You can say anything. It's all just supposed to add context and we're told it won't sway the judges. However, when it's presented to other court-appointed officials, like a junior Cafcass Guardian, you have to wonder if they also dismiss it in that way. My Cafcass experience was undeniably hostile and I suspect that was down to the many false allegations my ex-wife made in the reports the Cafcass Guardian read.

This verbatim reporting of testimony without challenge or a right to reply is fundamental to the processes of Family Court. This is because Family Law is unique in the legal world because unlike criminal law, contract law, tax law, intellectual property law, human rights law and so on. There is no singular cause or single event in a Family Case that is examined before the court and represents a breach of law. Family Law is about relationships, not breaking laws or breaching contracts.

As a result, Family Law is a sort of grey area where everyone has a say and then the judge, depending on their own biases and views, makes a judgement. If the judge is a racist, it goes badly for ethnic minorities. If the judge is a misogynist, it goes badly for the woman. If the judge hates the law firm representing one side because they were the law firm in his own divorce case, he'll find against them out of spite, perhaps. Who knows? If you Google 'Complaints about Family Court Judges' you will find page after page, thousands of news articles and campaigns to reform the system.

There is no burden of proof in Family Court like there is in criminal cases. In criminal law, you have to prove beyond reasonable doubt that someone accused of crime is guilty. In Family Court they use a different concept – the balance of proof – which is a lower standard. It's more like taking a view on what is most believable or likely. Legal experts will tell you this means the more extreme the claims one side makes, the less likely the judge is to consider it. You might say the judge in Family Court judges you based on the balance of probability, or the law of averages.

The problem there is obvious. Parental Alienation is not average. It's not common compared to other issues before the court. This is why I have written consistently in this book that when you claim alienation, it goes against you, you are broadly speaking dismissed as a complainer or as someone who is claiming Parental Alienation to cover up their own shortcomings. So when you claim Parental Alienation, the judges pretty much ignore it because it's not that likely, and very hard to prove.

I never threw abuse at my wife in the Family Court assessments. I accused her of Parental Alienation, but proving that was impossible. How could I? My kids had read private court papers, but my ex-wife claimed they were snooping in her study. My kids had read angry emails between us, my ex-wife claimed they had somehow got her password and hacked into her email. Both of those things were, in the eyes of the judge and the Cafcass Guardian, more believable than my wife deliberately sharing information with my kids to make them hostile towards me.

There were, however, two key pieces of information in the court reports that clearly showed my ex-wife had behaved in an underhand way, sinister way, causing me considerable hurt in other areas of my life.

The dead horse

Firstly, there was the issue of 'Horse-gate', the dead horse story. My former assistant Peter had told Elle I had him kill a horse belonging to an ex-girlfriend. He did it to test her loyalty, because he suspected she was a gold-digger and a con-artist. He said as much to me, but only revealed the horse story at a later date, after my ex-wife told the same story to the court-appointed consultant child psychiatrist when he interviewed us – me, my kids and my wife – making an assessment of our situation.

I had no idea what Peter had done. When I read it, I couldn't believe it. It sounded so stupid. It also sounded familiar – wait a moment, isn't that what happened in *The Godfather* movie?

Isn't that what happened to Shergar and Desert Orchid? Killing horses is something organised criminals do, like the Mafia. It is what made the story sound so ridiculous. I told Peter, and he admitted his part in telling Elle.

So how did my ex-wife know about it? In the same report, my ex-wife also told the psychiatrist that Elle was frightened of me, that I had threatened to burn her suitcase and she had helped her hide it from me.

This shows one thing. My ex-wife and my fiancée had a much closer relationship than I knew at the time. Not only that, but also Elle was telling my ex-wife wild stories about me. It also showed that my ex-wife was helping Elle make arrangements to flee the country in a hurry. Why else would you ask someone to hide a suitcase for them? What did she say to my ex? 'Will you help me hide a suitcase from your ex-husband because he's threatened to burn it'? And my ex-wife helped? Then I was robbed. The police must have spoken to my ex-wife about it, otherwise how would they know she was involved – which the inspector who investigated my complaint confirmed to me months later.

Consider that. My ex-wife was assisting Elle – a woman who stole a huge sum of money from me, who made false accusations against me, and repeatedly tried to steal money. That makes a decent case for the argument that she was working against me. She didn't warn me about Elle. I was the father of her kids, you would think she would want to protect me at least from events that could hurt them, wouldn't you? Her actions hurt me. Her actions show a degree of secrecy, and planning with another person behind my back. No matter what the reason, my ex-wife was involved with Elle, and Elle broke my heart, emptied my safe and hurt my kids.

The dead horse story was absurd. However, it also was read by the family therapist, and the Cafcass Guardian. I can only assume my ex-wife gossiped about it with other people too, it's hard to believe she would tell a psychiatrist about it in a court assessment but nobody else.

The dead deal

In that court assessment, my ex-wife also mentioned something else. Something that was equally as disturbing. While we were getting divorced, I was approached by a good friend of mine – David – who wanted to launch a car dealership. He had all the contacts with a major German brand, he had an excellent business plan and I thought it would make a lot of money. He needed finance, I was going to become his sleeping partner. At the last minute, David got cold feet and said he wanted to get finance from somewhere else, and the deal fizzled out. I was very disappointed, I didn't know why at the time. It seemed very odd. He went on to raise finance elsewhere, and in the end sold his new venture for £70 million. I would have pocketed £20 million from that if we had gone ahead with it.

In the court assessment where my ex-wife revealed she was involved with Elle, she also claimed that she had warned David off doing a deal with me because I was a ruthless businessman. That interference in my private affairs cost me £20 million. That's insane. However, what it also showed – as with Elle – was my ex-wife was involved in my life in a dark and sinister way. Without my knowing.

What was so odd about this episode with David was what

happened with his wife. She was my ex-wife's best friend. She was one of my ex-wife's supporters and gave an affidavit to the court during our hearings, explaining why I was such a bad father. It was the usual story – the same as her mother's affidavit, and her sister's affidavit, all of which were very similar and clearly orchestrated to make me sound like a Dickensian dad who makes his kids do extra tutoring all the time and never had any fun.

David's wife said in her affidavit that I wanted to do a deal with her husband, but he turned me down because he didn't require investors. She said I had offered him money, he refused, and she added *'I understand that this is an issue that has arisen in the proceedings concerning the children.'*

What? No it wasn't. It was nothing to do with the kids. I hadn't raised it. I had completely ignored it in fact. All I cared about was seeing my kids. Now, over a year after my ex-wife had bragged about scuppering that deal to the psychiatrist, here was her friend telling the story in such a way to make it seem my ex-wife had nothing to do with it? My ex-wife had clearly said she warned David off. Now his wife was saying that wasn't true. Why did it even matter? It sounded very much as though my ex-wife was trying to cover up her involvement in it. Because it would have shown her to be what? Manipulative? Vindictive? Capable of alienating me, perhaps?

What this shows isn't just my ex-wife interfering in my life behind the scenes, it shows her friend helping her to cover it up a year later. If my ex-wife had stood by her remarks, they would have passed by, but the fact she was now still talking about the deal with David makes her look guilty.

It makes the whole situation more bizarre. Warning David off wasn't a crime. It merely showed she was vindictive and hurtful. Covering it up a year later made her look highly capable of more.

Perhaps, after the revelations about Elle, my ex-wife became paranoid about me finding out more about her actions behind the scene. After all, she kept the online grooming of my kids a secret from me, she kept the magnitude of the self-harm a secret from me. She was a secretive person. And she was manipulative, clearly. So once again, I ask the question, does the person who colluded with the mentally ill con artist who robbed me and wrecked my life, and the person who scuppered a £20 million deal out of spite, could that person be called manipulative? Could that person be considered hostile to me or vindictive?

The answer, clearly, is yes.

My Ex-wife, the Alienator

My ex-wife was the person who suggested my kids should have their own representation. She was the person who involved Cafcass. She was the person who took the kids to therapists I objected to, and put them into the care of a private clinic. She was the person who told my children's GP not to share information with me regarding their self-harm and referral to that clinic for therapy. She was the person who was on the PTA at the school where the teachers shared information with her but I had to get a court order before they would share it with me. Actions which were a clear breach of my rights.

She claimed that all she wanted to do was support the kids. She claimed that she would do whatever the court thought was best. However, for someone who claimed to be so focused on the children and their wishes, she was very much involved in my private life. She was clearly closer to my fiancée Elle than I knew. She was clearly involved in ruining a multi-million pound business deal for me, and that's what we know of. Imagine if that's just the tip of the iceberg in reality.

She was described by two of the assessors who wrote reports before the court as someone who was still feeling a lot of hurt and anger towards me.

She went on a great length about what a bad father I was. The affidavits from her friends and mother went on about what a bad father I was too. About the onerous pressure of tutoring I put on my kids. About working long hours and never spending enough time with them. About taking them to the theatre instead of Disneyland, again.

Was she manipulating my kids to be hostile towards me? Was she trying to make me appear like a bastard before the court?

I never made any personal attacks on her. I had no involvement in her private life or business dealings. I alleged my kids were clearly at risk – and suffering difficulties – under her care and it was a safeguarding risk. They were self-harming and they had been targeted by an online abuser. That was a safeguarding issue as it took place in my ex-wife's home. I also alleged she was alienating me. I hadn't seen my kids for two years, she was doing nothing to help me contact them, and she was involved in my personal life in a sinister way. Was I right to allege that?

Did she manipulate David when he suddenly decided not to deal with me on the grounds my ex-wife told him I was ruthless in business?

Did she manipulate Elle when she took the suitcase, and agreed to help her flee the country?

Did she try to manipulate the court when she testified to the absurd tale of me having a horse killed?

What was that if not an effort to hurt me? Was she capable of alienating me? Of course she was, she was capable of wrecking business deals and helping someone leave the country with £300,000 of my money and empty my safe of cash. She was at the very least, capable of lies and gossip, and involved in my life behind the scenes in a sinister way that even the police had never seen before. Would she be capable of manipulating my kids to be hostile towards me? It was probably worth investigating, wasn't it, bearing all those things in mind?

My kids read court papers and in those papers read all the lies about the dead horse and so on. They also discovered the existence of the 'secret child' in those papers. They also read emails between me and my wife where I was angry. Could that have been manipulation? A deliberate attempt to influence them against me? I think it is quite obviously a yes.

Remember the Cafcass definition of Parental Alienation? Hostility that is unjustified and the result of psychological manipulation? I wonder if children who read court papers in which their father was described as a ruthless man who paid a thug to kill a horse would count as psychological manipulation?

My children became hostile towards me – and comparing their initial statements aged 11 and their last statements aged 14 it's absolutely clear that despite the fact I hadn't seen them for years, they had become a lot more hostile

– because of living with my ex-wife who described me as some sort of gangster, and was helping Elle to make plans to flee the country. Wouldn't that meet the definition of psychological manipulation by one parent against the other? If not, I wonder what would?

Did none of that raise a red flag with the courts? Did none of it make anyone a little bit suspicious that she was capable of acting in an underhand way when it came to me? That would be consistent with someone who was alienating me after all, and I had alleged she was alienating me.

Here was my ex-wife, whom I claimed was acting against me, and nobody took it seriously. Yet she helped the woman who stole from me. She interfered in my business dealings. And she consistently tried to cover up her involvement in my life – including allowing my kids to access damaging private information about me – and cover up the safeguarding failures that led me to fight for them to receive help through the courts in the first place.

In the beginning of my case, in 2015, my ex-wife said she would get my kids to send me a text and restart contact. By 2017, she claimed I was a bully. A man who had a horse killed. A man who was ruthless. A man who wasn't a fit parent. However, all the things she described in 2017, all the reasons why I wasn't a fit person to see my kids, they all related to things that happened before 2015, when she said she would help get my kids back in contact. Her story had changed beyond recognition. Mine hadn't. Mine was still the same.

To put it another way, it wasn't just my kids who changed the reasons for hating me between 2015 and 2017. My ex-wife also completely changed her version of events – and her assessment of me, too. My story didn't change. Hers did. My kids' did. I went from being a fit parent to being an unfit one according to her, yet nothing had changed. I hadn't seen my kids or her in the interim period.

Was that change in the degree of hostility toward me by my ex-wife and kids considered evidence of psychological manipulation by one parent against another? I would say it's practically a living definition of what those words mean.

Chapter 9:
The Cafcass problem

If you take a moment to listen to the stories of other alienated parents they mostly talk about the failure of Cafcass – the court-appointed child social workers and guardians who act as representatives of the children in Family Court cases – to help. In fact, the overwhelming opinion of most alienated parents is they positively made their case much worse. Cafcass and its shortcomings are written about extensively in the media and also in many damning opinions from legal experts, and even a hugely critical recent 214-page Ministry of Justice report. The failings of Cafcass are widespread and chronic.

This doesn't just affect alienated parents. The failings within Cafcass have placed children in harm's way. The problems within this troubled service will come as no surprise to most people, they stem from the usual lack of resources and recruitment shortages that can affect the public sector in a negative way. However, beyond these generic issues, there are also complaints about the prevailing culture within the organisation, which is often labelled as biased in favour of white, middle-class mothers to the detriment of men, ethnic minorities and working-class people.

I can't speak to those complaints, only my own. However,

if you do some research, you will find a broad cross-section of Cafcass clients have reported discriminatory biases against them on grounds of ethnicity, religion and gender. I experienced what I believe to be bias in my Cafcass experiences for sure. My experience of bias was the most common one reported in complaints, namely a bias against fathers and their issues.

Cafcass is an organisation staffed primarily by middle-class, younger women, and the complaint is often a lack of insight into the kinds of problems fathers encounter in children proceedings. I am always very careful not to leap onto bandwagons, or endorse the opinions of angry men against the mothers of their children, so I am reluctant to make sweeping generalisations but in my case I was treated with hostility from the moment Cafcass got involved. When I say hostility, I should point out that this only became apparent when I compared the transcripts of my Cafcass interview with my ex-wife's. I will address that later in the chapter.

For this moment, I want to focus on my shock at the opinion the Cafcass officer reached about my situation, and my shock at how directly this report influenced the final ruling in my Family Court case. It shocked me because the Cafcass Guardian completely dismissed the opinions of all other experts in the case of my children. Without justification. The guardian made no attempt to debate or discuss, there was no nuance or acknowledgement of complexity in the situation, it was a simple, perfunctory dismissal. My case was not alienation. My kids were justified in their hatred of me. My ex-wife was doing the right thing by supporting them. There was no reason for me to have contact with my kids. That was that.

Why is this so important? Because Cafcass makes the recommendations the Judge is obliged to follow in private law Family Court cases. If the Cafcass recommendation is to be challenged within the court, it requires additional procedures and hearings which make it expensive and complex to challenge. The upshot is, if you get a bad Cafcass ruling, it can wreck your case and you have little comeback to challenge it. That's what happened to me.

The law states clearly – the much quoted section 11 of the Children and Families Act, and the *presumption of parental involvement* clause – that courts are to presume that unless there is evidence to suggest otherwise the involvement of both parents after separation is in the child's best interests. It uses the word welfare, and the terms welfare of the child. It is a clear, unequivocal statement which leaves many alienated parents dumbfounded. In cases like mine, where there is no evidence to suggest otherwise, the welfare of the child is at stake without contact.

In cases where the child refuses contact, this should raise a serious question about intervention, where the case is investigated thoroughly by experts. You would expect Cafcass to fall into this category of expert investigation, however what you actually get is an underqualified junior with a caseload that prevents them from giving your case more than a cursory glance. What you receive is a report that is often filled with stock phrases and copy-and-paste sections which are all too familiar to the lawyers who read them day in, day out.

What you have is a low-paid, overworked junior civil servant with the power to express an opinion that is neither backed by experience or qualifications beyond those of your average graduate trainee in any field. That opinion will outweigh the expertise of people with advanced doctorates or decades of experience at the top of their chosen field of expertise – particularly those with a medical background.

This shocked me because the experts in my case – whom my children's guardian dismissed out of hand – were the head of a children's services charity, a consultant child psychiatrist regarded to be one of the leading lights in his field, and a family therapist with a long career and a doctorate in psychotherapy. The young Cafcass social worker dismissed their opinions – which in the case of the consultant psychiatrist were a diagnosis – and effectively made their role in proceedings meaningless. Three years of court interventions, heard before six judges with multiple court orders for assessments which found major issues with my children's wellbeing, were more or less erased by the opinion of one person with mere hours to spend on my case.

Also, let's not forget, their opinion was contrary to the guiding principle of the Children and Families Act. That act is being modified by a new domestic abuse bill that will hopefully introduce Parental Alienation to the statute, however at the time of my court case and as I write this, the act completely misses the concept of alienation. It does, however, underscore a number of times the importance of a relationship with both parents and maintaining that is the basis of all contact disputes.

Family lawyers all make the same observations about Cafcass. Cafcass deals with around 40,000–45,000 Family Court cases per year according to their statistics. That represents only around 40 per cent of the annual number of divorcing and separated families with dependent children according to government figures. That 40 per cent of divorces and separations account in turn for around 80 per cent of private law Children Act cases annually, dealing with issues surrounding contact for roughly half (50–55 per cent) of the children who are subject to a child arrangement order ruling by the Family Court.

What those numbers illustrate is clearly most divorces and separations with children never go to court. Cafcass get involved in the lives of half of the children with child arrangement orders, which account for around a quarter of the total number of children of divorces and separations in the country. It is fair to say these cases are disproportionally dominated by cases where there is domestic or child abuse, and safeguarding risks, i.e. problem divorces and litigation over contact. This could explain their bias toward looking for problem parents, as opposed to keeping an open mind.

Also, it is worth noting the numbers of officers. Cafcass has around 2,000 officers according to their own stats. They receive 40,000–45,000 Family Court cases per year, which covers cases for between 60,000–70,000 children. In addition to this, they deal with an additional 18,000–19,000 public law care cases. That's upwards of 30 cases per officer per year, giving them less than 8 working days at best to investigate and report on each case, spread over the average reporting time of around 12 weeks. Within this there are interviews to have, reviews of previous reports, standardised checks, holiday entitlements, sick days and so on. The open caseload is increasing year on year, according to Cafcass, by around 16 per cent and of course some cases like childcare orders are much more complex than Family Court disputes – involving police, welfare and local authority homes.

These figures paint a picture of a service that is overstretched. It's unrealistic to assume your case receives the same attention your lawyers gave it over a three-year period. Or the same time and attention other court-appointed assessments received, or the same time that you spend over the duration of a family court settlement trying mediation or therapy to sort out your problems.

Cafcass, in the view of most family lawyers, is overstretched and a finite resource with limited tools to assess each case. They usually make recommendations that relate to contact, they never recommend family therapy or constructive complex solutions. To a Cafcass officer, the case is decided with contact orders. Contact orders are a blunt instrument that can't deal with relationship issues that need more complex solutions. Often, family lawyers will ask for cases to be referred to the Local Authority social workers or private Family Arbitration rather than Cafcass because they have more latitude to order solutions like therapy or mediation.

Cafcass is a lottery. Depending on your local office, you might get an experienced officer who can make informed evidence-based assessments or a new recruit who has been on a short course with little practical experience in certain kinds of cases. For certain, we know there's very little understanding and even less professional training for cases where Parental Alienation is alleged.

The bottom line is once Cafcass reports on your case, the court is guided to rule in line with the report's recommendations. Appealing that report means a special hearing, which may or may not be granted. It's complex and expensive, and often will yield the same result because the Cafcass report is generated from a stock set of questions which don't allow for each case to be judged on its own unique merits so much as blunt, basic issues like safeguarding.

In my case, I was interviewed at their offices, with my kids' lawyer and two Cafcass officers present. My ex-wife was supposed to come to that meeting but was a no-show. She didn't call in. She didn't answer their calls. She completely blanked the meeting. That meant I never got the chance to raise my accusations of alienation and she never had to answer them before a court-appointed official.

She was interviewed at home, by the Cafcass Guardian. My children were interviewed at home too. I felt unfairly treated by that. If they had come to my home, and seen my kids' rooms and their toys, the home I had made for us at the farmhouse, I think they would have judged me differently. And I would have been more relaxed about it.

Did that make a difference? It's not uncommon. Where the mother and children often get visited in friendly, home turf environments, fathers don't. They get summoned for an interview, or over the phone. That is a very different experience on both the interviewer and interviewee side. Consider how different it is to talk to someone over a desk in a formal setting as opposed to in your kitchen. In matters where the person and their mood directly affect the report that is made. Surely that is an obvious flaw in a process that is supposed to be fair and objective to all concerned.

Finally, my children were represented by one single

Cafcass Guardian, not two. As I noted before, they both shared different opinions about restarting contact, about how they felt about me. They deserved separate representation. They were treated as having one opinion. They expressed frustration in some of the court reports of being treated like that. I wonder if they had different guardians, giving them advice as individuals, would the outcome have been different? Maybe.

What I do know for certain is with one lawyer representing both, and one guardian representing both, if one child didn't agree with the other or the prevailing mood of the room it would be hard for that child to raise its voice against three others. In that scenario, the wishes of that child are bound to get swept up in the aggregate decision making of the other child, the lawyer and the guardian. Of course, you might challenge why that automatically goes against me, the father, to which I would respond that the lawyer and the guardian were assigned at the suggestion of my ex-wife. I was against it on the grounds that the issues we faced weren't within the competency of children aged 14 at the time. Also, I believed they were being psychologically manipulated. Assigning them their own joint representation was a pointless exercise. My kids and I needed a way to reconnect, not another fee-earning lawyer in the mix to argue the same toss as my ex-wife's legal team had done for the last three years.

Who decides what is normal?

My children's Cafcass Guardian didn't match the experience or qualifications of the doctorates whose opinions she dismissed. She wasn't qualified to make a psychiatric diagnosis, or work as a family therapist. In fact, her familiarity with my case amounted to a couple of hours of interviews in which she described my children to be normal teenagers, very normal in fact. My ex-wife was a perfectly normal divorced mother, and I was a perfectly normal angry, blaming, aggressive bastard.

Normal? Consider that sweeping statement. What, precisely, is normal?

My children were receiving 24-hour care in a private clinic for anxiety and depression. One of them had been abused by an online predator, which resulted in a police investigation. The other had cut themselves many times, raising alarms and subsequent medical intervention. These were described as very normal teenage problems, in the circulated minutes of the interviews the Cafcass Guardian undertook with my kids, which was the underpinning of the final Cafcass report. My ex-wife agreed they were normal teenagers with normal teenage problems. The court-appointed child psychiatrist didn't think they were normal, he reported they were suffering from anxiety and depression. However, normal was the word that featured – and seemed to dominate – the Cafcass assessment.

I can't be sure if the Cafcass Guardian actually agreed or just wrote it down because they were too busy to form their own opinion. But in the interview transcripts, they stated and restated how normal the children were, in very strong terms. Normal, polite, chatty, enjoying social lives and school. A glowing report, in fact. The kids were doing great.

Even the reported testimony of the therapist they were seeing in the private clinic was glowing. It transpired, in the opinion of the Cafcass Guardian, that they weren't receiving therapy for anxiety or depression – which was their diagnosis. No, the Cafcass Guardian decided that they were receiving therapy to deal with stress over the acrimony between me and my ex-wife. The acrimony had made them anxious and depressed? Why was there acrimony? Because I was completely cut off from them and they were having problems and forced to fight in court against my ex-wife who clearly didn't want me in their lives.

It made no sense. What was clear was the acrimony – in Cafcass' opinion – was my fault. Again, that was clearly a dubious conclusion to reach. My ex-wife was also involved in the acrimony, after all, there are two sides in a court case. To blame one and not the other for the acrimony doesn't make sense.

Was anything in my case, or my kids' problems, normal? Not really. Very normal? No. I would argue under the circumstances, neither child's problems were normal teenage problems. Not normal at all. And the acrimony was caused by the fact I was over two years with no contact with my kids who professed to hate me. That wasn't normal either.

I argued my children desperately needed help, because they were collapsing academically and needed psychiatric therapy. In the opinion of the Cafcass Guardian, that was bad for my children's self-esteem and unfairly critical. How could it be bad for their self-esteem? I wasn't saying it to them, I was saying it about them to other adults. It only became bad for their self-esteem when they found out about it, which shouldn't have happened because it's wholly inappropriate to do so. Having said that, you can't help but be confused about what they were told when they were referred for therapy at a private mental health clinic. Were they told they were going for anxiety and depression therapy sessions because they *weren't* in need of psychiatric help? Were they told everyone goes to a clinic for therapy at 14? Were they told they were just normal teenagers with normal teenager problems, like self-harming and treatment in private clinics?

I can't imagine being in that situation and my parents not describing it as needing help. If they did, that would feel neglectful. Imagine it, *'I got sent to a mental health unit with a diagnosis of anxiety and depression. The social worker and my mother said it was normal'*. That sounds like something they'll be talking to a therapist about in later life, for sure.

Cafcass is unfit for purpose. Those normal teenagers were my children and I was in pieces with worry about them. Let's not forget they were 14-year-old children who had lived a privileged life and attended an expensive private school, not a couple of 17-year-old addicts living in a squat. They did not have normal problems, they had very unusual problems compared to most other 14-year-old children from any background, let alone a very privileged one.

It's a cliché, a myth perpetuated by people who work at the sharp end of society that serious social problems are everywhere and more widespread than you know. I fully accept that a lot might go on behind closed doors, but the truth of the matter is most people don't have any experience of the sort of issues that dominate social work, like addiction, crime, domestic violence and sexual exploitation. Any more than they experience the sort of issues police encounter, or firefighters, or paramedics. Normal for those professions is not the same normal for the vast majority of boring, law-abiding, working parents and their families. If it was, the newspapers and daytime TV shows wouldn't be full of cases like that, because it wouldn't be salacious or shocking to the average audience member, would it?

Self-harm affects a relatively small percentage of children, reckoned by charities that work in the area and various government statistic sources as around 13–15 per cent over a broad age range from 11 to 16. Which means nearly 85 per cent of kids in that age range don't self-harm. 13–15 per cent is not what *normal* means. Normal implies something that is usual or expected, a norm, not something that affects a small minority of the population. Normal would refer more accurately to the 85 per cent of kids that don't self-harm, i.e. they make up the majority or the average expectation of an event like self-harm happening within that cohort of children.

One of my children had been sexually exploited by an online groomer who asked for nude pictures and then attempted to blackmail them for more pictures. This is not a normal teenage problem either. It's reckoned from various charity studies to be a problem less common than self-harm, however higher than you might expect. Estimates of this sort of abuse – including failed attempts by groomers – reaches percentages of around 4–8 per cent of internet and social media using children. Again, that's not what normal means. Normal is the 90 per cent of kids who don't fall prey to online exploitation.

There are around 12 million children in the United Kingdom, around 3 per cent of them are in the social care system via local authorities, and around half that amount are estimated to be targeted by online sexual abusers through social media and the internet – according to various surveys and studies. That is a huge number of children, worryingly around 200,000 per year, however taken as a percentage of the child population it is not normal – or a norm – in the sense that word implies.

My ex-wife, in her interview with the Cafcass Guardian described these problems as normal, and the guardian agreed they were normal. I felt like I was an alien at that point, because my entire life experience was telling me there was nothing normal about it. Honestly, I find it almost impossible to believe a parent could accept self-harm and online grooming with a shrug and a 'oh well, that's kids these days' response. In one report, she even described the online abuser as a *'gentleman'* they met on Periscope. Calling a sex abuser a 'gentleman they met online' shows how my ex-wife showed a complete lack of concern over the seriousness of these problems. She consistently downplayed my kids' issues – and she did it because I had accused her of safeguarding failings.

They were not normal teenagers with normal teenage problems by any measure, yet Cafcass agreed with her interpretation. Their opinion is biased. My kids had received a diagnosis of anxiety and depression and recommendation for 24-hour care from one of the country's leading consultant child psychiatrists who was appointed by the court to assess their mental health. Neither my ex-wife nor the Cafcass Guardian were qualified to make the judgement of normal to the extent it could overrule a psychiatrist. The idea of it is absurd. But that is what happened.

This bizarre turn of events made me think the guardian was out of her depth and completely inept. That description of *very normal teenagers* with *normal problems* might make sense if your experience of teenagers and their problems is a very selective minority of kids. Which, of course, is part of the Cafcass problem. Their experience of children cases are not a broad cross-section of society. It's skewed towards kids with problems, in the same way it is skewed towards a high number of cases where the father is abusive and the mother is afraid of them. I am not criticising the work they do in those cases, however it should be obvious that if your entire caseload and experience is dominated by the worst and most difficult cases, your appraisal of normal will be worse than what most people consider normal to mean.

What is clear, is Cafcass represents an ever increasing caseload for low-paid civil servants who have to prioritise children at risk of serious harm over those who aren't. Which is probably a big influencer over the fact cases like mine get whitewashed with a report made of stock phrases and assertions that despite all the problems my kids endured, they were just normal teenagers with normal teenage problems. There are worse-off kids, with worse problems, and they get more attention than kids like mine.

However, for my children, the children of loving parents at an exclusive private school with all the educational and social opportunities those things provide and no hardships, their problems were very far from normal. They were not the kind of kids who were ever likely to end up in a foster home or council children's home. They were not the kind of kids who would come home to an empty house and fend for themselves, with no money to make ends meet. They were privileged kids with a very comfortable life. Their problems hinted at something much worse than deprivation, it demonstrated the documented psychological effects of alienation.

If you take into account the documented child behaviour problems associated with Parental Alienation – such as poor grades, behavioural problems, anxiety, depression, inappropriate sexual behaviours at a young age, eating disorders and so on – my kids were ticking many of the boxes that they could only be considered normal in terms of the normal problems children in cases of Parental Alienation experience.

Normal teenagers with normal problems, however, was the opinion the Cafcass Guardian put in their report. And the judge in my case, who was brought out of retirement and clearly spent less time reading my court papers than even the Cafcass Guardian, followed her recommendations to the letter and cut me off from contact with my kids, and left all hope of reconnecting with them in the hands of my ex-wife.

That recommendation was not normal.

I presented no safeguarding risks to my children, none had ever been raised, were raised during the cases or established subsequently. In the final hearing, my ex-wife claimed that she felt there were safeguarding risks. She claimed she didn't know what the word meant for the last three years of hearings, but now she thought there were risks arising from my strict parenting style.

I was never accused of anything, nothing specific. Just being strict, or angry, or blaming, or all the things Parental Alienation makes you appear to be. There was nothing that could be considered abuse or abusive, it was never an issue.

My children just didn't like my personality, and that was that. And my ex-wife just supported them and that was that. I had not seen my kids for nearly three years, but they had learned to hate me more for things they discovered – or were told – in the interim period between refusing to see me aged 11 and refusing to see me aged 14.

Their reasons for not wanting to see me were things that they had learned from reports they weren't supposed to see, and things said about me that were completely untrue. That view of me was described using the word alienation and the term parental alienation by court-appointed experts.

My final judgement was an indirect contact order, decreeing my kids have no contact with me, but I could write to them via my ex-wife. This judgement was made on the grounds my children were exhausted by the Family Court proceedings. Which was implied to be my fault because the proceedings were brought by me because my ex-wife wouldn't support contact. No acknowledgement was made of why my children had become more involved in the case than I wanted. My ex-wife had insisted the children get more deeply involved with their own lawyer and a Cafcass Guardian, which in turn led my children to express their exhaustion of being involved in the courts – I was exhausted too. This was something that I paid for, even though I didn't agree to it, because the court's alternative was the costs were met not by my ex-wife but by my kids' trust fund. I wouldn't allow my kids to lose out on their inheritance to finance their own legal representation against their own father.

It is unarguable that the children found their representation via a lawyer and Cafcass to be a burden. It dragged them into the legal process, to make decisions no child should be asked to make. It was a strain on two kids who were already struggling mentally with the whole process. It was cruel. This strain was the reason the judge made a ruling to stop the Family Court process. He acknowledged it was a shame, and expressed a hope that – in the future – I would work things out with my ex-wife and we could put a stop to the acrimony and re-establish contact.

That was, of course, a completely circular argument. If we were capable of working it out and re-establishing contact, we wouldn't have been in the Family Court. That ruling was in line with the decision of the Cafcass Guardian. It was not, however, a ruling in favour or against my claims of Parental Alienation. It was a ruling that regardless of all other factors, the kids had been through enough.

I wonder about that to this day. Was the unpleasantness my kids endured worse than losing their father? Will it be worse than the other things they could experience as a result, like difficult relationships or emotional problems in later life? What about guilt? Will they ever wake up and feel guilty over the way I was broken and battered by it? In cases where the alienated parent takes their own life, those effects can be devastating for the child in later life. It's nonsense to assume they won't look back on these events and question themselves over it. We all do that. Self-doubt and second guessing is human nature. I want them to know that they have nothing to feel guilty about. None of this was their fault. I love them now as I always did. I hope one day, they will come to realise that.

Ironically, in that one respect, the judgement in my case was actually normal. It is often reported anecdotally by family lawyers that – in acrimonious cases where both sides are entrenched and Cafcass gets involved – the judgement is to put a stop to the court action without a resolution because it's too hard on the kids.

Orders and rulings are made to either enforce contact or not, usually depending on whether there is contact ongoing or not. So in cases of Parental Alienation, it's quite normal for Cafcass to recommend – and the judge to rule – against a contact order on the grounds there is currently no contact and the kids don't want it. Similarly, in cases where parents are asking for greater access, it's denied and the status quo is kept. In cases where a change of residency is requested, it's denied and so on. I can't be sure, but the underlying theme seems to be whatever the situation you found yourself in that made you resort to the Family Courts in the first place, by the time Cafcass get involved it's a fairly safe bet to assume they'll rule to keep things as they are to save the children from further court-related stress.

The complexities of Family Court cases are such that it's a huge failure of public services to put a time-poor, underfunded agency like Cafcass in a position where they could be making tragic mistakes and life-changing decisions without the proper time and resources to do it properly. Which presumably is why alongside the many calls to reform the Family Courts, there are a chorus of parents, lawyers and politicians calling for reform of Cafcass. Those demands for urgent reform are, in my view, the only normal thing about the whole messed-up system.

Regardless of your own opinion of the proper role for services like Cafcass, let's not gloss over the fact they did – in my case and thousands like it – facilitate Parental Alienation and allow two children with anxiety and depression to become exposed to the direct pressure and stress of a court case. That is not putting the welfare of children first, nor it is upholding the principles of the Children Act to ensure a relationship with both parents where possible.

Can you prove Cafcass bias?
Yes, I think you can

I set out, in this chapter, to demonstrate the bias I experienced in my Cafcass experience, but then I hit a major problem. Bias is contextual, without reporting verbatim from the documents presented to court in depth, how can I show bias? Even then, it's a matter of interpretation. You would need to know more about the case, the background and so on.

Then it occurred to me that I could illustrate the focus of the report by counting the frequency of topics mentioned. It's reasonable to assume a report about my children and the problems between two parents would probably give roughly equal time to each point of view. I base that assumption on the fact I was interviewed, my kids were interviewed together, and my ex-wife was interviewed. So there were three interviews that were used by the Cafcass Guardian to write the final report.

However, that assumption was possibly faulty because my children were interviewed in my ex-wife's home when she was present. There are no notes from that meeting that were shared with me. These interviews – called protocol meetings – as far as I can tell from my documentation were only recorded as my ex-wife's interview and my interview.

As a result I never found out what they actually said, I only heard it second hand in the final report.

Nevertheless, I counted the number of times I was mentioned in the final report, the number of times my ex-wife was mentioned, and the number of times my children were mentioned. By mention, I mean, by name.

My method works like this: If the report is all about my kids and their wishes and feelings, you might predict their names to feature more than mine or my ex-wife's – a logical prediction as the report is about them, and both my interview and my ex-wife's interviews were about them. You would expect their names and pronouns to exceed mine and my ex-wife's by some considerable margin.

If the focus of the report was the deteriorating relationship between myself and my ex-wife, or if our positions were treated equally, you would probably predict our names to feature a similar number of times to the children. Perhaps that total number of mentions is less important than roughly equal numbers of mentions. It's reasonable to assume that if the report is fair and balanced, although the precise number of mentions per person might vary, my ex-wife and I would get roughly even number of mentions – showing equal attention, or a report that was objectively showing each person and their position had received the same kind of attention and scrutiny.

Finally, we should also assume the Cafcass Guardian will refer to herself as she is giving her recommendations and professional opinion in the report. As this is also the focus of the report – it is her professional judgement of the case based on her own investigations – you would expect words like 'I' and 'my' to feature quite frequently. In fact, you might predict they would feature at least as much as the other three parties in the report – me, my ex-wife and my kids taken as a pair (which is how they were interviewed, and represented in Court).

Report summary:

The report is 127 sentences long.

The report is 3,857 words long.

There are 1,376 operational words (the, a, if, do, and, when, it, has, this, that etc.) and details like reference numbers and so on.

There are 2,481 words that actually refer to me, my kids, my wife, our relationship and the Cafcass Guardian's professional opinion.

Mentions by name:

There are 444 mentions of the names or pronouns referring to me, my ex-wife, my children and the Cafcass Guardian herself.

220 (49.5 per cent) of the mentions are of my children / pronouns referring to them.

141 (31.8 per cent) of the mentions are of me / pronouns relating to me.

48 (10.8 per cent) of the mentions are of the Cafcass Guardian or pronouns referring to herself.

35 (7.9 per cent) of the mentions are of my ex-wife / pronouns relating to her.

Mentions by topic:

Court and Court Proceedings is mentioned 44 times

Contact mentioned 14 times

Psychiatrist mentioned 13 times (his reports)

School mentioned 10 times

Assessments mentioned 8 times

Harm mentioned 4 times

Family Therapist mentioned 3 times (her report)

My estranged child (sibling, secret child) is
mentioned 3 times

Parental Alienation mentioned 2 times

Self-harming mentioned 1 time

Grooming mentioned 1 time

Putting the numbers into words

What does this show? Is it a bias on the behalf of the Cafcass Guardian? Showing that might not be obvious however you can draw conclusions from comparing the number of mentions of people with the topics that come up most frequently. What they show is the focus of the author – the Cafcass Guardian. It also reflects the questions that were asked during the interviews with myself, the children and my ex-wife.

Firstly, who is the focus of the report? My children are mentioned the most, as they should be because the report is largely about them, and our interviews with Cafcass were dominated by discussions with them.

I get the next highest number of mentions. Compared to my ex-wife, I get over four times as much attention each as she does, closer to 12 times as much when my kids and I are taken together.

Without question it's therefore a fair and accurate

reflection of the numbers of mentions to say this report is not about my claims of alienation. Those claims addressed my ex-wife as the alleged abuser – and would require her to answer them and be scrutinised by the report. That clearly didn't happen. My ex-wife is hardly mentioned compared to me or my kids. In fact, my ex-wife isn't even mentioned as much as the Cafcass Guardian mentions herself and her own opinions.

My ex-wife did not receive any additional scrutiny in the report, even though she was the only one accused of domestic abuse through Parental Alienation. She was the only one who I alleged was failing in her duty of care to safeguard my kids properly. Again, this was never asked about or challenged with her.

So then, it's fair to say this report is mostly about my relationship with my children and the Cafcass Guardians opinion of my relationship with my children. Most of the 127 sentences are about me, and my kids' feelings about me. Not about their mother or their feelings about her. In a contact dispute, you would expect a more balanced approach. The number of mentions shows I was held to a higher standard of accountability than my wife by a long way.

The report overlooks some crucial facts of the case, i.e. I have not seen my children for three years, and I am alleging Parental Alienation against me by my ex-wife.

If you look at the topics that dominate the subjects covered in the report, the biggest ones by far is the court, and court proceedings. Taken together, these are mentioned over three times more frequently than contact, which was what I was fighting for in the three years of Family Court actions.

This goes back to the point I made earlier, that Cafcass is primarily focused on putting a stop to court proceedings because of the strain it puts on the children, rather than the reason for the court action – in my case, contact with my children. This report shows the Cafcass Guardian spent most of her time asking the kids how they felt about the court case, nothing more.

Most damning perhaps is the mentions of self-harm and grooming, which are only mentioned once in the entire report. If you imagine my panic at learning about those things happening to my kids, and the fact they were part of what drove me to press for court assessments of my kids and their deteriorating mental health, it's unthinkable they should receive less attention in this report than any other topic. And 44 times less attention than the number of court hearings and assessments the kids had been through.

The crux of my case was Parental Alienation. That was mentioned twice.

It was mentioned fewer times than the family therapist who reported that I was being alienated. It was mentioned fewer times than the Consultant Psychiatrist who used the word alienation to describe my situation.

However, perhaps the smoking gun of bias was the fact the discovery of my estranged child by another woman – something that my children discovered whilst under the care of my ex-wife, in her study – is mentioned three times. More than my alienation claims. More than the self-harm. More than the grooming.

Take a moment to consider that.

Something that unequivocally made me look like the

bad guy got more attention than my claims of Parental Alienation. Something that was private, and only my ex-wife and court-appointed officials knew about. My kids weren't ready to handle that information.

Without showing the report or quoting from it, it is fair to say that statistically speaking, this report spends more time talking about court proceedings, my children and myself than it does about their mental health, their problems, Parental Alienation or contact. It completely misses the point – and ignores the substance – of my claims.

Without showing the report or quoting from it, it is fair to say statistically it spends over four times more addressing my role in proceedings than my ex-wife. The Cafcass Guardian spends more time talking about herself than she does my ex-wife, in fact.

Without showing the report or quoting from it, it's fair to assume my children were asked a lot more questions about their hatred of me than they were about their feelings towards their mother. If she had been manipulating them – as I had alleged and is part of alienation – it was never investigated. The reasons for them hating me weren't challenged, they were simply recorded.

Perhaps that's why I am mentioned over four times as much as my ex-wife, because my kids were asked about me more than her. In a case where Parental Alienation is alleged, you would expect a more even approach to each parent and their role in the broken relationship.

The unarguable case is, this was supposed to be an assessment of my children to ascertain their wishes and feelings to be represented by their lawyer and their court-appointed social worker from Cafcass. What that assessment turned into was a one-sided report into my role in the court action, and my kids' feelings about court action. What it did not do, is investigate my claims of Parental Alienation. It did not address the state of the children in terms of their academic performance, or obvious problems with self-harm and grooming. And the one person who received the least scrutiny was my ex-wife.

There are many claims of bias levelled at Cafcass. In particular, bias against fathers compared to mothers. Does this report bear up to that accusation?

In this report, the father was mentioned over four times as much as the mother.

The father was interviewed in an office by two Cafcass officers and a lawyer that were appointed at the mother's insistence. The father paid for the legal representation the mother insisted was assigned to the kids, when he objected to that fee coming out of his children's trust fund at their expense.

The mother was interviewed in her home, by one Cafcass officer and the lawyer. The mother is mentioned the least in the report.

The mother who was accused of Domestic Abuse in the form of Parental Alienation. Parental Alienation – the father's accusation – was mentioned least, except for the terrible events that had happened to the children whilst under her supervision.

Those topics – in aggregate – were mentioned less than the existence of the father's illegitimate estranged child, the existence of which was revealed to the children while under the mother's supervision.

Does that sound like the report has an inherent bias of some sort? Does it favour the mother to be mentioned a fraction of the number of times that the father is? You can debate that all you like, but you can't argue that by being mentioned so much less her actions and role in the proceedings was given the same amount of attention as the father. In children proceedings, if one side received four times or more scrutiny from the court-appointed social workers than the other, would that suggest bias to you?

You would expect 50:50 wouldn't you?

Maybe you would expect more time to be spent on the parent with residency of the kids, who was refusing to facilitate contact with the other parent, wouldn't you?

That's right. I wasn't the one who had broken our mutually agreed contact arrangement. Our court-ordered contact arrangement.

I didn't stop bringing the children to see her for her allotted weekends.

I didn't stop bringing the kids to her house for the mid-week stay.

I wasn't the one who had primary care of them while they cut words into their thigh and sent naked pictures to an online predator.

I wasn't the one who shared her private personal information with them – and she has a very dark secret in her closet indeed.

I was the one fighting to see my kids.

However, when Cafcass gets involved, I am put under the microscope and my ex-wife barely gets mentioned in comparison.

That is a clear case of bias – which means (according to the Oxford English Dictionary) an *inclination or prejudice for or against one person or group, especially in a way considered to be unfair* and a *concentration on or interest in one particular area or subject.*

There is a clear concentration on one particular area or subject – the court proceedings. There is a clear inclination for one person or group – me as opposed to my ex-wife. With the irony being that my ex-wife dragged our children into the court proceedings knowing they were already suffering with anxiety and depression. Something a loving parent would never dream of doing, but someone guilty of Parental Alienation probably would.

I get this sense that alienated parents are set-up to fail in Family Court. We initiate proceedings, therefore we are blamed for causing the acrimony of a court case. This is a perfect bind. The resident parent can resist the court case, and when the children can become stressed and anxious because of the acrimony the abuser parent can blame the alienated parent for it. In my case, I never wanted my kids to have their own lawyer or guardian, this was my ex-wife's suggestion. It brought the children into the court proceedings more deeply than before. If it was a tactic, it worked well. By involving my kids with their own legal team, I became their legal opponent as opposed to my ex-wife's. It framed the conclusion of the case, and the Cafcass report, in a picture that made me to blame for court case, and therefore by inference, for my kids' suffering because of it. My ex-wife became a bystander in the case that without doubt, was about a dispute between me and her.

In effect, my kids became her shield against my claims of parental alienation, as surely as my kids became her proxy for hurting me through the alienation itself.

The Cafcass Bias

The Cafcass report was a tick-box exercise by the Cafcass Guardian. What I mean by that is this: If I levelled an accusation at my ex-wife or her behaviour, the Cafcass Guardian looked for evidence in my ex-wife's testimony to counter it. It was tit-for-tat, not an investigation or fact finding mission, a simple he-said-she-said.

That might sound reasonable, however it is not at all reasonable when you consider my interview with Cafcass was supposed to be an interview with both my ex-wife and me. The day before, we all confirmed with Cafcass and with each other that we were attending this critically important final interview with both parents. As the resident parent, my ex-wife was interviewed without me, and so were my kids, so the Cafcass Guardian spent more time with them than she did with me. That already suggests a cause of bias because they got considerably more time to talk about their side of the story than I did.

However, this meeting with my ex-wife and I both present was critical, because it afforded the Cafcass Guardian an opportunity to see us interact. In my ex-wife's interview she is at pains to point out she is only supporting her kids and will do whatever the court decides regarding contact. She sounds very reasonable, and she is never questioned about my allegations of Parental Alienation or my reasons for initiating court proceedings, which was my belief that the children were in an unsafe situation and suffering mental health problems as a result, which were diagnosed by the court-appointed expert. That was critical. My ex-wife said she supported the kids and they were fine, a leading consultant child psychiatrist diagnosed the supported, fine kids as being depressed and needing therapy.

The opportunity for me to state my case in that regard and the opportunity for my ex-wife to answer it – with the Cafcass Guardian present to see which one of us was being reasonable and which one wasn't – should be of paramount importance. How else do you make a decision about which side is more credible? If you only hear one side of the story at a time, you are left looking at a transcript and reading your own meanings into the words. If you interview the people together, you have a better chance to add some insights into who is trying to resolve the problem, and who is being stubborn.

My ex-wife did not attend the meeting.

She didn't answer her phone, she didn't respond at all.

This was a crunch meeting – a court-ordered meeting and seemed reminiscent of the one that was meant to happen with the kids, the consultant psychiatrist and I. That meeting never happened either. It was the meeting the whole Cafcass report was dependent upon in my mind. A chance for the Cafcass Guardian to hear my side of the story, my concerns about my children's mental health and my concerns about my ex-wife's safeguarding. Also a chance for my ex-wife to respond to the questions she was never asked in her interview, which related to my claims of alienation. It was a chance for her to explain why her nice, normal kids were diagnosed with anxiety and depression, and were self-harming and being internet groomed under her nose and she thought everything was just fine. To ask what kind of mother would drag her kids into a courtroom drama knowing they were already suffering.

I was worried. I thought something had happened to her. In my interview notes, it's reported that she had confirmed twice, and her solicitor had also told them she was attending. This made me even more worried. I called. They called. Nothing. I thought she had been in a car crash. Of course, it was never explained. My ex-wife missed a crucial meeting with the court-appointed social workers who would make a ruling that would decide my relationship with my children for the rest of our lives – and she missed it. Her participation in that meeting was vital. By missing it, the meeting turned into a one-sided interrogation where I expressed multiple times I was deeply concerned about my children, based on the evidence in medical assessments.

Those concerns were not addressed in the final report, other than as criticisms of me. I was according to the guardian – by referencing my children's therapy in a private clinic and the psychiatrist's diagnosis that put them there – labelling them. I was damaging their self-esteem by acknowledging they had problems. They were in a private clinic seeing a psychologist, and it wasn't because everything was completely fine with them. It is not a label, it was a truthful description. I was not labelling two people to discriminate against them, I was talking about my kids and their diagnosis. That word, *labelling* shows bias. It implies intent on my part, an intention to discredit in some way.

What you see in the report, as a result, is a facile

argument. It's based on three interviews, taken on three different occasions, which didn't ask one party about any of the accusations the other had made against them but did ask the other party in depth about the accusations made against them. Needless to say, the answers that found their way into the report featured a lot more of the person who was interrogated more. Hardly surprising is it?

For example, I alleged Parental Alienation, and as part of that said I suspected my ex-wife had deliberately chosen to share information with my children that affected their hostility towards me. In the report, it refers to this and counters it in the same paragraph by mentioning the fact I told my kids their mother had been involved with Elle and her attempt to steal from me. Those two things are not the same.

I did say that in the heat of the moment, and I regret it. I did not allow my kids to read confidential court papers which contained extremely private information that my ex-wife had elected to share with them, alone. Nor did I let them see court papers that detailed the break-up of our marriage, or sex life, or feature wild allegations that my ex-wife had paid someone to kill a horse or I had been some sort of raging sex maniac with prostitutes and so on. Losing your temper is one thing, permanently scarring a 12-year-old kid with graphic, adult material is quite another. However, in the Cafcass report, they are balanced out, one against the other.

Similarly, my claims of Parental Alienation are dismissed on the grounds that in the first court-ordered assessment, I told the consultant psychiatrist that my wife was a good mother. That was before I discovered the true extent of her behaviour behind the scenes, as it unfolded that my kids were in a mess. However, when I came to raise these issues and suggest there were real safeguarding concerns about my ex-wife's home on the grounds self-harm and online grooming were happening under her nose, this was dismissed as me contradicting myself over the earlier remark – made almost two years before – that I thought my ex-wife was a good mother. Again, in the mind of the Cafcass Guardian, one cancelled out the other.

Alongside these tit-for-tat dismissals, there were strangely weighted items that were in the report that made me sound unreasonable. For example, the Cafcass Guardian asked me to change the times I visited the children's school to receive my updates on their academic progress. She said my kids wanted me to go later in the day, so there was no chance I could accidently bump into them. They were anxious about this. To my mind, this wasn't a very useful suggestion on the grounds it wasn't up to me, the school had never given me an opportunity to select a time other than 3 pm. They said I could go at 3 pm on a specific date, and that was that.

Given the issues I had experienced with the school withholding information from me and being extremely difficult to deal with, I was reluctant to argue over timings with them. This was taken by the Cafcass Guardian to show I was completely unreasonable. Wait, it was just diary issues, wasn't it? Not some sort of trick to prove I was really a bastard? Was I being tricked here? I felt like it when I read that and realised the whole question was – by the guardian's own admission – a test to see if I was flexible enough.

What the Cafcass Guardian failed to report in relation to my school visits was the fact in over two-and-a-half years of visiting the school once every six weeks, I had never seen my kids. She also failed to report the school is massive, set over acres of land, so it was unlikely I'd see my kids anyway. Nor did she mention the fact that the school set the times, not me. All she reported was the children were anxious about my school visits and I was unwilling to change the time. In fact – how did they even know I wonder?

Worse, I also said I thought that would make the kids feel empowered to control my access to school. Bear in mind, they had allegedly refused to consent to share any information with me via the school regarding the self-harm and the grooming. I had been forced to get a court order to make the school share their safeguarding records with me. They shared them freely with my ex-wife, but not me despite my legal right as a responsible parent to have that information – which was proved and supported in court. Knowing how my kids were set against me, I didn't want to give them encouragement. I told the guardian my kids weren't capable of making reasonable choices like that, they were being manipulated.

The Cafcass Guardian recorded this as me not wanting to give power to my kids. She made me sound sinister. She said she found my thinking to be worrying. That I was making the situation more complex than it needed to be. What? I told her the school tells me when I can attend? What did she think I could do about it? And yes, my kids had asked their teachers to hide a police investigation into child abuse and hide the fact a bunch of kids had been cutting words into themselves at school, so no, I was not going to let them decide for me what I could and couldn't do when it came to getting reports from their school. That's not sinister. That is common sense.

Her judgement that I was trying to take power away from my kids, was bias. They had no power to decide when I could attend school, any more than I did. Worse, the fact she set that question up as a test was biased. She didn't tell me I was being tested. She didn't tell me how I answered the question would be important to her final finding, or how that information would be used. That is completely unethical. Even murderers are told that what they say might be used against them in a court of law. You can't make someone participate in a test without informing them. I did not consent to her test.

She reported it as an opportunity to demonstrate insight, which was absurd. The suggestion she made demonstrated she had no insight whatsoever into how things worked at my kids' school, or how the school had withheld information from me. That is bias. Realistically, the Cafcass Guardian probably had little experience of the kind of school that charges £25,000 per child, comparable to a junior civil servant's annual salary – and how high-handed and officious that kind of price tag makes schools like that.

Ultimately, I was labelled as aggressive and angry. And I was. I had lost my children. What was I supposed to be? Happy about it? Was I supposed to serenely lose the most precious relationships in my life and be cheerful?

Worse, the guardian repeatedly made me sound like some sort of fascist on the grounds I was trying to force my kids to see me.

I was not trying to force anyone to do anything.

I was trying to find a way to restart a relationship with my kids whom I hadn't seen for over two years. How sinister can it be to want to be there for your kids? To be a parent to them? I didn't want them dragged kicking and screaming so I could lock them in a room with me like torture. I just wanted to see them. To get a call or something. I was prepared to start small, but I wasn't going to accept never seeing them again as an option. That was, needless to say, the option the Cafcass Guardian suggested.

Her recommendation was for me to give up.

My reluctance to give up showed that I wasn't *child focused* enough, apparently. If I was, I would completely abandon them. That was the Cafcass suggestion.

As for my ex-wife, the criticism she had received in previous assessments, which labelled her as passive and so passive she wasn't helping the children, was reframed by the Cafcass Guardian as questions. The guardian prefaced the few things she said about my ex-wife that weren't unequivocally positive with phrases like *I wonder if she realises* … and so on. I got an unequivocal *he is like this, he thinks this, he does this.* She didn't once wonder, or express a scintilla of doubt about me, my actions or my motivations. She did nothing but wonder about my ex-wife.

The Cafcass Guardian's final recommendations were that the court proceedings had to stop. And no contact between me or my kids was to be ordered to protect my kids from further emotional harm and distress.

Protect my kids from emotional harm and distress? Like the emotional harm of being groomed or the distress of self-harming, which happened when they hadn't seen me for a year? How the hell did she reach that conclusion? What harm had I done to them? I hadn't seen them.

However, she went on to caveat that final statement with a note that if the court did order contact, it should be one way only (I could write to them) but only if I made no mention of their therapy, or their ongoing medical treatments and such. Basically, any of the things you might expect to make a parent frantic with worry.

If there was ever an accusation of bias to be made, it was here. Because the Cafcass Guardian said that if I were allowed leave to write to my kids, it would have to be via my ex-wife. She recommended that my ex-wife both read and assessed the letters, and decided if they should be passed on to my kids or not.

I have complained about this before in this book, but I am still shocked by the absurdity of that suggestion. I had accused my ex-wife of Parental Alienation. If that were true and she was alienating me, she wouldn't pass my letters on to my kids. If it wasn't true, I had falsely accused her and dragged her through the courts for three years as a result. In that case, putting her in charge of my contact would be bizarre because she would have every reason to tell me to piss off. This recommendation was either putting the abuser in charge of stopping the abuse, or putting the wrongly accused in charge of helping their accuser. In both cases, it's a completely unworkable solution that is bound to fail. So, putting the mother in charge of a situation that is almost guaranteed to fail the father's needs? Is that biased towards the mother?

Yes.

My experience of Cafcass was sadly, proof of all the clichés I'd heard before. All they did was recommend stopping the court proceedings without resolving the reasons that started them in the first place. That was predicted by the lawyers. And in their report, they showed a clear and demonstrable bias which glossed over accusations against the mother, and focused four times as much attention on the father. That bias against fathers was borne out to be true in my case.

In the next chapter, I will present a better model for settling Family Cases.

Needless to say, Cafcass will not be a part of that solution.

They did more harm than good and they completely missed the dramatic and negative change in the children from the point I was surgically removed from their lives.

Their reputation for doing more harm than good in cases of Parental Alienation and acrimonious litigation is justified in my opinion. But don't take my word for it, look at the numbers in this chapter and decide for yourself.

Chapter 10:
Creating a real solution to Parental Alienation

So far in this book I've spent just shy of 70,000 words doing a post mortem on my experiences of the Family Court, Cafcass and the broader failings of the system when you find yourself caught in a messy battle for contact and claim Parental Alienation. I have also told my story in a thematic way, to unpack the issues in my life and relationships by explaining how they related to different people and institutions that were involved in my story.

It has given me a chance to discuss the experience of Parental Alienation without a laborious *War and Peace* length account of what happened in chronological order. The reason I approached it in this way was simple – everything has led to this point, where I want to design a better way to deal with Parental Alienation.

By now, you are familiar with the failings of the Family Court, of the highly variable and underused role of the school in messy contact situations, and the biased, ineffective one-size-fits-all approach that characterises the way Cafcass operates. You are also familiar with the endless Catch-22 loops that I have been caught in, the way that Parental Alienation has no status in law, no definition, no way to measure it.

The circularity of the situation I found myself in is systemic, by which I mean, the system makes it impossible to resolve cases of Parental Alienation.

When you consider my case, and the typical issues alienated parents report, the problems become clear:

1.   You can go for years without seeing your kids, your kids can claim to hate you for reasons that only emerged in the years you have been estranged, through things they learned about you from others. Yet somehow, you are ultimately held responsible for your children's feelings towards you instead of the people responsible for shaping their opinion of you.

2.   Despite there being no safeguarding issues – in my case I had a DBS check and no safeguarding allegations against me – the children claimed to be afraid of you, even though they haven't seen you and weren't afraid of you before. You can supply the courts with photos and videos of you and the kids having a great time on holiday, only to be told that years later they have panic attacks at the thought of seeing you driving down the street.

3.   When you assert your children need professional help, you are accused of negatively labelling your children, even though they are receiving the professional help you said they needed.

4.   When the children are reported to be caught up

in serious problems, you are told it's normal.

5. When you get a psychiatrist to assess your kids he diagnoses them with problems arising from not seeing both parents, the courts and Cafcass say that the court proceedings and assessments are the problem, not the non-contact. Non-contact is a documented cause of mental health problems in kids.

6. You are told you need a cooling-off period, you are then said to have alienated yourself by breaking off contact.

7. You are told that you are angry and aggressive after years of not seeing your children, and that's why your kids don't want to see you – as opposed to it being a result of not seeing them.

8. You are told your children's wishes and feelings come first, and that means if they don't want to see you, that's what you must accept even if the reason is you took them to see a West End Show instead of Disneyland Paris.

9. You are told the guiding principle of the law is that it is important to have a relationship with both parents in cases where there are no safeguarding issues, then in the same breath told your children don't want to have anything to do with you and that's that.

10. You are told the guiding principle of the law is that it is important to have a relationship with both parents in cases where there are no safeguarding issues, but you are excluded from

contact without any safeguarding issues, whilst they reside with a parent that you have made safeguarding allegations against. Your children have been self-harming, groomed online and are receiving therapy in a clinic while in the care of that resident parent, however no safeguarding concerns apply to the care of that parent.

11. You are told that the only way you can hope to restart the relationship with your kids is to stop trying to have a relationship with them at all.

12. And in the final judgement, they place the person you have accused of alienating you from your children in sole control of contact between you and your children, without any investigation into your claims against them.

I could go on, but let's face it, the whole thing is bizarre. It's like falling out of reality into a parallel world where no matter what you do, it is taken to mean the opposite. Where whatever you do seems to make things worse. Where everything you think proves your case, disproves it even more in the eyes of the court.

It makes you paranoid, it makes you second guess yourself, it tortures you with what-if thoughts about making different decisions in the past.

It's like living in *The Twilight Zone.*

Except, *The Twilight Zone* is a TV show where the normal rules of reality don't apply. The failings I have listed above are systemic. They can be fixed. The law can change. Procedures can be improved.

I think it's time for a reality check for the whole messed-up system.

Family Court: Kicking your case into the long grass

One thing that persistently reminds me of the sheer gap between reality and Family Court ordered reality is the complete lack of foresight about what happens next on behalf of the professionals involved.

The Family Court kicks the issues that come before it into the long grass. That's all it is geared up to do. The problems it tries – and fails – to solve are lifelong relationships. You can cut off contact, but you don't cease to be parent and child. A meaningful resolution is the only thing that will be a proper, sustainable fix to the relationship issues. Sooner or later, there will be fallout that the children have to deal with as well as the adults in the courtroom. Fallout that could be devastating in terms of life outcomes. From suicides to abusive relationships and addiction, the children and adults of Parental Alienation don't just hurt while the case is ongoing, their whole futures can be adversely affected, sometimes with the most tragic outcomes possible.

It is heart-breaking to consider everyone within the Family Court process is preoccupied by winning the case or ruling one way or another to put an end to it, that the real reason you are there – the long-term relationship between you and your children – is left completely unresolved and potentially, made more complex and traumatic for everyone a few years down the line. The focus of the process is warped by the various legal demands of the two sides and counter measures, rather than the central issue you petitioned the court to solve. In my case, although I hadn't seen my kids and it was to the detriment of their emotional wellbeing and mental health, that issue was overlooked and was decided on how stressful the court proceedings were.

Consider that.

The court decides, with Cafcass's recommendation, to stop the stress of the court proceedings and the distress of your children. They completely ignore the risks of what non-contact will do to those children in their lives moving forwards. They completely ignore the fact they are reducing the nature of your contact – in many cases like mine where the father pays maintenance and school fees – to a financial relationship only.

But when it ends it will create a significant change of circumstances for the children and your ex-partner. And that means more hardship, and more pain for all concerned. That's the problem lurking in the long grass for the kids. Basically, they don't decide your case and put an end to the pain and acrimony, so much as put it off for a few years until the children are adults, but by then, the Family Court is no longer responsible for fixing the mess they helped create. As far as they are concerned, their work is done.

My children had their own legal representation. My ex-wife also had her own legal representation. The rulings that were made, on aggregate, resulted in me financing their lifestyles. In the divorce and subsequent extra hearings my ex-wife received millions, and my children benefited from the creation of a large trust fund. My ex-wife receives maintenance for the children, and I also pay the kids' school fees which amounts to another hefty six-figure sum over time.

As we know, my kids don't want to have anything to do with me.

And as we also know, my ex-wife supports their wishes and feelings in this regard.

But I wonder if my kids' lawyer or my ex-wife's lawyer have prepared them for the reality check of that financial arrangement ending? They might want nothing to do with me in person, but they have never stopped having a relationship with me financially. It's a strange thought that they might have never questioned the nature of that financial relationship. Maybe they think their school feels and lifestyle is financed by my ex-wife? Who knows? Whatever they think now, I wonder what they will think when they all have to finance themselves? Or how well they can do it? I am their father. I will never stop being concerned about things like that. It's a parent's job.

In the testimony one of my kids gave in a court assessment, they used money as one argument about why they never wanted to see me again. Specifically, they complained bitterly that the maintenance I paid my ex-wife is less than the average UK salary – which relative to my personal net worth, seems low. That was their argument. That was clear manipulation by my ex-wife, who had obviously shared just one part of the equation to make me look bad. What my children had not mentioned during this interview was that they lead a privileged life and attend a private school. They also have a huge seven-bedroom house where they live with their mother and another large house where they spend time with me plus a fabulous holiday villa in Spain. They lead a privileged life and all they seemed to know was that I paid monthly maintenance equal to the average UK wage. Surely this statement from a 12-year-old kid should raise an eyebrow – sadly not in the confused world of the Family Courts.

One of my claims of Parental Alienation came from this observation. It seemed to me unarguable that my kids were being manipulated into thinking something that wasn't true and made them hostile towards me. After all, how could my kids complain I was mean about money? How did they know how much I paid? I hadn't seen them for over two years at the time they said it. I had certainly never discussed amounts with them. Clearly someone else did.

Whoever had discussed finances with them had misled them into thinking I was paying less than half than I did – not to mention the multimillion-pound settlement! That person had made me out to be the bad guy to my kids. Misrepresented me to encourage hostility. It's the definition of psychologically manipulating someone to be hostile, i.e. lying to them about who is paying their bills. It's unarguable.

One of my kids complained to the court-appointed assessor that I was mean and controlling, and put my ex-wife into financial hardship by paying her so little monthly maintenance. I mean, quite apart from it being untrue, it's quite absurd to say someone with millions in the bank and a huge house valued in excess of £2 million (mortgage free) is in financial hardship at all. That's a very twisted view of the world. It either shows huge naivety on the part of my kids, who think you can be poor living in a multimillion-pound home, or something more akin to my ex-wife and family making me sound like something I was not – mean and vindictive at the expense of my own children. Again, it sounds to me like manipulating the kids to be hostile towards me over something that's not true.

Regardless of the alienation that implies, what concerns me is what happens when my maintenance ends, and it will, when my kids turn 18. At that point – next year as I write this book – they will be faced with something I very much doubt they have considered, which is paying for themselves. Be it for university fees, college, a year out, vocational training or whatever they want to do, my children will suddenly face the real world and I don't know if they are prepared for it. I would be happy to fund that for them, for sure, except I can't pay anything for two legal adults if they aren't prepared to see me, talk to me or even acknowledge I exist.

What, I wonder, will be the impact of that?

More pain for us all, I expect, one way or another.

While they were children, my kids never had to confront the reality of their choices or consider their actions – arguably they couldn't even begin to – because they were being manipulated into behaving like that. However, my ex-wife, her lawyers, my kids' lawyer and the Cafcass Guardian all knew that one day, those two children would face a major turning point in their lives as a direct result of the Family Court ruling. They knew my children would lose the financial safety net that has shaped their experience of life. And they did nothing to warn them.

I have written that Parental Alienation is like watching a slow moving car crash. You scream and shout about the problems that are coming for your kids, and nobody believes you. Even when respected researchers from world leading research universities find the same. Even when experts in Parental Alienation say the same. Even when court-appointed experts say the same. There are more life problems coming too – relationship issues, eating disorders, drug and alcohol problems – and yet again, nobody is thinking about that future, they just want to make a ruling and move onto the next case.

That is why the system needs a reality check. Not simply because it is out of touch or not fit for purpose, but because it's a system that is geared up entirely around short-term fixes or fudgy compromises that in the long run will make more pain for everybody concerned. My kids will one day suffer more problems, most likely, because that is what happens to children who grow up in alienated families. They had tough lives and problems.

However, supposing we had been treated with a long-term view. Suppose we were ordered to fix our broken relationship. Then my kids would most likely have never suffered anxiety or depression, and the other problems they encountered. We would be stronger together, as all families are, even separated ones. We could share the burdens of life as a family and support each other as we should, and as a parent wants to support their own kids.

The Family Court, Cafcass and my judge didn't stop my kids from suffering by ending our court action with no contact, they just kicked it into the long grass so they could suffer a whole lot of different pain and problems a few short years down the line. And now, there is more pain looming on the horizon as my kids with problems turn into adults with problems, with all the issues adulthood can bring. That is the human cost of the broken process.

Turkeys don't vote for Christmas

Of course, the urgent need to reform the courts isn't just about the human cost – although that is the most important issue. It is also all about money. It's a business.

Do you wonder why so many people complain, year in, year out about the Family Courts? You might assume that everyone complains about the court cases they lose, regardless of the sort of court. Prisons are full of people who complain about the courts, no doubt. However, Family Court and its associated bodies like Local Authority Children's Services and Cafcass receive so many complaints from within the system itself. But no matter how many people complain, little seems to change and the reason for that is simple. It's a lucrative business to be in.

The Family Court system represents a vast marketplace, predicted to be worth more than £2 billion by 2024. Divorce cases generate the highest volume of work, but are declining year on year. The other market trends are disturbing. Private Children Act cases – like mine – are increasing rapidly. It's not surprising that as divorce cases fall and complex children cases continue to grow. Law firms are looking towards the growth areas and technology as important new strategies for the industry.

In other words, reforming the Family Courts to address the obvious shortcomings of the system – particularly in regard to drawn out litigious battles and Parental Alienation – isn't in the financial or business interests of family lawyers.

Turkeys don't vote for Christmas, and lawyers aren't going to petition the government to put themselves out of business.

The root cause of the problem is – in my opinion and that of many lawyers and commentators – judges. Judges are almost a law unto themselves, no pun intended. Every solicitor and barrister will advise you if at all possible, to settle out of court. This is why most legal disputes never even make it into a formal court hearing. Both sides know that in a complex case of claim and counterclaim, their chance of winning is low, and variable. It depends on the judge. Even in cases which appear to be clear-cut, you have at best a 70 per cent chance of winning. There is no case, no matter how plain the facts, that a lawyer can guarantee a result. The random element of the judge comes into play every time.

In the time it has taken me to write this book so far, one prominent Family Court judge – Robin Tolson – has resigned, describing the courts as both *'incapable of meeting users needs'* and complaining that there is *'not enough time or money for the necessary and deserving; and a tendency to concentrate resources on the unnecessary, complicating the simple and pandering to agendas which are at odds with reality or a diversion at best.'*

To his first point, he's commenting on the fact there is a growing chorus of people demanding reform of the Family Courts, including 120 MPs demanding reform of domestic abuse legislation – which will potentially make Parental Alienation an offence for the first time on the statutes. More than that, there are campaigning charities, petitions and thousands of complaints filed against the Family Courts. The concept of No-Fault Divorce – in which there's no case of fault on either side, so no need for a court case – is only about to become law as I write this book. Reform is slow, and ongoing. However, the cause of this constant pressure to reform is as Tolson says, because the court isn't capable of serving people in the modern world.

To his second point, about resources being concentrated on the unnecessary and pandering to agendas that are at odds with reality, we can decode that to mean one thing: too much money is spent on reports and court orders and too little focus is on the facts of the case. Again, I would agree. I paid for my kids to have their own lawyer, only for that lawyer and Cafcass to recommend the answer to me not seeing my kids was best served by not seeing my kids. It made no difference to the situation that caused the court case. It was a ruling, but not a judgement in the sense of judging the situation and resolving it.

It left me with only the option to appeal, which would mean more expense and more time, neither of which would help me with the actual problem of rebuilding the broken relationship with my kids. We needed counselling and mediation, not more lawyers' fees and court dates to argue the same toss I'd argued for over two years.

In my world – finance – we use a lot of data-driven algorithms to make decisions. In some cases, I found myself reducing the endless letters to and fro between the lawyers, and the endless reports that led nowhere, with a simple algorithm that could solve the problem of alienation, based on the following questions:

Does the parent want to see the child?

Does the child want to see the parent (wishes and feelings)?

If no to either of the above, are there any safeguarding reasons why there should be no contact?

If no to either of the above, are there any material circumstances preventing contact (parent lives abroad, parent can't afford travel etc.)?

If yes, then it needs assessment of the issue that is preventing contact by a safeguarding expert.

If no, then mediation is the next outcome to prevent alienation.

However, his opinions to one side, Judge Tolson's resignation illustrates the judge problem very well. Over 130 family lawyers and campaigners had signed an open letter to the president of the Family Court Division demanding action over a ruling by Judge Tolson. The High Court judge who eventually overturned his ruling described it as *'manifestly at odds with current jurisprudence'*. In other words, he disregarded facts in the case which were found to be an error, and therefore, meant his judgement was wrong.

Legal practitioners often complain about Family Court judges in the same way that ultimately forced Tolson to resign; there is just too much volatility in the system.

While the statutory criteria within the Children Act encourage judges to exercise their discretion, the lack of rules and structure means the breadth of that discretion can be drawn very widely. For example, the exact same case might have a completely different ruling in two next-door courtrooms with different judges on the bench.

This issue is compounded by the fact that judges are overwhelmingly white, male, and aged mostly over 50, with many over 60. Given many of them started their legal careers in the 1970s or 1980s when the law and social attitudes were very different, they inevitably possess bias, especially subconsciously, something society would refuse to accept were it not for the secrecy of Family courts.

In cases where people's lives and happiness are at stake – which is how it feels to lose your children through Parental Alienation – there should be fewer mistakes, bias, and greater consistency of outcome.

In my case, I saw six different judges in under three years. There's no consistency in that. No judge who could see the facts of the case develop as the case went on. Instead, they were always starting from scratch and playing catch-up with months and years of claims and details.

The last judge I saw was a Deputy District Judge, who had come out of retirement to help deal with the Family Court's backlog of cases. What he knew of my case was limited to the time he could spend reading the court papers, which wasn't much. He said I was a stockbroker. I am not a stockbroker. It's a small thing perhaps, but I was deeply concerned that the man deciding my future had the wrong occupation down for me. It made me think he had merely skimmed my papers, decided that I was an angry parent who was pushy and strict, and then lazily followed the Cafcass report recommendations to the letter.

This judge went on to surmise that because I had my kids tutored for the Eleven-Plus and the entrance exam for their highly selective school, that life with me would be unreasonably spent doing school work and extra lessons – even though the extra lessons fell away post the Eleven-Plus exams in the autumn of 2014. He took exception to this, for some reason. It was a handful of hours of tutoring per week that had ended long before our argument over Elle and my ex-wife.

He also dismissed my claims that my kids had crashed academically – by reading their latest school report. Not any of the previous ones, making comparison impossible. How can you judge a crash without comparison? You can't – it's a sample set of one! Worse, he saw no evidence my kids were struggling academically. One of them was in the bottom 25 per cent of grades in every subject. Again, that's not a fair reflection of her abilities or previous grades, but you can't decide that without seeing more than one school report.

There were other issues the judge raised which were bizarre or banal. I was shocked. Why do Family Court judges get it so wrong and make such wildly variable judgements? The answer is it could quite literally be anything.

A 2009 study of Israeli parole hearings showed that people who appeared just after breakfast and just after lunch had a 65 per cent chance of having parole granted than those who came just before a meal break or a snack, where the odds of parole dropped to almost zero. This raised a lot of questions about the role of food and mood in judicial proceedings, or in other words, bias.

However, that report was widely debunked a few years later by another study that showed that the best lawyers would always manage to get their slots scheduled earlier in the sessions than the poorest parolees who represented themselves and usually came last in the session. As a result, the lunch-dinner problem with court rulings was nothing to do with snacks and was all to do with the scheduling habits of the best lawyers. So it wasn't about bias, it was about affording a better lawyer than the others.

But what about justice? Isn't that the point? Should any of that stuff matter? Justice is supposed to be blind, and equal. Not governed by how deep your pockets are or how hungry a judge may be. In my view none of this should matter in Family Court, or any other. Why should it be that if you get a good lawyer, or pick a better time slot, or get a judge who has skim read your files, the facts of the case become less important in determining the outcome? That isn't justice, it's a lottery.

The Family Court lottery works on multiple levels. A good lawyer and a good barrister might win the day or not, depending upon other factors. In my case, my lawyer told me that if my court case was a football match, we were starting 2-nil down without a goalkeeper at half time. That was because I was a man, I worked long hours in London and it would be assumed I was typical workaholic with no time for parenting, and I was alleging Parental Alienation against my ex-wife who had residency. That, in my barrister's opinion, was a huge disadvantage because the courts usually find in favour of the mother and the kids.

I would like to point out my barrister was a woman, not some cigar chomping old public school boy with an outdated attitude towards women.

She was also a realist – although my previous lawyers had decided to drop her.

The bottom line is most men in Family Court struggle to make their case, especially once Cafcass is involved. The overwhelming majority of social workers are younger women from middle-class backgrounds, the majority of cases they deal with involve abusive men or men who don't pay their maintenance or absentee fathers and so on. As a result, there are a lot of assumptions and presumptions that go against you if you are male. That again, is how the system works.

So we have a number of problems to fix to make the Family Courts work. We need to eliminate the huge variability of the judge and judgements, we need to address the costs, and we need to rethink the system of assessments to make a meaningful outcome that benefits the children the most predictable result. That means we need to begin way before court is an option too.

Here's a suggestion for a better system …

A family relationship process for divorcing and separating families

Assuming 50:50 shared care

There is a clear mechanism that facilitates Parental Alienation and shapes the bias inherent in the court system against non-resident parents, and that is the current prevailing idea that one parent has residence, and one does not. If both parents had statutory 50:50 shared care after separation or divorce, then it is much harder to alienate one parent over the other. It's simple, really. The more time one parent has with a child, the closer their bond becomes and the greater that parent's influence over the child. If that was regulated to be equal, then it would minimise the principal mechanism by which alienation – and acrimonious litigation – come about.

Clearly, this would need more thought. Breastfeeding infants, for example, clearly need more than 50:50 time with their mother. Children under nursery age or school age have different requirements for care at home, which could make 50:50 shared care seem very complex to arrange for working parents or parents where one works and another stays at home. There are many workarounds for this, from adjusting the default shared care options to accommodate working parents and younger children and infants. There should be an established statutory right, however, to balance the care of children over school age with both parents.

In my case, there were times when my ex-wife went on holiday and left my children with the in-laws. I could have had them come to stay with me. I had retired, I could have had them 50 per cent of the time quite easily. If I had, there would have been little opportunity for my children to become so full of hatred. The same is true in reverse, of course. Were I the one doing the alienating, it would be much harder with a 50:50 arrangement.

The underlying point of addressing basic contact expectations is dismantling the basic legal assumption – and the de facto reality – that the resident parent effectively becomes the person who grants contact to the other. This is usually mothers facilitating access every other weekend, plus another day for the father. This is a double-edged sword because it prevents mothers from returning to work if they want to, in the same way it tends to drive fathers to work without receiving the same considerations for childcare, so they find it harder to manage their childcare obligations. It should therefore be mandatory for employers to recognise employees with 50:50 contact arrangements and make it easier for them to manage their responsibilities.

These are the real-world, practical arrangements that cause stress and disputes. If the courts assumed 50:50 shared care, and workplaces adapted their employment policies to enable more flexible working for shared care parents, it would reduce the incidents of litigation cases and massively reduce the opportunity for parental alienation to occur in the first place. 50:50 shared care is already on the statutes in a lot of countries worldwide, so we know it is a workable system. It seems like an obvious and relatively simple shift in favour of a safer system.

Practical advice and training before splitting

In Denmark, which has a higher divorce rate than the UK but also regularly tops surveys for happiness and wellbeing among its citizens, couples who want to divorce have to take a training course before their marriage can be ended. Part of that course is learning about the requirements to make proper provisions with the children for contact, and how to communicate with your kids. In Norway, divorcing couples must obtain a certificate of mediation before their divorce can be granted. Again, this is to ensure a better transition for the children and couples into shared care.

What this shows to me is a huge improvement over the British system, which works after the fact. In my case, you can't go to Family Court until you have tried mediation.

This is pointless, because if you are fighting over contact arrangements, mediation is too late. Mediation should happen before you divorce, and ideally before you move out. That way the whole family can be guided into separation and shared care in a more effective way. This should prevent a lot of issues further down the line, or identify risks prior to litigation, including Parental Alienation, early enough to do something more effective about it.

This has got a track record in other areas of life. Since the UK began prenatal classes, incidents of childhood illnesses and neglect have fallen. The creation of Sure Start Centres for children in poor areas have helped to reduce crime rates, school absenteeism and employment outcomes for young people and single parents. There is no argument to be made against better provision of services, and for the 120,000 or so separations each year, this would be a much better use of resources than failing organisations like Cafcass.

A school code of conduct

As soon as you divorce or separate with children, there should be provision of notification to schools and clear lines of communication for parents with their local schools and nurseries. For pre-school age children, this should trigger when they are registered with a school. The code should make it absolutely clear what parents are entitled to in terms of communications, and clarify the grey area that exists over safeguarding information and access to it. More importantly, it should prohibit the sharing of information with one parent but not the other. If you have parental responsibility, you should have sight of the same information at the same time by law. In the days where most school communication is via email and apps, and easy to audit, there is no reason why one parent should be excluded from any communications no matter how trivial or serious.

We also need to reform the application of data privacy laws in these cases to a basic level. If the child allows access to one parent, if that parent shares responsibilities with another parent, the child cannot exclude that parent on the grounds of privacy. Being competent to decide who knows about an issue is too complex for a child to decide and speaking as a parent whose children were caught up in police investigations over serious crimes and self-harm, I had an absolute right to know about their wellbeing and safety. Data privacy is not designed in its intent to prevent parents from safeguarding their kids properly. In my case, had I not been informed and my kids were at home, they could have been at risk – as they were in my ex-wife's home where the online grooming allegedly took place.

Schools should play a key role in sharing information between parents, not take arbitrary and possibly unlawful decisions to exclude a parent from vital safeguarding issues on the grounds of the Data Protection Act and its application to children under the age of 12.

A family tribunal system

At the heart of the problems, as I have made the case before, is the unfit Family Court process. So let's scrap that and treat this issue like other complex, relationship based disputes are treated, with a tribunal system. As all lawyers will tell you, Family Law is not like criminal or civil cases where a clear breach of a statute or a contract is the issue. Family Law is about relationships, and judging relationships requires more than just the opinion of a fee-based older man who is directed to rule in line with whatever a junior social worker with less than eight days to investigate the entire history of the case and interview the individuals involved.

A tribunal is similar to a court, except the bench is comprised of three experts who address different aspects of the case and evidence before them. This is a much fairer system because it means there is less chance of human error – like not following best practice or modern standards (like the Tolson example) – and three times as many eyes to read the reports and information offered to the tribunal.

You will find tribunals are highly effective in many relationship-based disputes. In employment law, employment tribunals normally match an employment judge with a specialist for employers' organisations – like a professional body, and a specialist for employees' organisations – like a trade union. In mental health tribunals, the judge is matched with a psychiatrist who is independent from the hospital where the patient is being treated, and a specialist layperson who is an expert – often someone who has been a patient, service user or support worker. On the similar format – but larger – for Parole Boards, a public protection advocate (like the judge) sits alongside the prisoner, the prisoner's lawyer, probation officers, prison officers, psychologists and so on. There are many more examples I could share, but they all blend a cross-section of the society that makes up the purpose of the hearing. It is not a court case before a solitary judge.

The reason I suggest this change is simple. You cannot assess a complex relationship like a separated family in the course of acrimonious children proceedings without a number of different perspectives. The Family Tribunal should pair a salaried Family Court Judge – not a fee earner – with a clinical specialist like consultant child psychiatrist or clinical psychologist, and a divorced parent who has been through training to help mediate disputes fairly.

It should be mandatory that every case undergoes a fact-finding mission by the court, not through Cafcass or local authority child services but through a neutral body like a local children's charity, who deals with a broad range of cases not a majority of cases where there are safeguarding concerns or allegations of abuse – like Cafcass.

The tribunal should then assess the case with one goal in mind, restoring healthy contact for both parents with the children, which is in the child's best interest. It's simply unacceptable to argue that a failure of contact comes second to the child's wishes and feelings. That is because without a concerted effort to repair relationships and order parent-child mediation and family therapy, you will never be able to stop Parental Alienation.

The children, if deemed competent enough to have their own representatives, should also have to participate in the proceedings. This would be to enable the panel to judge the child's mental health, and ask questions directly rather than rely on reports from external court-appointed professionals.

Additionally, there should be a clear hierarchy of opinion when determining the child's best interests and course of action. That hierarchy should put the most senior mental health professional in charge of assessing the child's mental health, it should put the most senior counsellor in charge of assessing the wishes and feelings of the child. It should subordinate those opinions to that of a social worker regardless of their qualifications or experience. If the social worker holds a doctorate or similar, then their opinions should be considered within the context of the tribunal panel like the others, as an equal voice, not as the main report upon which the judge will rule.

Finally, the judge should not be able to rule without a majority of the panel ruling with them. It should be unanimous, however in a split decision, there should be a right to appeal for all sides in the dispute. The ruling should always be an outcome designed to facilitate the relationship as well. That means contact. It must never determine non-contact or indirect contact via the opposing parent – or something equally as damaging to the future relationship between the parties – unless there is a safeguarding issue.

The tribunal should also adopt a no-fault approach, like divorce, to solving the issues wherever possible. It would stop a lot of alienation issues if the acrimony was replaced with a fair principle that if one parent wants to see their kids but the kids and the other parent won't do it, that there's a need for therapy – not a legitimate reason to cut a parent out of a child's life. This is not about the parent's right to a family life, it's about the child's need for a healthy future without the problems proven to affect adolescents in cases where one parent leaves the family at a young age.

Capped costs and legal aid

There aren't any statistics published about how many Family Court cases end because one side runs out of money or legal aid. However, ask family lawyers the question and they will all have a story or three of cases that ended prematurely because one side could no longer appeal or afford the fees.

This has to change. We need to cap fees for children cases based on a means test. I was lucky, I could afford to pursue all the options at my disposal, but most people can't. It is scandalous that in the case of losing your kids, unlawfully through abuse, you should have to self-finance. Can you imagine if the guy who burgled your house got off because you had to afford your own prosecution? Or could you imagine the boss who sexually harassed you getting off because you couldn't afford the legal fees and had no award for costs likely?

Parental Alienation and children litigation is not suitable for self-funding. In fact, I would argue that the fees earned in this £2 billion market are the reason it keeps growing. If we adopted a new system, we could drastically reduce the costs.

A pre-divorce mediation service would divert a proportion of cases away from the courts before they even filed.

A tribunal system – as is the case in employment tribunals – would probably use an organisation similar to the Arbitration and Conciliation Service (ACAS) to attempt to make settlement out of court the first, best choice. In cases where that failed, the tribunal system would replace many of the court hearings that a typical case entails. For example, it took six hearings to review my case. There were my initial contact travel issues, then two court-ordered psychiatrist reports, an order for family therapy with a therapist that failed to make any progress, a court order to get the school to release safeguarding records to me, a court-ordered assessment by Cafcass and a final hearing and ruling. The tribunal approach would combine all of that into one process, massively reducing the costs and the timescales involved.

It would also remove the process of both sides having to agree on a professional to make an assessment, and agree on the questions they were allowed to ask. It strikes me as absurd that the child's mental health or wellbeing is not assessed by the court itself in Family Court. The separation of roles between experts, social workers, lawyers and judges makes the process slow and expensive. It also creates the lottery effect because in the end, it all comes down to a judge making a ruling which might lead to more court appearances, more reports and more expense. Or none at all through dismissal that leaves the issue of contact unresolved.

Capping costs is complex, but maybe just reducing the complexity and cost of the current system by putting all the right experts together will be enough to make justice – and a better quality of life for divorced or separated families – something that is an expectation, not a 30–70 per cent gamble with the lives of your kids.

A framework of assessments and measures for Parental Alienation

The last piece of the puzzle is a modern statute on domestic abuse that identifies Parental Alienation, and defines it more precisely. This would enable the research and assessment work necessary to make it something that can be proven without the endless circular debates I have experienced. It would also mean if parents claimed alienation before the tribunal, there would be an agreed process to assess the claim and act accordingly.

There is a point where alienation might take many forms, it might be deliberate or something that one parent does without realising it is Parental Alienation. It's a hugely complex area but without question, until there is a universal legal definition of what it is, a measure to show how it works and an assessment framework to make a reasonable judgement, it will never go away.

In my case, I haven't seen my kids for almost six years.

In our case, we have all suffered, my children from internalising and externalising problems like anxiety and behavioural issues that are complex and life-limiting in their long-term impact on careers and relationships.

This was never anyone's wishes or feelings.

This was never listening to the voice of the child.

It was a complete failure to recognise Parental Alienation or even acknowledge its existence in my case.

Until the law catches up, as it did with consent and the case that ended Judge Tolson's time on the bench for falling so badly behind on modern legal practice, all messy divorces risk damaging the lives of more kids, more parents committing suicide and more life-altering trauma for the entity the courts were designed to protect – the family.

This is why we need reform at all levels to replace the Family Courts and put families and their happiness before the fee-earners and civil servants who dominate proceedings.

Chapter 11:
My kids and their story

In a way, this whole book is about my kids and their story. However, the truth is, an alienated parent doesn't know their child's story, not really. You have a strong sense of it, no doubt, but you can't possibly know it for sure because it has happened in your absence. The only possible explanation of how your child or children decided to cut you out of their life – beyond the basic assumption of being manipulated by the resident abuser parent – is an explanation you have to piece together from court reports, endless legal letters and wishes and feelings work that is shared with you. It is like trying to see a big picture from looking through a pile of jigsaw pieces that only partially fit together. You also have to doubt some of it – if not all of it – because it's not necessarily your child's opinions anyway. It's what they have been influenced to think.

To my mind, when my children refused to see me during the assessment with the consultant child psychiatrist, that was a massive failing of the system. Here was an opportunity for an expert in his field to assess our actual relationship in person. They refused. I suspect my ex-wife encouraged them to refuse it, or her lawyers. Without a chance to observe us together, how could anyone really understand their animosity or otherwise toward me? They wouldn't even converse with me? Shout or scream at me? Anything? No. They edited me out of their lives as though I never even existed – blocked.

Your children's story is obscured by the many voices and people who form the paper trail between you. Those people are being paid and in most cases, by the hour, to generate more paper. It's like a fog of legalese and reported speech from one side or another, which feels more like gossip or rumours than a meaningful account of events. You have to make judgement calls on what is the child's opinion, the lawyer's advised opinion, the grandparents' opinion, whoever else influences or collaborates with the abuser parent's opinion. Somewhere though, in the pile of court documents and emails, your kids are telling their story. You just don't know how to start unpicking it from all the noise and misdirection of the other people involved in the process.

Ultimately your children's story is an interpretation, made partially through guesswork but mostly by trying to cross-reference the things they say in court reports with dates and times. If you can construct a timeline, you can begin the painful process of sorting through the jigsaw pieces and seeing what fits.

I have done this many times over, and in the process of writing this book I have done it all again. Every time I try to forensically assemble a narrative of what happened to my kids when I wasn't there, I spot something new. When you are an alienated parent, this is normal. You become – to an outside observer at least – obsessed with trying to explain precisely what happened to make your kids cut you out of their lives. However, the answer is always the same – your ex-partner did it. The problem with that answer is proving it. We are all partially responsible for something within a relationship. Relationships are a dynamic interaction between people, never completely one-sided. How can you possibly prove someone else was responsible for your children's wishes and feelings?

In my case, I had to first deal with uncertainty that somehow I had made my kids turn on me. I know it's not true. Compared with most divorced parents and children with good relationships, we were fortunate. It's normal for divorces and arranging child contact to cause some conflict between parents and kids, and I think that was the same for us towards the end of our relationship. However, in reality we argued rarely and laughed plenty.

I certainly had more time and more resources than most divorced dads which made it easier for us to go out on day trips and holidays, or share our time together in a really positive way. I also had the support of good friends, and my kids had access to tutors and my assistants to facilitate a resolution over the usual flashpoints for divorcees – like arguing over transport or homework and all those normal parenting issues. However, I have to accept the unarguable fact that I can't be objective about my relationship with them – or anyone else. Nobody can.

Objectivity requires a third-party perspective, which leads us back to the start of this chapter.

It's another circular catch-22 problem. If I can't be objective, I can't be sure of my role in proceedings. Or can

I? Is there a way? Perhaps there is.

Other people's opinions of my relationship with my kids, and my ex-wife's relationship with them are abundant in the reports and assessments, but it's hard to piece together the children's story from them, for all the reasons I have just outlined. However, there are also some things that are obvious without any reference in the many reports, statements or wishes and feelings work. Those things only become clear when you apply Occam's razor to it – also known as the Law of Parsimony – which basically means the simplest explanation is most likely the right one.

So what is the simplest explanation for why my kids cut me out of their life? How is it possible to prove I was alienated?

As far as the courts were concerned, my allegations were merely circumstantial and I had alienated myself by agreeing to a cooling-off period, and pursuing my court action to see my children. There was no evidence to support my claims as far as Cafcass were concerned, nor the Deputy District Judge who made the final ruling to end my legal challenge. Ultimately, my children's wishes and feelings were to cut me out of their life, and that was that. My ex-wife was just a bystander who was supporting her children in their heartfelt plea to never see me again.

But there was evidence of my relationship with my kids. Evidence that can be seen, heard and shared. The normal evidence of daily life in the digital age – images, texts, videos and emails. Not just mine, but lots of other people. Moments, captured on camera, of me, my kids and our life together. The people in those videos were happy. Those children weren't anxious or depressed. Those kids didn't look like they hate the man they call Daddy and said *'I love you'* to. They were close. You can see it. You can hear it.

Certainly, my experience with Elle hurt us all badly and I accept it was a tough few months. But families suffer tragedies, bereavements, sickness and accidents and they recover. Families are resilient, parents' and children's relationships are resilient too. Every day, you read stories in the newspapers and magazines of families who come through much worse than that. The bond between a parent and child is incredibly strong and has longevity – particularly the bond between younger children and parents. The bond visible and audible in the family movies is strong too. We were so happy, once. Something terrible must have happened to drive us apart forever, and I don't know what it was.

This means that whether you believe my claims of alienation or not, there is clearly something missing from the story told in the paper trail of the Family Court. That something is the missing piece of the puzzle, the force that turned our hurt over Elle and our cooling-off period into my kids completely cutting me out of their life forever.

It's not about the reasons they gave – which changed significantly over the three years of court reports and interventions – it is about what's missing from that. There is nothing in their reasons for never seeing me again that couldn't be fixed. Nothing we couldn't have worked out. Nothing that was so final, or fixed, or immovable, or terminal that no force on Earth could change it or repair it. We live in a world where even murderers and war criminals get the chance – through prisoner rehabilitation programmes around the world – to seek forgiveness from their victims and their families. Surely a divorced dad like me could get the same opportunity to seek forgiveness or closure for making whatever mistakes I had allegedly made?

My children wouldn't even give me a chance to repair our relationship. They cut me off, completely, without even attempting a reconciliation. I didn't even get a hearing. I didn't even get a chance to try and rebuild our relationship.

Think about that for a moment.

Whatever you did, would you expect it to be final? To be an absolute dead end for that relationship? That you would never get a chance to explain yourself, or apologise or ask why? That's not how society works. That's not how humans relate to their lives or each other. Consider how much discussion and to and fro occurs, not just informally but in civic life, school and so on. We very rarely are allowed to cut anyone off like that.

Criminals get trials. Legal action offers appeals. Disputes have mediators. Marriages have counsellors. Politicians hold surgeries for their constituents when they plan to put a motorway through the middle of it. Companies hold meetings for their staff over redundancies or job cuts. You can appeal parking tickets. Sports have judges and referees, video replay systems and hierarchies of judges. Doctors give second opinions. Social media provides an endless forum for discussion and debate. You can complain about products to trading standards. You can write to the ombudsman for almost everything from telecoms to your electricity prices. We live in a world where the right to reply, the right to a hearing, the opportunity to debate and talk about issues is a fundamental expectation of normal society.

The only place you can cut people off completely is when you block them on social media.

I was blocked, just like a Twitter troll.

Except I wasn't a troll, I was their dad – a loving dad.

Subsequently, my children have never communicated with me as part of the court process. The children were never – not once – obliged to tell me to my face why they would never see me again, or address me directly in writing, or video. They never got so say their piece to me, only about me. It seems almost unthinkable.

I did exchange text messages with one of them – before my ex-wife changed their telephone numbers – during the cooling-off break and before the first round of school-based counselling was done. We texted each other about a planned ski trip at Easter that was, clearly, not going ahead. I wanted it to, and so did my child – however they didn't want to go without their sibling, who was dead against it. I accepted it. My child said, 'I love you Daddy'. It gave me hope.

Then, just a couple of months later, with no contact, my ex-wife reported to the counsellor that the children were traumatised over being asked – as part of the counselling – to text me. What happened in those two short months to make it all so different?

We hadn't been in touch, I had neither seen nor spoken to them.

That was the last time we communicated.

Later in 2016 the family therapist who attempted to assess our relationship and begin a process of rehabilitation asked me to make a short video for my kids. It was less than three minutes long. I apologised, unreservedly, for whatever it was

I had done. I genuinely didn't know what it was, except the argument over Elle, but at the direction of the therapist I did it. I made it positive. I made it as friendly and gentle as I knew how. I sent it and I prayed they would respond.

The therapist informed me they refused to watch it.

My kids hadn't seen me for over a year. They were attending family therapy. They refused to even look at me or hear my words. They weren't even slightly curious to hear what I had to say. They wouldn't even see their father. That, again, shows there was a piece of the puzzle missing. How could they be so angry with me? So determined to cut me out of their lives that I couldn't even attempt to apologise or make amends?

This was before my kids had learned about my estranged child, apparently. That was a major reason they gave for cutting me off, also. I was cut off at this point too, but for other reasons – like being mean over money with my ex-wife, and saying unkind things about the woman who broke my heart and robbed me.

I raise the discovery of my estranged child because it loomed so large in the final reports and judgement. My kids were devastated by it, apparently. The only person I had told was my ex-wife, and I told her because I was worried the child's mother might turn up at her home or try to contact the children, because she had met them and knew them reasonably well. I trusted her to protect our kids from harm.

Was that discovery – which my ex-wife claimed happened in 2016 – made earlier? It was central in every report from December 2016 onwards, so the fact it wasn't mentioned before means I have to assume it wasn't. In which case it's another unknown. What happened to make them cut me off so completely for nearly two years before they learned about their estranged sibling?

I would like to use the rest of this chapter – and this book – to address that final missing jigsaw piece.

What happened to my kids, to make them hate me so?

The answer, I think, proves my case for Parental Alienation beyond any reasonable doubt.

The simple explanation is told in pictures and video

Something that shocks me to this day is the complete lack of evidence for the many accusations that were made against me, and at the same time the complete lack of attention paid to any of the evidence I offered to support my allegations of Parental Alienation.

Now of course, the knee-jerk response to that statement – as I have noted before when talking about the need to reform the Family Court – is judges tend to dismiss all that supporting information anyway and rule on the balance of probabilities of what one side or the other is alleging. In my case, the balance of probability is never going to support alienation claims because Parental Alienation is an unusual event compared to the vast majority of children cases. It is rare, and so therefore, tends to be discounted in favour of more common reasons for parental estrangement like one parent being unable to connect with the children for some reason.

In my case, as we know, there were no safeguarding issues or concerns. In my final judgement, the Deputy District

Judge – just out of retirement to help clear the backlog of cases – found no reasons why I wasn't fit to receive a direct contact order except for my attitude to education and tutoring. And the one time I tapped my kid on the top of the head to get their attention when they were misbehaving with a group of friends late one night. And an alleged incident in 2012, where I was supposed to have put one of them on the doorstep in the snow dressed only in their underwear, which never happened.

The judge made it sound like I would chain my kids to a desk and make them do homework non-stop in their spare time. He made me sound like a violent brute with a cruel streak. He also asserted that tutoring was unnecessary when the children were doing fine at school – except one of them was coming in the bottom 25 per cent of her class for every subject, when before, she had been described as an academic and a bright, intelligent child. He also felt I was out of touch, strict and too focused on their mental health and the interventions they needed for their deteriorating state. Those problems were indirectly my fault, in his judgement, because I was the one driving the court action. Although none of this was a factor when the children and I were in a relationship.

The problems I predicted, that are documented in academic studies as a result of absentee parents and alienation, were the result of my attempts to prevent those same problems from happening according to the judge and Cafcass too. It was – as I have shown time and again in the pages of this book – the circularity of the Family Court and the never-ending loophole of Parental Alienation.

Put simply, I was locked in an acrimonious court battle

because I was the cause of acrimony. And my children's wishes and feelings to never see me again were because of the acrimonious court proceedings, even though the acrimony happened *after* they broke off contact, which was *before* the court case even began. It was a self-referencing paradox. They cut me off *before* the court case, but also *because* of the court case? It's not possible without a time machine.

The judgement did not address the vast gulf between the man and children they described in the reports, and the happy people in the dozens of pictures and movies. The assumption made by the court was fundamentally flawed and plain lazy. The assumption was my kids hated me and I was punishing both them and my ex-wife with court proceedings. It was true that I was frustrated and angry, they were anxious and depressed, and those things were assumed to be our natural states as opposed to specifically because of the separation and the abuse it represented. But so much had changed, so much time had passed, it didn't explain who we were and how we were before all of this.

How could they possibly observe us as a family, as father and children, before the break-up? The answer is digitally, there was an abundance of that evidence. I thought it would save the day. I was wrong.

I gave Cafcass, my ex-wife's legal team, and my children's legal team each a USB stick loaded with images and movies of us on holiday, playing, at my house, all sorts. There were over 50 videos, pictures, all showed a truly wonderful relationship full of joy and love. These were dated from 2009 to 2014. I mean, what parent didn't have a phone, iPad or a camera full of pics by then? Surely this was enough to show a different side to the one presented by my kids and ex-wife?

The USB stick showed two bright, happy kids having fun in the sun and living a great life in and around London with their dad. They showed family friends. They didn't show two anxious kids, desperate and miserable, forced to work endless hours by some austere father. I was a parent, not a monster and those files proved it. In particular, the files unequivocally called my children's accounts into doubt and my ex-wife's too. For example, the holiday in California, at Christmas where my wife said they were miserable and called home all the time (they didn't have phones then), saying they missed their family. I had video and pics of us having a great time. Laughing. Fishing trips. Playing in the sun. They were not miserable.

They also reported to their therapist and others that they barely knew the man they called Uncle Matt in that holiday film. The man who saw them most weekends, one of my oldest friends who loved them like his own. They loved him too. That was inexplicable. We stayed together in California. Matt arranged an au pair – called Stella – who the kids loved and emailed for a year afterwards like pen pals. If you saw that footage, and read the testimony of the man they called Uncle Matt, you would know something was seriously wrong with their memories. They were having a great time in those pics and films – and Uncle Matt was there to see it with me.

Uncle Matt used to take them out on trips. He would see them all the time. We all went fishing and shopping and had a blast in California. But just a few years later, they could barely remember him? Described him as someone they liked but wasn't important to them? What did that mean?

They remembered California, they said they hated it. They said Santa had forgotten them, apparently. As I recall, Santa arranged for presents well in advance. Santa made sure they had gifts to open on Christmas Day, Monopoly, Rubik's Cubes and a telescope each, as I recall. They had to be easy items to pack and bring home on a flight, so nothing too big, but they didn't miss out on Christmas for an instant. I had pictures to prove it.

The first missing jigsaw piece is the unseen force that turned those children who are laughing and playing in all the home movies, who made me cards and sent me messages, who clearly had a very healthy relationship with me and my family friends, into two kids who suddenly cut me off and denied having a relationship with their Uncle Matt. What unseen force could do that?

Matt was very upset by it. He said, *'I love those kids and they love me. What they are saying is impossible. You don't just forget someone like that, not after all the time we spent together.'* What happened to make them forget all those good times? What made them describe a wonderful holiday in California as something miserable? What made them forget the man they called Uncle Matt and saw week in, week out for years? Why would they describe the scenes where they are obviously having a great time as miserable?

Sadly, that question was never asked but I know the answer.

Nobody looked at the pictures, or watched the videos. My ex-wife's barrister claimed he couldn't open them. I offered to show him how a laptop worked, and do it for him. He declined. It was clear nobody else looked at them either. Because if you saw those films, and looked at those pictures, you couldn't continue to fight a case based on the position that my kids didn't like me or I was a stern disciplinarian. The kids in those movies love me. And we are having the time of our lives.

Something or someone must have distorted their reality and influenced their dread of me. Their anxiety. Their fear of even seeing me. Something or someone had influenced them – and it couldn't be me because I hadn't seen or spoken to them.

The simple explanation is told in the difference between the kids in the movies, and the kids in the court

Another dear friend – Maxine – who my children loved and even one time dragged into my ex-wife's house to show their bedroom and toys to her – was also forgotten. Again, she became someone my kids claimed they barely knew.

Except, like Uncle Matt that wasn't true. They knew her well. They saw her a lot. We were platonic friends, we had known each other for years working in very similar fields. She would stay over, we would go on trips. And my kids loved her as she loved them.

Maxine last saw the children in 2015, at a court hearing where they were to attend too. I had bought gifts for the kids – Christmas was coming – and I desperately hoped they would see me or my old friend and agree to at least text me or something.

They agreed to see her and not me. She saw them, and emerged from the meeting in shock.

Maxine always called the kids *'her little peanuts'*. She said they were bright and effervescent. People always did. They were. Another dear friend – Toph – who had known me for most of my adult life and saw them the day they were born, described them as charming and polite, funny and engaging. They were. My kids were fun, bright, engaging children who charmed everyone. But when Maxine emerged from the court hearing rooms, she described two very different children. They were quiet and withdrawn. They looked down at the floor. They barely spoke to her.

They were with their grandmother, who was very stern at the meeting.

At first, when Maxine entered the room, both kids went to give her a hug then stopped themselves very self-consciously, looked at their grandmother, then withdrew.

They hardly spoke.

These were the same children who were described by the Cafcass report as chatty and polite? Maxine was devastated. She was convinced they were under duress. She described their grandmother's presence like they had a handler there to make sure they didn't say or do anything without checking first. She described feeling very awkward and intimidated by the situation. As she put it, *'It wasn't like seeing my two little peanuts. They were different children.'*

In one of the court reports, the kids described their Uncle Matt and Maxine as people they liked, but weren't important to them. They talked of my sister as being closer to them. However, I know for a fact they hardly saw my sister in comparison. I have a difficult relationship with my sister, who remains friends with my ex-wife and barely even keeps in touch with me. For my children to say she's closer to them than the man they called Uncle Matt and my friend Maxine, despite seeing her less and certainly never going on holiday with her or on trips out in London and so on, feels unbelievable. It sounds like brainwashing.

That distance they created feels like my kids didn't merely cut me off, they cut my friends off too. They erased our whole life together from 2009 to 2015, and replaced it with a story of miserable kids having a miserable time. It stretches the credibility of their wishes and feelings to a point that warrants further investigation. The kids in the home movies, the kids who my friends remember, were different children from the ones who were assessed by the courts. They were different in their demeanour. They claimed different memories. They were performing differently academically. They had behavioural problems the kids in the home movies never had.

Something had happened. The missing jigsaw piece was missing from that part of the picture.

The only alternative is they were faking it for years.

Faking it from the age of six?

Faking it, weekend after weekend, holiday after holiday, year in, year out from the age of six until they were nearly 12?

Faking it so convincingly that people they had known and seen regularly over a period of three to five years became diminished in their eyes to a point where only their mother's friends and associates mattered when assessed just a year later?

Faking it so well that, even after our cooling-off period began, I still have texts saying *'I love you Daddy'*? Texts they sent, faking our relationship because just two months later sending me a text made them angry and distressed?

They were not capable of faking it like that. No child is.

Something happened to change their minds.

Can anyone believe they spontaneously reinvented themselves to be unrecognisable to the people who knew and loved them, and the videos of their former selves that fill up the hard drive of my computer. If that was the case, and they just spontaneously transformed into different people, then something must have happened to cause it. People don't just change like that.

Whatever happened to my kids, it is missing from the records. It is missing from the assessments, and certainly missing from the Family Court ruling and Cafcass reports. They never even asked the question. They never reviewed the images and movies I gave them. They never considered the heartfelt pleas of the friends who loved my kids and mourned their loss as I did.

The truth of why they changed their minds so much might never be known, but when you consider there were multiple witnesses and a whole heap of family home movies that presented two very different children and showed a lot of very happy times – compared to the withdrawn, anxious children who remembered those events and their participation in them completely differently – it was, at the very least, worthy of investigation.

To add colour to that view, the children's tutor – who knew them aged 10–11 – described them as highly intelligent and socially skilled. And she described the tensions she experienced with my ex-wife, arising from the fact that my ex-wife didn't think education was a priority for the kids, because they were rich. I include this statement because tutoring is the one issue that the judge cited in his ruling as a bad thing for the kids. Also, in one of the court assessments of the children, my children say they hated the tutor and called her *'The Witch'.*

The tutor was young, a professional with a career working with kids. She was lively and engaging, with fashionable clothes. She drove an Audi sports car. She was cool. I have many pictures of her and the kids, laughing and having fun at the X-Factor live show and at my retirement party in the City. They liked her. They had fun. The Witch? It seemed like a strange nickname for two 11 year olds to give someone like that who was so much younger and cooler than her parents. My ex-wife – who terminated the tutor sessions – also called her the same nickname. Coincidence? Of course not. My kids learned that nickname from my ex-wife.

My ex-wife was against tutoring, and so was her family. In my ex-wife's statement to the court, and her family and friends affidavits to the court, they all mentioned the detrimental effects on the children of tutoring. Tutoring is commonplace for around a quarter of secondary school children in the UK. It is not slavery, it's education. My ex-wife, who was not a qualified person nor were her family and friends, was of the opinion that education was unnecessary for wealthy people. She felt my kids were lucky enough that they didn't need to work as hard as ordinary kids. The fact she could only afford that opinion because of the money she received from divorcing an ordinary working class boy like me represents a level of irony that is almost unbelievable.

The tutor was a *witch*, my focus on education made them

miserable, their tutoring to pass their Eleven-Plus and the entrance exams to a highly selective private school made them unhappy? That's a very neat little fantasy there. Oh, those poor kids with their tutor and their private school!

How about this version ... My kids are part of a very privileged group of children who attend a school that costs £25,000 per year plus expenses, and like a quarter of all the kids in the country and more like a third of London kids, have extra tuition to get better exam grades and a better chance at university at the end of it. *'Oh those poor kids'* sounds beyond stupid when you put it like that.

After the final judgement I saw the tutor – we are still friends – and we had lunch. Afterwards we went for coffee. She went into the local café to order take-out and emerged shocked and upset. She said my kids were in there, and they had shouted abuse at her. I looked over at the window and there they were, in the window, shouting obscenities and making obscene hand gestures like a pair of football hooligans.

I went inside – the last time I saw them – and told them their behaviour was completely unacceptable. They hurled abuse at me. It was horribly embarrassing and deeply upsetting. I barely recognised my own kids in those angry, foul-mouthed youths. I reported the incident to the police. The police investigated and made my kids write letters of apology for their behaviour. My children told the police they reacted like that because they had a court injunction to stop me from coming near them in public. That wasn't true. There was no injunction, no civil law case limiting contact or anything else. All that existed was an indirect contact order regarding me contacting them on a regular basis. There was nothing in place that meant if they flicked me the v sign and shouted fuck off out of a café front window on the high street, I couldn't tell them to stop.

Why did they think that? Why did they tell the police that? Who had told them that I was subject to the same kind of injunction they apply to stalkers? I'm guessing my ex-wife.

People think reporting them to the police like that was harsh, but I believe it was right. I believed if I didn't, my ex-wife would use it against me. I lived in a world where a hug would become a headlock. If I reported this event, it couldn't be escalated into new threats or accusations against me.

Three people bore witness to our lives together and were a part of it – Uncle Matt, Maxine and the tutor – were just three of the witnesses who wrote statements for the court, and wrote letters to the professionals involved expressing their deep concerns for the children. There were more. My assistant Peter wrote to the court. Toph wrote to the court. As did Kate my housekeeper, and also the mother of my estranged child, in support of my case. Less than a year later, the kids had transformed in their mood and demeanour. They all testified that the kids they knew had changed dramatically. In less than a year, the kids had transformed into anxious children who were afraid of me. Within two years, they couldn't even bear to look at me on video.

What the hell happened?

These witnesses to the life we had before the split described my kids as bright, bubbly, clever, chatty, vivacious and so on. The children who were assessed by the courts were anxious and depressed. That transformation is predictable, along with self-harm and inappropriate sexual behaviours, and academic decline. It's predictable based on studies into separated families where the father leaves the home, it's predictable based on expert insights into Parental Alienation and messy litigation.

However, as I have written time and again, my claims of Parental Alienation were dismissed. They weren't even investigated. The change in my children was attributed to the court action I was pursuing, and the acrimony between me and my ex-wife. It is barely believable, but that is what happened.

That hypothesis of my kids and the reasons for their wishes and feelings to cut me out of their life was directly contradicted by a huge amount of home movies and photos, witness statements and circumstantial evidence that clearly showed my children had no reason to cut me off and never let me back into their lives.

The reasons they gave were reasons that emerged after we had split. Reasons that – like the self-harm and online abuse – my kids learned about while they were estranged from me and in the care of my ex-wife, against whom I alleged Parental Alienation. They were hostile towards me, unreasonably hostile to a point where they wouldn't even let me apologise. They did so in a fog of claims that made events where they were on film laughing and playing sound miserable, with people they are hugging and kissing whom they claimed to hardly know.

Something happened to change their minds and their memories of people and events. And it wasn't the acrimonious court case that hadn't even begun when they cut me off. It couldn't be just that even when it had.

Something or someone had influenced them.

The simple explanation is visible in the difference between the kids in the court, and the kids in my ex-wife's witness statements

It's no secret that unscrupulous lawyers put words into witnesses' mouths. It's a common component of continuing professional development for barristers and police investigators to examine witness statements to note similarities that suggest the witnesses have been coached by someone – such as the defendant or a lawyer – to make their witness statements and testimony match too closely to be coincidence. There is an old adage, that if you ask ten witnesses of a car accident what happened, you will receive ten differing accounts. It is suspicious if statements share too many similarities.

The reason for this isn't just conventional wisdom, it's psychological. Our accounts of events always reflect the idiosyncrasies of our perspective of an event. Some people might describe a red car hitting a blue one, others might remember a Ford hitting a Honda. Some might recall a screech of tires, others, the crunch of broken glass. Witness statements focus on one thing over another, we recall things differently based on our interpretation of the memory, which changes over time depending on the way we remember it. This is why we love holiday snaps and movies so much, because everyone knows that memories fade and change over time.

My ex-wife, her mother, her sister and best friend all supplied statements to the court. As I did, and my friends. And these statements were all similar, too. My friends at a big picture level, described me as a loving father, my kids as bright and enthusiastic and described us doing things together like holidays and trips out. They described the events in the pictures and movies, and many like them. But they were not the same account by any means. My friends didn't know each other very well. The man my kids called Uncle Matt had met Maxine only a couple of times. They weren't friends with one another beyond their association with me. Other witnesses, like my housekeeper or personal assistant, or the tutor, or Toph were people who knew me and my children but not each other. This is reflected in the variance of details and focus between their statements.

The same is not true of my ex-wife and her statements. Her mother, her sister and her best friend, like my ex-wife, talk about me working too much and being an absent parent. They all mention my children's tutoring and how onerous it was for them. My ex-mother in law claimed they were forced to work every day and were only allowed a day off doing extra homework on their birthdays and Christmas! Which was insane! They all mention me changing arrangements without notice. They all reference my kids as being much happier without seeing me. They all mention my children becoming anxious when it was time to see me. One even talks about my home not being child friendly, even though she never even visited it once. Their accounts are similar in tone and content. They reference things that they had never seen or experienced.

Their accounts were too similar to be a coincidence.

They also describe my children as happy and relaxed. They describe my children as much happier without me in their lives – that in itself is shocking as it suggests they all felt that me being in my children's lives previously was a negative. They describe my kids in glowing terms, and they don't mention their problems. They don't mention their anxiety and depression – which occurred without seeing me and was diagnosed by a consultant child psychiatrist two years after they ceased all contact. They don't mention the change in the kids' demeanour that is so obvious to my friends, and is so obvious when you see the home movies. They paint a completely different picture of the children from the two kids who stared at the floor and barely spoke to my friend when she saw them in court.

The principal difference though, is the fact my friends' statements all talk about my relationship with my kids, something they had all experienced first-hand. My ex-wife's statement and her affidavits from family and friends all refer to something none of them had ever experienced. It is bizarre to make sworn court statements about something you haven't experienced first-hand. Not to mention impossible.

My ex-wife, her family and friends don't talk about her relationship with the kids. No. They talk about mine – consider what that says about their intentions.

The father's statements talk about the father-child relationship. The mother's statements talk about the father-child relationship. The mother-child relationship isn't discussed. What does that show?

I believe it clearly shows the intent of both sides.

It shows my intent to challenge the prevailing story that my kids had good reason to hate me. And it shows the intent of my ex-wife to show that they did.

I wonder why she didn't provide a set of statements that

said she was a great mother? That talked about her role in the kids' life? About the things she did with them? I believe the statements she supplied were coached, or steered, by my ex-wife to establish a set of reasons that justified my kids' wishes and feelings to cut me out of their life. Did it work? Yes. Like a charm. The Judge and the Cafcass report certainly dwelled on the same themes as those affidavits, of me being an overbearing, stern parent who forced his kids to do extra tutoring and who made them sick with anxiety at the thought of seeing me. It never challenged that opinion by asking anyone to explain why they were laughing and playing on a fishing trip, hugging people and saying I love you.

The difference between my statements and hers, in fact between everything I said in the court process and my ex-wife, was this: I spoke about myself and my relationship to the kids. She didn't. My relationship with the children came under intense scrutiny, hers didn't.

It is not beyond the realms of possibility, under those circumstances, to consider that my ex-wife was fighting her side of the lawsuit with the intention of showing the court why I shouldn't have a relationship with my kids, because my relationship with the kids was all she ever talked about.

Which means it's not beyond the realms of possibility to consider that she was manipulating my kids, assisted by her mother, sister and friends, to cut me out of their lives.

I think that is what happened to my kids.

Is the simple explanation that what my kids did to me is what they think I did to their estranged sibling?

All the reports after the discovery of my children's estranged sibling cite that information as a huge event in their lives. It isn't mentioned in the first consultant child psychiatrist report in 2016, but was in the 2017 report. So it happened at some point in between, I guess. At this age, the children were 14. They talk of the event in catastrophic terms, and it makes me sound like a complete and utter bastard that cut a child out his life. You have to wonder if that became their justification for cutting me out of theirs.

I didn't cut the child out of my life. I had broken up with the mother, and I had no desire to father a child. In fact, she told me she couldn't have children. The whole thing was a mess. I didn't want to become a father like that, I didn't believe in having kids outside marriage. It felt like I was being forced into it. Regardless of how you judge my actions in that regard, I felt I was fair. I met my responsibilities by paying towards the child's education and maintenance.

The child's mother wrote an affidavit to the court supporting me and confirming she knew my kids and I was a good parent too. We had no hard feelings, it was just an unsuccessful relationship. We had sorted it out.

You can't force someone to become a father, any more than if the mother had wanted an abortion I could have forced her to become a mother. I did not abandon the child. I never even met it. It has benefited in its life, I hope, from the financial support I have given it. The child and the mother aren't living alone in poverty, they are happy and comfortably off as part of a new family. The mother wrote to the court, on my behalf, expressing how we had come to an amicable arrangement. She also knew my kids, and spoke of our close relationship. She supported me.

The only person who knew about the child was my ex-wife. And she knew before the split with my children. She was very conflicted over it. She wanted to tell the children because she believed they had a right to know about their unborn sibling. I didn't. Finding out something like that can be very confusing for a child of nine (their age at the time). I didn't feel they could handle it. I also believed telling them would mean involving the child's mother, as it was her decision too. It was so complicated, I decided it was best to wait until the children were old enough to handle it.

Fast forward just under two years, and Elle left me. Then shortly after, my kids and I suffered the breakdown in our relationship. We kept in touch a little, via texts and email for a couple of months, and then they cut me off completely. And cut me off forever.

I can't help but wonder what justified that in their minds?

Then I consider how an 11 year old might judge what would be a just and proportionate way to punish a man who had a child and never saw it. There is a childish symmetry about how they might empathise with their estranged sibling, and how they might feel justice was done by treating me the same. But they didn't know about the child then, did they? They didn't find out for over two and a half years, according to my ex-wife. I can't help but wonder about that.

If they didn't know, it means they cut me out of their life completely because I was too strict over schoolwork, or because I lightly tapped one of them on the top of the head to stop them from jumping off the bed at midnight with their over-excited friends. Or because I once told one of them off over not wearing winter clothes when it was snowing. Or because I took them to the wrong treat in London instead of a theme park or whatever.

Again, there has to be a missing piece of the jigsaw there.

Did they know about the child? That would explain their hostility toward me, I suppose. They certainly knew about it – and made it the major reason for never wanting to see me again – when they were assessed for the final time aged 14.

So they cut me out of their lives over the fact I had another child.

They cut me out of their lives also over my meanness to their multimillionaire mother, my ex-wife, to whom I only contributed around £80,000 per year in maintenance and school fees. And who sued me over money I paid into the kids' trust fund and used the courts to force me to pay it to her instead.

They cut me out of their lives over the way I was unkind to Elle, who stole vast sums of money from me and falsely accused me of abuse. Elle who was also in contact with my ex-wife who helped to hide a suitcase on her behalf shortly before she fled the country.

The child, my meanness to their multimillionaire mother, my cruelty to the con-woman called Elle and my relentless obsession with helping my kids pass their Eleven-Plus and do better at school. And taking them on lavish luxury holidays.

They cut me off for that? It is beyond belief.

In fact, none of it really makes sense.

My children's reason for cutting me off changed so much from the argument to the judgement years later, it's impossible to know what is really true.

My children's descriptions of events and people in their life before we split changed so much it's impossible to believe them.

My children's decision to cut me out of their life completely is also impossible to work out.

I am, honestly and without hubris, a very successful man and well connected. Connected enough to get my kids a backstage interview with a famous ballerina and arrange a private viewing of the Crown Jewels. Connected and successful enough that I took them on holiday at a hotel where they ate breakfast most mornings with a high-profile member of the British Royal Family. Connected and successful enough that I could help them do anything they wanted in their lives and careers.

And I love them with all my heart, and would do anything for them except allow them to think they don't need to work and make a contribution to society like most decent, hardworking people.

My kids cut me out of their life completely, for reasons that either don't stack up, or seem trivial, or are the result of them learning private things about me without any possibility for me to discuss, explain or apologise to them.

Do you believe, having read this far, that their decision was right? Were they right to never offer me a second chance? Were they right to completely cut me out of their lives, and to shake with fear at the very mention of me?

Do you believe it was the court action that made them

anxious and depressed, or was it Parental Alienation that did it?

Do they sound like normal, healthy teenagers to you?

Is it possible in your mind that my kids were influenced by their mother, and her family, to view me as some sort of monster?

I think my ex-wife was so angry and vindictive she hurt me the only way she could. She couldn't damage my reputation or hurt my business interests, and even after taking me to court for millions of pounds I was still wealthy. The only weak spot I had was my children and access to them.

The only thing she could take from me was my kids.

And why?

Why would my ex-wife have been motivated to do this to me, when I was about to marry a beautiful woman and start a new family, which was all my kids could talk about?

If Elle and I had married and started a family, I genuinely think my kids would have asked to live with us too. I am sure of it.

But then my dream with Elle became a nightmare.

And my world fell apart, then I lost my kids.

My ex-wife got the money and the kids, and I ended up completely alone.

That is practically the definition of Parental Alienation.

You have read my story.

All I ask is that you make up your own mind, on the balance of proof, like the Judge did when he put my ex-wife – whom I had accused of domestic abuse and cutting me off from my kids – in charge of contact between me and my children.

A letter to my children

To my darling children,

I will always be here and I will always love you – that will never change. I miss you more than words can say and it seems so wrong for us to be apart. To say something that could be misunderstood would be a mistake so I simply say that I truly hope you read this book. I truly hope it shines a light on the reality of our relationship, our love for each other, and my endless quest for us to be together again.

Love always, Daddy

* * *

END